CHOOSING & WORKING WITH YOUR ADVERTISING AGENCY

William M. Weilbacher

NTC Business Books
a division of *NTC Publishing Group* • Lincolnwood, Illinois USA

This edition first published in 1991 by NTC Business Books,
a division of NTC Publishing Group,
4255 West Touhy Avenue,
Lincolnwood (Chicago), Illinois 60646-1975 U.S.A.
Manufactured in the United States of America.
Library of Congress Catalog Card Number 90-060619
0 1 2 3 4 5 6 7 8 9 BC 9 8 7 6 5 4 3 2 1

Contents

Exhibits

Foreword

The advertising agency business and the game of golf, as far as I'm concerned, have one thing in common. They both can give either high pleasure or high pain.

Very few business experiences come close to the genuine ecstasy of winning a big account or the deep depression when you lose one.

If I had my way, users of this book would have to prove they had thoroughly read Chapters 1 and 2 before they could proceed. In my judgment, far too many advertiser–agency relations are severed before they should be.

Nonetheless, if the decision is to look for a new agency, then I would urge the prospective client to use this book as it is written. Proceed step by step, do not jump around or cherry pick. The procedures should be followed scrupulously because they are written in a thoroughly professional manner by a thoroughly professional author. I should know. I have been on the winning side and I have been on the losing side when Bill Weilbacher has been involved.

Louis T. Hagopian
Chairman Emeritus
N. W. Ayer, Inc.

Introduction

This is a book about how to select, compensate, and develop an effective relationship with an advertising agency. It is designed to help advertisers who are choosing an advertising agency for the first time, as well as advertisers who are replacing an incumbent agency or adding another agency or agencies. It will also help advertisers who have settled their agency relationship but wish to review or revise agency compensation arrangements or improve the effectiveness of the relationship.

Companies that select an agency for the first time—or add another agency—simply make that decision and proceed to search. The decision to change agencies is another matter. Companies should not change advertising agencies simply for the sake of change. Of course, there are some instances in which a company has no choice but to fire its agency and select a new one. But in many instances the dissatisfaction of a company with its agency can be corrected by a clear-eyed appraisal of the causes of this dissatisfaction. This is especially true when the case of the dissatisfaction is the agency compensation agreement.

Changing an advertising agency is costly in terms of time, money, and the disruption of ongoing marketing and advertising programs. And there is no guarantee that a newly selected agency will turn out to be any better than the incumbent. Companies should resist the temptation to look for a new agency until they are satisfied that all avenues leading to a resuscitation of the existing relationship have been thoroughly explored.

When it is necessary to select an advertising agency, the process employed should be orderly. This process is the focus of this book. The agency selection process described herein is designed to make sure that all qualified agencies are considered in the selection process and that unqualified agencies are eliminated—early on. In addition, the selection process provides guidelines and procedures for narrowing the search to the few most qualified agencies and, ultimately, for selecting the agency that is best fitted to do the job for the advertiser.

In the final analysis, the success of the agency selection depends on the subsequent success of the relationship between advertiser and new agency. That relationship should enrich the advertiser through increased sales and profits. The better and more productive the relationship, the more it will contribute to increased sales and profits. That is why it is so important to make sure that the agency search is totally successful—and that is the purpose of this book.

PART 1

When to Find
an Agency

Do You Really Need
an Advertising Agency?

Most businesses are not totally self-sufficient. They depend on outside professional help, such as lawyers, public accountants, architects, public relations firms, and advertising agencies. Ordinarily, companies hire outside counselors for one of two reasons:

1. It is too expensive to employ top professionals because they command high salaries and prefer to work for specialized firms. These firms can pay more because they can charge more for their services. In addition, they can give their employees broader experiences in the field.

2. Specialized professionals and the companies that employ them can offer more expertise, a larger perspective, and a greater variety of services than in-house employees.

Firms hire advertising agencies for both these reasons. It is difficult and expensive to hire advertising professionals, because they prefer to work in advertising agencies. Furthermore, advertising professionals bring a breadth of experience from their agency background that guarantees better solutions to advertising problems than employers are likely to get from their own advertising employees.

Of course, firms that have no need to advertise—or choose not to—do not hire advertising agencies. Other firms, usually with modest advertising programs and requirements, may receive advertising services from advertising media or buy them from non-advertising agency sources. And some firms set up in-house agencies to service their advertising needs.

However, most advertisers prefer to use an outside advertising agency because they believe that agencies provide better, more efficient, or more effective advertising than other sources.

What Does an Advertising Agency Do?

It is easy to say that an advertising agency makes advertisements, and let it go at that. Some advertisers seem to have this view. For example, the director of sales and marketing for one large airline, in briefing several prospective agencies who were soliciting his account, said:

Look, we're just about the same as our competitors. We fly the same planes. Our pilots are just as experienced. We recruit and train our stewardesses in exactly the same ways. Our reservation systems are just like theirs. Our prices are usually competitive. And we treat our customers at our terminals just as they do. Don't waste your time trying to find a difference. Just go out and make some ads and bring them back. If I like your ads, you get the business; and if I don't like them, you don't.

However, most advertisers understand that when they hire an agency, they are entering into a two-sided relationship. They also understand that the more they put into the relationship, the better their advertising is likely to be. Given this insight, it is important to understand what an advertising agency does and how its work relates to the total process of creating successful advertisements. This knowledge will also tend to clarify the advertiser's role in the advertising process.

One of the truisms of the advertising agency business is that no two advertising agencies are exactly alike, nor do any two agencies provide exactly the same services to their clients.

Some agencies develop a particular character because of either the special skills of their principals and key employees or the unique needs of their clients. Most agencies acquire specific personalities as a result of both these factors—special agency skills interacting with particular client needs.

Although most advertising agencies differ in one or more respects from their competitors, they all provide four basic services:

1. Strategic advertising planning
2. Creation of advertisements
3. Placement of advertisements in advertising media
4. Billing advertisers for placed advertisements and paying of the advertising media

These four basic functions of the advertising agency can best be illustrated by showing how they fit into the overall process of developing and implementing advertising programs.

Chapter 1

The Agency Role in Developing Advertising Programs

The Marketing Context for Advertising.   The work of the advertising agency is carried out within the context of the total marketing activity of the firm. That is, the advertiser determines the content and direction of a total marketing program for its products and services. Within this total marketing program, the purposes of the advertising program are determined, and specific advertising strategies and plans are developed and then executed.

Strategy is nothing more than an expression of intended action. It is a statement of how a goal is to be accomplished. Ordinarily, advertising strategy begins with a statement about what advertising must convey in order to maximize the sales potential of a product or service. If advertising can be developed without attention to—or agreement about—what the advertising is supposed to do and how it will do it, well and good. Most advertisers believe, however, that it is critical to the development of superior advertising to have some agreement about what the agency intends to do—*before* it does it.

The advertiser and its advertising agency interact in this process: The advertiser tends to dominate the development of overall marketing goals and strategy, although the advertising agency usually participates. However, as advertising plans and executions are developed, the advertising agency becomes more important and dominant in the advertiser–agency relationship. It is the agency that ultimately produces finished advertisements and media placement programs.

The Advertising Process.   The entire advertising process consists of the following series of seven steps.

Step 1. Determine marketing objectives or goals. Before specific marketing strategies and programs can be developed, it is necessary to know what they are supposed to accomplish.

The advertiser must specify the objectives or goals of its marketing programs in terms of dollar sales, unit sales, or market-share objectives, or in communication terms, such as desired levels of consumer product awareness or knowledge.

Advertisers are primarily responsible for setting marketing objectives or goals, although advertising agencies may participate in their determination as well.

Step 2. Develop general marketing strategies to accomplish marketing objectives or goals. Marketing strategies state specifically how marketing

4

goals will be accomplished through a variety of marketing means. These marketing actions include the following:

- Designing, redesigning, or embellishing products or services
- Pricing products or services
- Selecting the product, service line, or assortment
- Organizing, stimulating, and compensating direct-selling efforts
- Designing and implementing sales promotion and merchandising programs
- Designing and implementing advertising programs
- Using other marketing activities to achieve marketing goals

Marketing strategies not only dictate the kinds of individual marketing actions that will be undertaken to achieve marketing goals. They also dictate how these actions will interact to produce the most efficient mix of marketing activities to achieve marketing goals.

Once again, the major responsibility for developing marketing strategies lies with the advertiser rather than with its advertising agencies. However, the agency will certainly participate in determining the general role that advertising will play in achieving the company's objectives.

The agency may also participate in marketing strategy decisions involving product/service design, price, product/service line or assortment, direct-sales organizations, sales promotion programs, and whatever other marketing activities the advertiser uses to achieve its goals. Many advertisers make a point of requesting the agency's help in the development of these non-advertising strategies.

Step 3. Develop specific advertising strategies. Advertising strategies are statements about how marketing goals will be achieved through advertising.

Specific advertising strategies will be developed to give direction to these four key elements of an advertising program.

- *Determining the core advertising message.* The core advertising message is the *vital essence* of the product or service to be advertised, expressed in consumer terms. It is the simple statement about the product or service that will have most meaning to the broadest group of consumers. Sometimes this vital essence is called the product or service "positioning," and sometimes it is called the "creative strategy" of the product or service. Whatever it is called, the core advertising message implies a distinction between all of the things that *could* be said about a product or service, and

5

the one or two things that *must* be said about the product to gain maximum consumer allegiance.

Advertising agencies identify and refine core advertising messages.

• *Identifying the advertising's target audience.* The target audience is that group of people or firms to whom the core advertising message will be meaningful. It is the audience that can be expected to take some sort of action as a result of having received the core advertising message.

Advertising agencies identify target audiences.

• *Determining how the target audience and the core advertising message will be brought together.* It must be decided how the core advertising message will be delivered to the target audience. This is the general question of the selection of appropriate, targeted advertising media.

Advertising agencies determine how target audiences and core advertising messages can be brought together through advertising media.

• *Developing the tone of voice of the advertising.* Advertising varies widely in its tone of voice. It may be declamatory, strident, argumentative, assertive, straightforward, refined, remote, or even cool. Each advertising campaign must assume the tone of voice that is appropriate both to its core advertising message and to its target audience.

Advertising agencies develop the tone of voice appropriate to individual advertising campaigns.

These four specific advertising strategies define *what* will be said to *whom, when* it will be said, and *how.* These advertising strategies are the templates with which specific advertising programs are formed. Strategic planning is the first of the basic services that advertising agencies always perform for their clients.

Step 4. Create advertisements. Once advertising strategies have been developed and both advertiser and agency agree to them, the agency proceeds to create the finished advertisements.

• First, advertising ideas are developed in rough executional form. These early advertising ideas should be completely compatible with all of the advertising strategies. That is, the rough executions of advertising ideas must express the core advertising idea; they must be compatible with the target audience; they must be capable of delivering the core idea to the target audience through advertising media; and they must be compatible with the tone of voice with which the advertiser wishes to convey its advertising messages.

• An important part of the development of advertising ideas is the determination of the media that will best present them. The development of the advertising usually is geared to the advertising medium in which the final advertising will most likely appear. Sometimes a particular execution of a particular idea dictates the final advertising medium choice. But, in any event, the working through of advertising ideas in rough media formats is the beginning of the process through which advertisements are finally developed.

  • The agency then decides which of several rough advertisements are to be presented to the advertiser.

  • The rough advertisements must then be approved by the advertiser. Once they are approved, the advertiser authorizes the agency to proceed to final production within an agreed-upon budget.

  • The advertisements are then produced in final form.

Step 5. Develop media programs. A plan of advertising placement will have been developed by the agency, before or at the time the creative work is initiated. This plan will identify the advertising media and specific individual units that will be purchased to reach the target audience. The plan will also include an advertising placement timetable. This timetable will indicate exactly how the advertising budget will be expended, by units of media, over time. The entire plan will be submitted by the agency to the advertiser for approval and expenditure authorization.

Step 6. Negotiate contracts for the placement of advertisements in advertising media. Following the approved media plan, the agency will execute contracts for space and time, negotiating for favorable media rates.

Step 7. Verify and pay media bills. As the advertising actually appears or "runs" in advertising media, the advertising agency receives bills for the advertising. The agency verifies that the advertising has, in fact, appeared as the bills reflect, then bills the advertiser. Finally, the agency pays the advertising media.

This review of the advertising process indicates the respective roles of both advertiser and agency. Most advertisers retain responsibility for setting marketing goals and basic marketing strategy while depending heavily on an advertising agency (or agencies) to provide the four basic services—strategic advertising planning, advertisement creation, advertising placement, and billing/paying—as described in the foregoing paragraphs.

Additional Advertising Agency Services

Many agencies provide other services in addition to the basic four, including marketing research, sales promotion planning, public relations and

7

publicity, package design, direct mail marketing, yellow pages service, sales meetings arrangements, merchandising, and other kinds of peripheral advertising services. Although only the largest agencies are likely to offer a full list of such services, most agencies try to provide some additional services beyond the basic four, in order to keep pace with competition and to broaden their revenue base. When an agency says that it offers "full service," it means that it offers the four basic services, plus at least several of the additional services listed earlier.

Some agencies that offer some or all of these additional services as part of their basic service to the advertiser are compensated for them under their agreed-on compensation arrangement. However, most agencies expect to receive additional compensation when they are asked to provide some or all of these extra services to their clients.

Other Sources of Advertising Services

Specialist Advertising Agencies

In addition to the full-service, general-line advertising agencies, there are also agencies that specialize in particular kinds of advertising: recruitment, help-wanted, medical, classified, industrial, financial, direct-response, retail, yellow pages, theatrical/entertainment, investment, travel, and so on.

Specialization occurs in such fields for a variety of reasons. Often, as in recruitment advertising, for example, specialized media or media uses are involved that require knowledge and expertise not ordinarily found in a general-line agency. In other cases, such as medical or industrial advertising, the subject is technical and requires that writers and artists have training in order to write meaningful advertising messages about it.

Such specialist advertising agencies are also usually "full-service," in that they offer all four of the basic advertising agency services in their area of specialization—plus other, peripheral advertising services related to their area of specialization.

Limited-Service Advertising Agencies

Some advertising agencies limit the amount and kind of service they offer. Such agencies usually offer only one or two of the four basic services. For example, although some agencies that specialize in "creative" also offer strategic advertising planning service, their basic interest is in the creation of advertising. Similarly, some "media-buying services" offer media planning service but concentrate on media buying, placement, and billing.

When the advertiser chooses to use limited-service advertising agencies, it must assume some of the advertising planning and coordination activities that are routinely handled by the full-service advertising agency. Thus, the advertiser who uses limited-service agencies usually takes greater responsibility for the strategic planning function, gives greater strategic direction to specialist creative or media agencies, and exercises greater control over the product of these specialized agencies, ensuring that their separate activities are well-ordered and -coordinated.

Non-Advertising Agency Suppliers

Many non-advertising agency suppliers can help the advertiser prepare advertising. Some advertisers, especially those who believe their advertising activities to be too infrequent or on too small a scale to justify the use of a full-fledged advertising agency, avail themselves of the services of these non-advertising agency suppliers.

Perhaps the most numerous of the non-advertising agency suppliers of advertising are the media themselves. Newspapers will help advertisers design advertisements that are to be typeset by the publication ("pub set"). Some magazines accept "pub set" advertising if type specifications are included with the order. Many radio stations will help with the preparation of radio copy and supply staff announcers, standard sound effects, and production facilities. Many television stations will help with the preparation of copy and provide staff announcers and production facilities. Direct-mail houses will help in the preparation of direct-mail pieces and in the selection and testing of lists.

It is often convenient and relatively inexpensive for an advertiser to use such media services. However, there are two major disadvantages. First, because media usually do not provide professional copywriting service, the advertiser must often depend on the help of novices and amateurs. Second, the use of one medium for creative help commits the advertiser to the use of that media facility, eliminating an objective appraisal of all available media, as would be routinely provided by most advertising agencies.

In addition to the media, there are a variety of non-advertising agency suppliers that specialize in the physical preparation of creative materials, usually for local use. These suppliers—typically small, one- or two-person operations—are often inexpensive and convenient. Whether they can supply the professional expertise available from a full-fledged advertising agency is for the advertiser to decide.

In-House Advertising Agencies

Finally, some advertisers choose to set up an advertising agency function within their company. Sometimes the in-house advertising agency is established to provide the four basic advertising agency functions. It may also specialize in one or more advertising functions, such as planning and creating advertising or media planning, buying, billing, and paying. Advertisers who choose this option believe that the in-house agency can provide services equal to or better than those available from full- or limited-service agencies. In addition, some advertisers believe that they can provide such advertising services to themselves at a lower cost than would be charged by an outside agency.

In sum, after deciding that it needs the services of an advertising agency, the advertiser must then decide what kind of advertising agency is best for its needs: a full-service advertising agency (either general or specialist), a limited-service agency, a non-agency supplier of advertising agency services, or an in-house agency.

This book will assume that the advertiser has decided on a full-service advertising agency, be it general or specialist. This does not imply a bias against limited-service advertising agencies, in-house agencies, or non-agency suppliers. Indeed, much of what follows is directly applicable to the search for the latter kinds of agencies. However, advertisers who believe they should or can depend on non-full-service suppliers of advertising tend to be special cases, which must be dealt with individually.

For example, advertisers who can use limited-service suppliers usually are relatively large companies with strong internal advertising staffs often supplemented by a limited-service *de facto* in-house agency. Such internal staffs often are (or can become) expert in adapting their specific advertising service needs to the characteristics and peculiarities of outside, limited-service suppliers. It is difficult to generalize about these relationships. At the other extreme, small and sporadic advertisers tend to depend on non-agency suppliers, which fulfill their specialized and limited advertising needs.

Advertising Accounts That Advertising Agencies Don't Want

Many advertisers assume that there will always be advertising agencies eager to win their advertising account. Although this is usually the case, advertisers should be aware that there are some accounts that many, if not most, advertising agencies are not particularly interested in handling.

First, agencies do not want accounts that they believe will be unprofitable. Advertising agency compensation is generally determined in one of two ways. (This topic is covered in considerable detail in Chapters 9 through 12.) In the traditional method of agency compensation, a 15 percent commission is granted to the agency by the advertising media against gross media bills. Under this system, if a media bill is $10,000, representing time or space purchased by the agency on behalf of its client, the medium bills the agency for $10,000; the agency bills the client $10,000; the agency remits $8,500 to the medium; and the agency keeps $1,500 from the transaction to compensate it for its services. (Although the "traditional" commission allowed by the media to advertising agencies is 15 percent, the trend in recent years has been to lower the rate actually paid by advertisers to a level below 15 percent or to replace the flat rate with a scale of rates that decreases as media billings increase. See Chapter 10.)

The second system of agency compensation is the fee method, which has become increasingly popular in recent years. Under the fee method, the agency and client negotiate a fee that will compensate the agency for its services. A great many variations of this approach have evolved, but all have two characteristics. First, the agency and client negotiate an agency compensation that differs from the agency compensation that would be yielded by the "traditional" 15 percent agency commission. Second, the agency rebates commissions earned if the negotiated fee yields an agency compensation that is less than the earned commission, or the agency bills the client for additional compensation if the fee yields a higher level of income than that thrown off by earned commissions. Negotiated fees are especially popular with advertisers whose business is either not advertising dependent or requires extensive agency contacts with dealer, franchise, or trade organizations in behalf of the advertising program. Also, negotiated fees are popular with very small advertisers who require more service than commissions earned on their account will pay for.

An unprofitable advertising account is likely to be one in which many individual advertisements must be created and placed at relatively low media cost per insertion. An unprofitable account may also be one in which there is a relatively small advertising budget and in which the advertiser insists on the commission method of compensation. An unprofitable advertising account is likely to be one in which the advertiser insists on staffing and service levels that exceed the commission compensation but resists additional fee compensation. An unprofitable advertising account is, in summary, usually an account that does not fairly compensate the agency, either by fee or commission, for the totality of work that is required in servicing the account.

Many agencies are reluctant to solicit advertising accounts that have the reputation of being difficult to handle because of the manner in which finished advertising ideas and advertising work are evaluated. Agencies are also reluctant to deal with advertisers who have a reputation for making capricious and unprofessional demands for the continuous revision and reworking of advertising materials.

Finally, agencies are wary of advertisers who impose a *de facto* "If I make money, you make money" philosophy on the relationship. Such advertisers cheerfully agree to whatever compensation arrangement the agency proposes. Then if the advertised product—a direct-response record/cassette offer or an independently produced movie, for example—prospers, the agency receives payment. If the product fails, however, the agency is left high and dry, with only the courts to turn to.

An advertiser must, of course, be what it is: It would be naive to suggest that an advertiser should change the nature of its business or that it should change the way it runs its business to suit prospective advertising agencies. Nevertheless, the advertiser should understand that to the extent that its business has characteristics that will not appeal to all advertising agencies, it may have to settle for less than first-rate agency service when it selects an agency.

When a company begins to spend any appreciable amount of money to advertise, it is natural that it begin to consider whether or not it should have an advertising agency. In making this decision the company must know what advertising agencies do and what they do not do. In addition, the fledgling advertiser should become informed about the different kinds of advertising agencies that have evolved, as well as the several variations on the basic full-service agency that have come into existence. With this information and understanding, the advertiser can then decide whether it really needs an advertising agency or whether some sort of limited-service, in-house, or non-advertising agency supplier will fulfill its needs.

Should You Change Your Advertising Agency?

In Chapter 1, we assumed that the advertiser is looking for a full-service agency for the first time. However, this situation obtains only for new companies or for established companies that, because of growth or a change in marketing policy, wish to alter their advertising methods. Most advertisers who set out to choose a full-service advertising agency do so as they are dissatisfied with their current agency and want a new one.

The replacement of an advertising agency should not be undertaken lightly. It is costly in terms of executive time; it is bound to produce an awkward transition period that may last for many months; and, in the end, the new agency may be no better than the one it replaced. The advertiser should be sure that the dissatisfaction with the current agency cannot be alleviated by changes in agency staffing, compensation, or the amount and kind of agency service; or by other changes that will remove the cause of dissatisfaction without the trauma of an agency change.

Experience indicates that there are eleven common sources of advertiser dissatisfaction with advertising agencies. Five of these sources of dissatisfaction almost inevitably require a change in agency, but six of the eleven causes usually can be eliminated by forceful advertiser or agency action.

Sources of Advertiser Dissatisfaction That Necessitate Agency Change

Disagreement on Basic Marketing Strategy

When an advertiser fires its advertising agency, the most common reason publicly given is that the client and agency could not agree on basic marketing strategy. In fact, this reason is so frequently given that it may simply be a convenient way to save face for both advertiser and agency in a potentially embarrassing situation.

Certainly, however, many situations arise in which the advertiser and agency have a genuine difference of opinion about how to market a product. Because the advertiser must ultimately determine the basic marketing goals and strategy for its product or service, the actual disagreement with basic marketing strategy often arises on the agency side. There are two main areas of disagreement.

- The agency may not believe that it can create effective advertising under the advertiser's marketing strategy.
- The agency may believe that there is a better marketing strategy than the one held by the advertiser.

Whatever the situation, a "disagreement over basic marketing strategy" implies a genuine disagreement between advertiser and agency, in which the agency does not accept the client's fundamental marketing view of the product.

If both parties remain adamant, the relationship should be dissolved. The advertiser is then free to seek out an agency that will accept its view of how the product is to be marketed and advertised.

Advertiser Growth

It is not uncommon for an advertiser's business to grow so big that its first advertising agency simply cannot keep pace with its burgeoning service requirements. This situation has developed, in recent years, with imported cars from Japan and several fast-food chains. The typical pattern is that the advertiser starts on a relatively small scale and in a relatively limited geographic area. As sales and market coverage expand, the advertising agency also expands. But when a modest regional advertising account becomes a national account of considerable size, the agency is simply not able to offer the scope and quality of professional service required.

The advertiser needs sophisticated media planning and buying, especially of national television. It needs well-founded and broad-scale market analysis and research. In order to satisfy a variety of individual marketing substrategies, it needs a depth of creative service to provide a variety of different campaigns. An account that had originally been easy for the agency to handle has gradually become extraordinarily complex and demanding.

Typically, there is an interim period during which the agency tries to catch up with its client's growth. The agency may be reorganized during this period; it may establish offices in new geographic areas; often it extends its staffing by bringing in experienced specialists from larger advertising agencies.

Sometimes the agency grows successfully with its client, but more often it does not. As a result, the client becomes increasingly dissatisfied with the performance of the agency. At the same time, the client becomes aware that there are larger full-service agencies that are already staffed and organized to service its account comfortably and professionally.

Finally, the advertiser makes the reluctant decision to move to one of these larger agencies—for the sake of its business and despite the historic ties with the original agency.

Agency Growth

Of course, this process may work in reverse. An agency may open its doors with one or more relatively small clients. However, if the agency is good (and lucky), it may grow even though the original clients—through no fault of the agency's or the clients'—stay relatively small.

As the disparity in size develops, the agency may well decide to stay with its original client, even though it has become unprofitable to do so. The relationship may continue in this way, with the advertiser very satisfied with its successful and growing agency. The agency maintains the relationship for reasons of loyalty, in spite of its inadequate profitability.

Trouble may develop, however, if the agency has the opportunity to solicit another, larger account in the same product or service category. Many agencies have found it difficult to forego the opportunity to trade up from a small, unprofitable or marginally profitable account to a larger, potentially very profitable account, no matter what the history of their current client relationship.

Competitive Conflict

Sometimes an agency must resign an account because a competitive conflict develops. Competitive conflict is most likely to become an issue in three distinct situations.

An Agency Merger. When two advertising agencies merge into a single agency, competitive conflicts often exist between the clients of the merging agencies. Typically, one of the competitive accounts, usually the smaller,

15

is resigned by the merged agency. Agencies usually assume that such a resignation will be the normal upshot of such mergers. One of the first questions that potential agency merger partners discuss is the degree to which such conflicts exist between their clients. If there are extensive potential conflicts, a proposed merger may not be viable.

An Advertiser Merger.   When two advertisers merge, the result may be competitive conflict that affects their advertising agencies. The merged company may have brands that compete with other clients of the agency. Unlike the situation created when agencies merge, advertisers are unlikely to pay much attention to the competitive effect that the merger of their companies will have upon the agencies. If conflict results from the merger, one or more of the agencies will usually be discharged.

A Client's New Product Development or Acquisition.   An agency may service two clients whose businesses, once quite different, have become sharply competitive. This may occur because of overlapping new product development or acquisition. The new or acquired product may become so important to the advertiser that it feels uncomfortable with an agency that handles the business of a competitive company, even if a direct product conflict is not involved. For example, an agency might handle a major cigarette brand for one tobacco company and a fast-growing soft drink brand recently acquired by a second tobacco company. One or both of these tobacco companies may decide that it is undesirable to deal with an agency that handles business that competes with an important division or subsidiary, even though no direct competitive conflict is involved. Thus, the agency may lose one of its accounts because of secondary or corporate conflict.

Product conflict seems much less likely to be a cause of dissatisfaction among business or technical advertisers than among packaged goods advertisers. Perhaps this is because advertising is relatively less important to such advertisers or because specialist agencies in these fields have perfected methods of isolating potential conflicts in agency operations. In any event, one is much less likely to hear that a new agency has been chosen in the business or technical fields because of account conflict.

The Advertiser–Agency Relationship Wears Out

Sometimes the advertiser and agency simply grow tired of each other. The advertiser no longer perceives excellence in the work of the agency. The agency no longer seems able to respond with fresh and enthusiastic creativity to the problems of the advertiser. Vitality gradually seeps out of the relationship and neither side seems able to rouse itself to overcome this tendency.

Whatever reason given publicly for the inability of the agency and advertiser to work together, the real reason is that the relationship has simply worn out. This is the reason that when an advertising account is put into review and the incumbent agency is invited to join in the competition, it rarely retains the business. When the advertiser–agency relationship turns sour, it is best to look for a new agency.

In all of the preceding situations the advertiser's dissatisfaction is overt. When there is disagreement on marketing strategy, one partner has outgrown the other, competitive conflict occurs or the relationship wears out, the advertiser almost inevitably will seek a new agency.

There are, however, other sources of advertiser dissatisfaction that do not always require that the incumbent agency be fired and a new agency appointed.

Agency Problems That May Be Resolved

Compensation Disagreements

A basic cause of dissatisfaction in the advertiser–agency relationship is often agency compensation. The advertiser may feel that it is paying the agency too much. The advertiser may feel that if it received just the agency service wished or needed, and no more, total payments to the agency might be reduced without reducing the effectiveness of the overall advertising program. On the other hand, the agency may believe that it is required to give more service than it is paid for, and therefore it is operating at a lower level of profit than it wishes or at a loss.

The basic problem is that it is very hard to put a labor rate value on an advertising idea. There is no time frame within which advertising ideas are created. An idea of great potential advertising leverage may occur to its creator in almost fully developed form in a matter of moments. Yet, mediocre advertising ideas may require time-consuming meetings, extensive revisions, and several research evaluations.

Thus, the labor rate value of second-rate advertising ideas is likely to exceed the labor rate value of superior advertising ideas, possibly by a substantial amount. Furthermore, a superior advertising idea is likely to have far greater economic value than a second-rate advertising idea.

17

The historic resolution of this compensation problem has been the system of 15 percent commission on media billings. No one, as far as is known, has ever been able to justify the commission system in either economic or labor rate terms. The system is simply a classic compromise: As long as they can make a profit, agencies are willing to work for an amount that advertisers are willing to pay, regardless of the amount of actual work involved. Advertisers accept the commission system in the hope that the friction-free environment thus created will lead to a strong and steady stream of advertising ideas.

The appeal of the commission system has deteriorated in recent years for a variety of reasons.

- Some agencies, including many with a good track record for producing superior advertising ideas, are willing to work for less than 15 percent.
- Some accounts generate such large media billings that no agency—no matter how service-oriented or how productive of superior advertising ideas—could justify compensation based on the full 15 percent commission.
- Advertisers have become increasingly cost conscious and increasingly confident that they can, in fact, get adequate advertising for less than full commission.

As reduced commission and labor-based fee agency compensation arrangements have grown in importance and have been widely publicized, they have led to dissatisfaction with traditional compensation arrangements in a significant number of advertiser–agency relationships. Advertisers fire agencies because they are unwilling to work at a specified level of compensation. Agencies resign accounts because they believe that they are being unfairly compensated.

One major food company recently changed its agency compensation arrangements from commission to labor-based fee, without making an agency change. However, it discovered that a great deal of work was required to find an equitable fee basis of agency compensation. For years, that company and its agencies had defined what the agency would do—in breadth of creative presentations, media analysis and backup work, research, and client entertainment—on a day-to-day, situation-specific basis. The result was that different brands received distinctly different levels and kinds of agency service. The service seemed to depend largely on past practices and on the personalities of the client and agency people working on the brand at any given time. The problem was solved, but it was more difficult than expected.

The company had to specify exactly what agency service *all* brands required. Deciding on a standard level of service—in the creative, media, research, and account management areas—that everyone could agree on was not easy. But it was accomplished, and the fee was then based on direct agency costs for providing this standard level of service, plus agency overhead and profit. Although many client and agency people were quite certain that the new arrangement couldn't work, all were required to try it for a year. After some difficult moments in the early shakedown period, both sides eventually came to agree that the new arrangement was both better and more professional than the old.

Clearly, then, advertisers and agencies must agree on agency compensation, for the relationship depends on such agreement. This is, in principle, a negotiable issue. Reasonable people should be able to decide on a satisfactory level of compensation. If they are not able to do this, the advertiser–agency relationship will dissolve.

The fact that so many advertiser–agency relationships founder on the agency compensation issue suggests two conclusions.

1. Neither the fee nor the commission system of compensation will, *in their simplest forms*, provide a solution to most agency compensation problems. Each advertiser–agency relationship must develop a unique solution to the problem of agency compensation, which is based on a variety of factors that are unique to each advertiser–agency relationship. These unique factors include the size of the advertising budget, the nature of the advertising program, advertiser specification of agency tasks, the importance of new product development in the relationship, the role that advertising research plays in the relationship, and so on.

2. Any agency compensation plan will be improved if it includes incentive payments for the agency based on the quality or productivity of the agency's creative work. If it is hard to put a labor rate value on an advertising idea, as noted above, this suggests that labor cost should not be the sole basis for agency compensation.

The agency *should* be fairly compensated for the work that the client requires it to perform, but the question of agency compensation should not end there. If the creative work of the agency is very sales productive, the agency should receive extra compensation. This possibility encourages the agency to produce superior work on a routine basis. It also directs questions of agency compensation away from agency labor costs and toward a continuous, objective appraisal of the value of the agency's work to the advertiser.

Agency compensation is negotiable. It is an issue that can be addressed at any time in an advertising–agency relationship. However, when the advertiser selects a new agency it is a question that *must* be addressed. Agency compensation should be addressed and decided upon *before* the final agency selection is made. The general topic of agency compensation, as well as its particular importance in agency selection, will be discussed in detail in Chapters 9 through 12.

Inadequate Agency Staffing

Advertising agencies are supposed to staff their accounts with competent people. The account executives should have some experience in the product or service for which advertising is to be prepared. The creative and media and research people should be competent professionals and should also have some background experience with the account product or service. The agency is responsible for making sure that these people will work well together as a team to produce and place advertising that will achieve the advertiser's marketing goals.

The advertiser has some responsibilities, too. It should familiarize the agency people who work on its account with the intricacies and peculiarities of its business and its products or services. The advertiser must also specify exactly what, if anything, it expects from the agency beyond basic advertising service.

Finally, the agency is responsible for finding people who can develop comfortable and professional relationships with client peers. The "chemistry" that exists between agency and client representatives is absolutely crucial to the well-being of the advertiser–agency relationship. And it is the agency's responsibility to make sure that this chemistry develops in a way that is acceptable to the client, not only at the time that the advertising account is assigned to the agency, but throughout the life of the relationship as well.

An advertiser may become dissatisfied with the personnel who have been assigned to its account. Before deciding to look for another agency that will supply "better" people, the advertiser should identify exactly what it is about the incumbent agency personnel that is unsatisfactory.

If the agency people are not professional, they can always be replaced with those who are. If the agency people have not achieved good chemistry with the advertiser's people, they can be replaced with people who will. Often enough, however, the problem with agency personnel derives from the advertiser's failure to give them adequate information about its business or its failure to tell them exactly what it wishes them to do, or both. If the advertiser has failed to fill its responsibility to the agency, it is unlikely that an agency change will solve the problem.

If the advertiser knows what has led to the dissatisfaction with agency personnel, it is entirely possible that the problem can be solved without resorting to an agency change.

Agencies survive by keeping very close tabs on the effectiveness with which their people serve their clients. This is a function of agency management. Often agency personnel problems have little or nothing to do with the excellence of the advertising work that the agency is producing for its clients. One very successful advertising agency president attributes the success of his agency to its willingness to change management supervisors on any account that develops any discernible client dissatisfaction.

Look, my management supervisors are responsible for three things: good advertising, good client relations, and profit. We know how to do good advertising and we know how to make a profit—all our management supervisor has to do is follow the rules and he's home free. But it's up to him to keep our clients happy. And it's up to me to know when he isn't. An unhappy client means a new management supervisor in our shop. We don't fool around with changes on the crew: we change at the top, and all the management supervisors around here know it.

Inadequate Advertising Ideas

Sometimes advertisers are dissatisfied with their advertising agency because the advertising ideas that the agency produces seem ineffective. Perhaps the advertising does not seem to generate enough sales; perhaps it does not perform well on copy tests or other research measures; or perhaps the advertiser, its salespeople, or its customers do not like the advertising.

It is certainly the prerogative of the advertiser to assess the quality of the advertising ideas presented by the advertising agency. If the agency consistently presents ideas that are unsatisfactory, the advertiser will be disgruntled and dissatisfied. The crucial question is, of course, whether the advertiser has made clear how it intends to evaluate advertising ideas. The more clearly stated the basis of evaluation—judgmental, research-based, or whatever—the more likely the agency is to develop effective advertising that the advertiser will like.

If evaluations of advertising ideas are capricious or irrational, it will be hard for the agency to know exactly what kinds of ideas will be acceptable. Of course, it may be argued that the advertiser may set whatever criteria it wishes for the evaluation of advertising, capricious or not, rational or not.

Advertising professionals tend to agree that advertising works best when it is developed in an explicit framework based on knowledge (of market, consumer, competition, etc.) and when this knowledge has been translated into overt strategic plans. Although agency relationships may be terminated because advertising ideas are inadequate, it is unlikely that an advertiser will ever find a satisfactory advertising agency unless it makes explicit exactly what it means by a "good" advertising idea.

When the advertiser thinks that it is getting nothing but inadequate advertising ideas, it may be in its best interest to explore exactly what it means by this before concluding that the only solution is to replace the advertising agency.

It is up to the agency, of course, to convince its clients that its advertising is likely to be successful in the marketplace. Many advertisers judge agency work less on its intrinsic merit than on the ability of the agency to explain why it will work. So it is important for the agency to think through the rationale for the work that it presents and to do this on a consistent, day-to-day, and month-to-month basis. After all, if the agency doesn't know why the advertising is likely to be effective, who will?

Thus, when the advertiser thinks that it is getting nothing but inadequate advertising ideas, it may be because it failed to make its criteria clear, or because the agency cannot demonstrate why its advertising will succeed. Frequently, it is possible to resolve advertiser concerns about advertising excellence simply by focusing on these two issues.

Inadequate Agency Service

A somewhat more ephemeral concern is the advertiser's complaint that it simply is not getting adequate service from its advertising agency. Inadequate agency service can have a wide variety of meanings.

In the first place, agency service may reflect the size of the advertising account. The service a client receives depends fundamentally on the amount of revenue that it generates for the agency. Small advertising accounts receive less service than large advertising accounts. This usually means that the account gets fewer agency people, more junior people, and relatively less time. From the agency side, this is simply a matter of economics. The smaller the compensation from an account, the less the service that can be made available to it.

The only solution to the advertiser's complaint of inadequate service is for advertiser and agency to agree on a level of compensation so the advertiser receives the desired quantity and quality of service and the agency receives the profit that it feels it must have.

The same kind of service dissatisfaction may develop with large accounts. Advertisers may be disgruntled because they believe that they are not getting as much service as they deserve—or need—given the level of commission or fee income the agency receives. The basic question is in defining exactly how much "service" is required from the agency. This problem has two facets.

First, most advertisers receive considerably more service than they realize. Advertisers rarely see or are aware of *any* traffic, production, accounting, or art personnel who work on their accounts. Advertisers rarely see *all* of the research, media, creative, or merchandising people that work on their accounts. In fact, about the only agency employees that advertisers ever see are those assigned to their accounts, along with the senior creative, media, and perhaps research people who work on the business. So, the first issue in identifying the proper service level for larger accounts is that advertisers almost certainly do not know the total amount of service they already receive from the agency.

Second, there is the question of establishing just what level of service the advertiser *should* have, though this may be hard to figure out for four reasons.

1. First is the question of the quality of agency personnel assigned to the account. One or two truly professional and service-oriented account executives can seem to provide a very high level of service as much through their verve and style as for the true content of their accomplishments. Such service "aces" may, in fact, provide relatively little more effective service than their less charismatic peers, but in the assessment of service the residual impression in the advertiser's mind may be more lasting than the basic facts.

2. There is, in addition, the question of exactly what the notion of service has come to mean in the minds of individual advertiser employees. Often the idea of agency service becomes confused with a concept of catering to individual advertiser employees. Does the agency entertain enough? Does the agency entertain in the choicest places? Does the agency deliver good tickets to shows and sporting events? Does the agency entertain the marketing people at an annual Christmas party or at a summer sports day?

In short, the concept of agency service, which should be concerned only with everything necessary to deliver a superior advertising product, may be misinterpreted by some advertiser employees to mean the provision of a wide range of personal amenities and accommodations.

3. Agency service quality depends not only on *what* is delivered to the advertiser, but also *when* it is delivered. An advertiser may be totally satis-

23

fied with the service received, but the difficulty may arise in the promptness of the service.

As advertising agencies have grown large and become bureaucratized, the overall quality of the service available to advertisers has improved dramatically. This is, in fact, undoubtedly the reason that big advertising agencies tend, inexorably, to grow larger. Whether this excellent service is always delivered as it is needed—to the proper recipients and within a context of an understanding of the advertiser's problems—is another matter. Often a service "ace" on the agency side as account manager or supervisor will know how to cut through whatever bureaucratic inertia and fog may exist in order to revitalize the sense of service that the advertiser feels its agency must develop.

4. In the final analysis, the definition of what service the agency should provide *must* be supplied by the advertiser. Frequently, when an advertiser complains that it is not receiving adequate service from an agency, it has never specified exactly what it means by adequate service. It is left to the agency to decide what it must do to adequately satisfy the advertiser.

If the agency must guess what kinds of service the advertiser wants, it is almost inevitable that it will guess wrong at least part of the time. One of the curious reasons why many advertisers do not provide more explicit direction for their agencies is that they apparently fear that by doing so they may limit the total range of service and/or accommodation that the agency provides. Such advertisers apparently feel that they will get more for their money by letting the agency infer their service needs as broadly as possible rather than by imposing any restraints on the process. However, this implies that the advertiser does not know its real service requirements and that it is willing to settle for an agency definition of them.

The only way for an advertiser to be fully satisfied with agency service is for the advertiser to define what it wants and then discuss this with agency management. This is not a topic on which an advertiser need be arbitrary and inflexible. It's likely that the best agency service arrangements come about when agency and advertiser work out solutions to the problem jointly. Certainly, an agency should not be fired for "poor service" until both agency and advertiser have tried to determine what the advertiser's real service needs are.

Top Management Indifference

It is almost inevitable that the chief executive officers of advertiser and agency will meet periodically. Presumably, they meet to discuss the relationship between the two organizations and the status and prospects of the business to which these organizations are dedicated. The advertiser top-manager's interest in these meetings varies in intensity in proportion to his business's dependence on advertising. It also varies with his involvement in the advertising process and with how much he feels he has in common with the agency president or chairperson.

These two persons will have met at the original solicitation of the account by the agency, or, if the client chief executive is new, they will have met at an indoctrination presentation by the agency. Certainly, at this original meeting, or shortly thereafter, the two parties should have reached an understanding of their roles in the relationship. Will the client chief executive officer review advertising materials before they are released? How often does the advertiser chief executive wish to review the total performance of the agency, if at all? What kinds of reports does the advertiser expect from the agency chief executive, and should they be verbal or written? How frequently should these officers meet, and in what setting, with what other participants, and for what exact purpose?

There must be some sense of the relative roles of the top managers in every advertiser–agency relationship, no matter how formal the actual relationship. If there is no such agreement, the agency is vulnerable to the advertiser top manager's charges that he or she is being ignored by agency management and that agency performance is below par because its top management is not sufficiently involved with the agency work.

Agencies are fired because of such lack of agency top management attention, whether real or imagined. It is not uncommon for substantial accounts to move to agencies where a close relationship exists between client and agency chief executive officers.

This move need not happen if the agency chief executive intentionally works to make sure that a healthy and substantial contact is maintained with the advertiser's chief executive.

The chief executive officer of one large food manufacturer has this to say about the attention he gets from the president of one of his advertising agencies.

That fellow calls me for lunch every two months or so. If I'm busy, he suggests dinner, and if I say no to that, he asks if he can come to see me at 8 A.M. some morning. He keeps at me. It's not that I don't want to meet with him. Of course, I do. I have other things to do, but he keeps at me till we meet. And, also, when we do meet, he gives me the impression he knows our business, knows it well, and has a real interest in it. He's *well informed*. I don't know how he does it; it must be a trick of some sort. He can't be that well informed about *all* of his clients, but he pulls it off, and I give him credit for that. And somehow or other, I always come out of our meetings with some kind of new idea, too. That guy is really good, and I'm certain his agency is, too.

Agency Changes because of Faltering Sales

As we have seen, advertisers may discharge their agencies for a variety of reasons. Up until this point we have been discussing advertiser dissatisfaction with the relationship itself rather than with the end result of the marketing process.

Just as the managers of professional baseball teams are fired—sometimes without logical reason—when their teams do not win consistently, so, too, advertising agencies are fired when the sales of assigned products falter, or do not reach the sales goals.

Unless all the other product marketing activities are effective, there is always some irrationality—if not downright hypocrisy—involved whenever an agency is fired because brand sales are not satisfactory. Of course, the agency may have gone stale on the brand. There may seem to be little agency inclination to make any attempt to solve the sales problem. And, of course, the agency may have become defensive about the quality of its creative work and its other contributions.

Even if all these charges are true, firing the agency is not the only solution. At the least, the agency may be given an opportunity to form a new account team or a new creative team or teams to work on the business. The agency also may be given a period of grace within which to improve its work and, presumably, its client's sales. For even if the advertiser does decide that it can no longer tolerate its present agency, there is no guarantee that another agency will find the golden fleece that will lead to a genuine increase in sales. In fact, there is little evidence that an agency change, in the absence of other marketing reforms, is likely to resuscitate a faltering sales curve.

The Agency Fires the Client

So far in this chapter, the assumption has been made that the advertiser is about to initiate an agency search because of dissatisfaction with some aspect of its agency's performance. However, advertisers do not have the exclusive prerogative to terminate advertiser–agency relationships. Agencies also resign accounts for a variety of reasons, most of which have been described or suggested in the preceding sections. Agencies resign clients occasionally for matters of principle when basic differences on marketing strategy arise. Agencies resign clients when competitive conflict forces them to do so, when they believe themselves to be inadequately compensated, when they outgrow the client, when personal chemistry becomes so bad that there is no choice but to resign, and when the opportunity for a larger competitive account presents itself, with the promise of substantial increases in billing and profits.

When the agency resigns, the advertiser must seek out a new agency. Similarly, as we have seen, there are other circumstances in which it is almost inevitable that the advertiser will seek a new advertising agency. When an irreconcilable difference over marketing strategy occurs, the advertiser must seek a new advertising agency, unless it switches to the agency view and changes its marketing conception of its product. If the advertiser outgrows its agency, it will almost always look for a new one. If there is an impossible conflict, a new agency must be found.

Caution in Changing Agencies

In some circumstances, as we have seen, the advertiser–agency relationship may be troubled, but this does not mean that the only solution to the problem is to find a new agency. It may be possible to reach an amicable and reasonable settlement in respect to agency compensation. It may be possible to improve agency staffing or to find ways to stimulate new and superior advertising ideas. Agency service may be improvable. Agency management interest may be revivable. Sales may be improved as a result of new creative work from new creative teams, and a general shoring-up in the marketing activities for the faltering brand.

Before an agency change is made, it is certainly important to explore the possibility of improving the existing relationship. There are several good pragmatic reasons for the advertiser to take this point of view.

1. First of all, the fault in the relationship may lie with the advertiser rather than with its agency. No advertiser should ever change an agency unless it is sure that the agency is at fault. If the advertiser is primarily at fault, no agency—regardless of its record or the persuasiveness of its case histories—is likely to resolve the underlying causes of advertiser dissatisfaction with the advertiser–agency relationship. In other words, a new agency cannot, in this situation, guarantee better performance than the incumbent agency.

2. Most advertising agencies handle most of their accounts with modest success, if not distinction. Therefore, an advertiser might wonder, before firing the agency, just what it is about its account and the way it is handled that leads to its dissatisfaction. Is the account more difficult, is its

marketing conception more sophisticated, or are its people smarter or more demanding? In short, if its agency can do good work for *some* people, why can it not do good work for *it*? It makes good business sense to know the answer to this question before going on to another agency.

3. An agency change is disruptive and wasteful. Inevitably, time is wasted. Old agency services, some of which the advertiser may not even have been aware of, must be instituted in the new agency. New agency people must be found to do jobs that now seem complex and elusive, yet previously seemed to be done effortlessly by the veteran employees of the old agency. In the process of changing agencies, business opportunities are lost. Furthermore, a new kind of advertiser–agency relationship evolves that is usually somewhat better than the old one in some ways, somewhat worse in others, and, on balance, usually neither much better nor much worse.

Veteran marketing executives, especially those who have changed agencies more than once in their careers, apparently prefer not to change advertising agencies if they can possibly avoid it. The price, in terms of professional time lost and organizational disorientation suffered, usually seems to them to be too high. They would prefer, it appears, to negotiate, to compromise, and to find a basis of reconciliation that will provide better service from their existing agency—rather than to hope that an outside agency may do better.

A senior marketing executive in a cosmetics firm recently asked me to help him identify four or five agency creative people with proven track records in the development of cosmetics copy. He said:

The agency has run dry. I'm simply not getting the kind of creative work that will move our brands ahead. It looks as if the only thing for me to do is to change agencies, but I don't want to do that. That is just a great big pain. It takes three months to do, and then another three months passes before I'm any better off than I was before. The whole thing is a crap shoot. So I think, "How can I keep the old agency and make it do better?" One way is to find superior creative people and suggest to the agency that they should look them over, because I think they are the kind of people who might solve our copy problems. I don't know; maybe the agency would be smart enough to take the hint and save me all that trouble.

Despite such sentiments, trade press records document the continuous turnover of advertising agency accounts. Many of these turnovers are unavoidable. Though theoretically avoidable, many are not amenable to negotiation. In these cases, the advertiser must find a new advertising agency. The process of finding a new agency is covered in Part 2.

The Advertising Agency Search

Beginning to Look for
an Advertising Agency

No one knows for sure how many advertising agencies there are in the United States. One reason for this is that many firms provide some limited kind of advertising service, but relatively few firms are full-service advertising agencies. For example, the Department of Commerce has estimated that there are 20,000 business enterprises in the United States that may be called "advertising agencies," at least in a restricted meaning of that phrase. The *Adweek Agency Directory for 1988/89* lists "more than 8,000 advertising agencies, public relations firms and media buying services." The widely used *Standard Directory of Advertising Agencies* lists a total of 3,588 firms that proclaim themselves to be advertising agencies.

Yet an authoritative listing of advertising agencies—that provided by *Advertising Age* in its annual U.S. Agency Income Profiles—included only 533 firms in 1989. (See Exhibits 3-1 and 3-2. Firms 1-500 reproduced here.) Although 533 firms is a far cry from the 20,000 firms estimated by the Department of Commerce, the 8,000 plus listed in the *Adweek Directory,* or the 3,588 listed in the *Standard Directory,* it is at least clear that every one of these 533 organizations is a *bona fide* advertising agency in one of the senses used in this book. (See Chapter 1.)

It seems almost certain that each of these available lists—that available from the *Standard Directory,* that produced by *Adweek,* and that developed by *Advertising Age*—must include one or more agencies that would satisfy every advertiser's need. The advertiser's problem is to determine just how to identify the advertising agency that is just right from the many that are available. How should the advertiser proceed to accomplish this objective?

Exhibit 3–1.   The Top 100 United States Advertising Agencies in 1990—Ranked by Worldwide Gross Income

U.S.-based agencies by domestic gross income

Rank 1989	1988		Agency, headquarters	U.S. gross income 1989	1988	% chg	U.S. billings 1989	1988	U.S. employees 1989	1988
1	1	✓	Young & Rubicam, New York	409.5	372.8	9.9	3,114.8	2,791.8	4,066	4,717
2	3	✓	Saatchi & Saatchi Advertising Worldwide, New York	395.2	326.3	21.1	2,778.9	2,209.6	1,760	1,975
3	2	✓	BBDO Worldwide, New York	373.6	340.5	9.7	2,656.0	2,414.3	3,375	3,598
4	4	✓	Backer Spielvogel Bates Worldwide, New York	310.7	282.7	9.9	2,158.0	1,964.2	1,370	1,322
5	5	✓	Ogilvy & Mather Worldwide, New York	305.1	281.1	8.6	2,104.4	1,874.9	2,636	2,732
6	9	✓	DDB Needham Worldwide, New York	302.9	244.4	24.0	2,386.3	1,929.3	3,025	2,786
7	7	✓	Leo Burnett Co., Chicago	288.8	263.4	9.6	1,945.3	1,765.0	2,222	2,083
8	6	✓	Foote, Cone & Belding Communications, Chicago*	280.5	273.7	2.5	1,871.2	1,825.8	2,832	3,081
9	8	✓	J. Walter Thompson Co., New York	266.5	257.5	3.5	1,851.0	1,787.9	2,484	2,427
10	10	✓	Grey Advertising, New York	240.7	227.9	5.6	1,605.3	1,520.3	2,067	2,015
11	11	✓	D'Arcy Masius Benton & Bowles, New York	232.3	209.6	10.8	2,055.3	1,794.2	2,341	2,288
12	12	✓	Lintas:Worldwide, New York	224.9	201.7	11.5	1,499.9	1,345.4	1,781	1,917
13	13	✓	McCann-Erickson Worldwide, New York	209.1	197.0	6.1	1,394.8	1,314.0	1,767	1,889
14	14	✓	Bozell Inc., New York	155.4	150.3	3.4	1,165.0	1,090.0	1,643	1,665
15	16		Wells, Rich, Greene, New York*	132.5	125.1	5.9	883.0	833.9	860	829
16	15		NW Ayer Inc., New York	128.8	127.8	0.8	859.1	946.7	980	1,337
NR	NR	✓	Campbell-Mithun-Esty, Minneapolis (BSBW)	115.9	105.6	9.8	859.8	783.0	1,155	1,227
17	17	✓	Ketchum Communications, Pittsburgh	112.9	102.1	10.6	854.9	726.0	1,229	1,360
18	20		Chiat/Day/Mojo, Venice, Calif.	106.0	77.0	37.7	785.0	603.5	935	812
19	18	✓	Ross Roy Group, Bloomfield Hills, Mich.	97.7	85.2	14.6	651.1	568.1	1,046	955
20	19		Della Femina, McNamee EWDB, New York	87.8	84.4	4.0	728.7	660.5	851	991
21	21		Scali McCabe Sloves, New York	79.0	71.8	9.9	590.3	559.7	717	706
NR	NR	✓	Tracy-Locke, Dallas (BBDO)	55.6	54.5	1.9	404.6	408.0	625	654
NR	NR	✓	AC&R Advertising, New York (S&SAW)	45.8	44.2	3.6	369.1	355.6	436	469
22	25		Admarketing Inc., Los Angeles	44.9	40.4	11.1	252.0	224.5	133	138
NR	NR	✓	Ogilvy & Mather Direct Response, New York (O&M)	44.2	41.0	7.8	305.0	272.0	488	471
23	27		W.B. Doner, Southfield, Mich.	44.2	37.0	19.4	309.0	268.7	523	500
24	22		Lowe Marschalk, New York	44.0	46.0	(4.3)	297.3	305.0	363	400
25	23	✓	Hill, Holliday, Connors, Cosmopulos, Boston	43.9	43.1	2.0	293.1	287.4	408	421
26	28		Earle Palmer Brown, Bethesda, Md.	40.1	36.2	10.8	310.5	271.1	469	446
NR	NR	✓	Wunderman Worldwide, New York (Y&R)	38.7	39.9	(2.9)	262.4	266.1	352	295
27	26		Jordan, McGrath, Case & Taylor, New York	38.5	38.5	0.0	315.0	300.0	282	283
NR	NR	✓	McCaffrey & McCall, New York (S&SAW)	38.2	41.1	(6.9)	254.2	297.9	407	413
28	31		Telephone Marketing Programs, New York	37.8	29.6	27.9	252.1	197.1	716	651
29	30		Levine, Huntley, Schmidt & Beaver, New York	37.1	32.1	15.7	250.3	216.4	245	250
30	29	✓	Ally & Gargano, New York	37.0	34.4	7.6	316.0	295.2	230	220
31	24		Laurence, Charles, Free & Lawson, New York	34.6	41.5	(16.5)	275.2	302.0	322	334
32	39		Hal Riney & Partners, San Francisco*	33.8	23.0	46.7	225.0	200.0	238	183
33	38		TBWA Advertising, New York	33.2	23.1	43.8	221.6	154.1	265	165
34	33		Nationwide Advertising Service, Cleveland*	31.0	27.8	11.5	206.8	185.4	398	376
NR	NR	✓	Bernard Hodes Group, New York (DDB)	30.5	30.7	(0.6)	203.1	204.4	393	419
35	32		HDM, New York	30.3	28.6	6.1	247.3	228.9	373	277
NR	NR	✓	Ammirati & Puris, New York (BBDO,DDBN)	29.5	28.0	5.4	220.0	210.0	260	260
36	35		Tatham-Laird & Kudner, Chicago	27.6	26.0	6.0	230.1	217.0	254	285
37	34		Direct Marketing Group, New York	25.7	26.1	(1.5)	149.6	152.9	625	637
38	37		Warwick Baker & Fiore, New York	25.5	24.0	6.3	170.0	160.0	NA	NA
NR	NR	✓	Sudler & Hennessey, New York (Y&R)	24.6	20.6	19.6	164.0	137.2	215	193
39	40	✓	Evans Communications, Salt Lake City	24.0	22.1	8.5	160.0	147.5	356	336
NR	NR	✓	Rapp Collins Marcoa, Chicago (BBDO,DDBN)	23.8	23.7	0.3	226.0	236.3	340	328
NR	NR	✓	Fahlgren & Swink, Parkersburg, W. Va. (Lintas)	23.6	18.9	24.8	157.5	126.2	340	284
40	43	✓	Dailey & Associates, Los Angeles	23.3	19.6	18.4	155.2	131.0	196	185
NR	NR	✓	Cato Johnson Worldwide, New York (Y&R)	22.6	19.0	18.7	150.5	126.8	308	230
NR	NR	✓	Thompson Recruitment, Los Angeles (JWT)	21.6	16.7	29.5	144.0	111.0	360	260
41	42		Keller-Crescent Co., Evansville, Ind.	21.3	22.0	(3.4)	106.5	110.3	546	561
NR	NR	✓	Kallir, Philips, Ross, New York (DDB)	21.2	17.7	20.1	168.0	163.2	206	215
NR	NR	✓	Martin Agency, Richmond, Va. (SMS)*	21.1	16.9	24.4	140.5	113.0	225	195
NR	NR	✓	Doremus & Co., New York (BBDO)	20.9	25.6	(18.5)	148.0	181.0	249	305
42	44		Griffin Bacal, New York	20.7	18.4	12.3	162.7	143.9	177	176
43	49		Thomas G. Ferguson Associates, Parsippany, N.J.	20.6	16.9	22.1	120.7	102.1	120	110
44	55		GSD&M, Austin, Texas	20.2	15.3	32.1	150.8	124.1	234	171
45	41	✓	Bloom Cos., Dallas	20.0	22.1	(9.5)	168.2	182.6	255	263
46	54		Wyse Advertising, Cleveland	19.9	15.7	26.5	140.4	105.8	275	231
47	45		Geer, DuBois, New York	19.5	18.0	8.3	130.0	120.0	201	190
48	48	✓	Rosenfeld, Sirowitz, Humphrey & Strauss, New York	19.1	17.4	9.5	127.0	116.0	176	124
NR	NR	✓	Clarion Marketing, Greenwich, Conn.(DMB&B)	18.8	16.4	14.5	125.2	109.6	133	126
49	58		Richards Group, Dallas	18.7	15.1	24.3	125.1	101.4	194	166
NR	NR	✓	Kobs & Draft Advertising, Chicago (BSBW)*	17.7	13.7	29.8	116.9	90.2	146	136
50	47	✓	Rubin Postaer & Associates, Los Angeles	17.4	17.5	(0.6)	143.1	128.7	157	148
51	51		Ingalls, Quinn & Johnson, Boston	16.9	16.2	4.5	137.1	133.4	202	219
52	53	✓	Davis, Ball & Colombatto Advertising, Los Angeles	16.8	15.9	5.8	147.4	135.7	201	215
53	52	✓	Eisaman, Johns & Laws, Los Angeles	16.7	16.1	3.7	124.0	111.5	216	199
54	57		Weightman Group, Philadelphia	16.5	15.2	8.6	110.0	101.4	203	210
NR	NR	✓	Lavey/Wolff/Swift, New York (BBDO)	16.1	12.7	27.3	107.7	84.5	159	135
NR	NR	✓	Fallon McElligott, Minneapolis (SMS)	16.0	16.5	(2.9)	131.3	131.4	145	130

Source: *Advertising Age,* March 26, 1990, pp. S 14-15. Reprinted with permission from *Advertising Age.*
© Crain Communications, Inc.

Exhibit 3–1   (Continued)

Rank 1989	Rank 1988		Agency, headquarters	U.S. gross income 1989	1988	% chg	U.S. billings 1989	1988	U.S. employees 1989	1988
55	63		Bayer Bess Vanderwarker, Chicago*	16.0	13.0	23.0	105.0	84.9	159	150
NR	NR	✓	Lewis, Gilman & Kynett, Philadelphia (FCB)	15.9	17.3	(7.8)	106.0	115.0	210	218
56	59	✓	Cramer-Krasselt, Milwaukee	15.8	14.0	13.4	108.6	96.5	188	181
57	56		William Douglas McAdams Inc., New York	15.6	15.2	2.5	107.0	107.0	163	159
58	61	✓	Avrett, Free & Ginsberg, New York	15.5	13.3	16.7	128.8	112.0	102	75
58	66		Long, Haymes & Carr, Winston-Salem, N.C.	15.5	12.0	29.4	103.5	83.6	205	181
NR	NR		Klemtner Advertising, New York (S&SAW)	15.5	12.0	29.2	121.1	90.2	135	125
60	46	✓	McKinney & Silver, Raleigh, N.C.	15.4	17.9	(13.9)	102.9	119.5	107	122
NR	NR	✓	Medicus Intercon International, New York (DMB&B)	14.8	12.6	17.6	133.5	113.5	160	158
61	85		Weiden & Kennedy, Portland, Ore.*	14.7	9.3	58.1	98.0	62.0	98	65
62	135		Tarlow Advertising, New York	14.6	6.1	139.9	109.2	39.9	74	27
63	62	✓	Lois/GGK New York, New York	14.4	13.3	7.9	99.7	99.4	95	95
64	126		Partners & Shevack, New York	14.2	6.5	118.5	144.5	52.0	102	65
65	50		Tucker Wayne/Luckie & Co., Atlanta	14.1	16.7	(15.5)	104.5	119.7	172	187
66	71	✓	Asher/Gould Advertising, Los Angeles	14.0	11.0	26.9	93.0	75.0	99	91
67	75		Margeotes Fertitta & Weiss, New York	13.7	10.6	29.1	88.8	68.7	95	75
NR	NR	✓	Creswell, Munsell, Fultz & Zirbel, Cedar Rapids, Iowa (Y&R)	13.6	11.9	14.3	90.5	79.0	196	190
68	60	✓	Cabot Communications, Boston	13.1	13.7	(5.0)	91.2	95.5	125	161
NR	NR		Rumrill-Hoyt, Rochester, N.Y. (S&SAW)	13.0	11.3	14.6	86.6	75.6	168	166
69	82	✓	DCA Advertising, New York	12.8	9.8	30.9	94.0	71.2	142	137
NR	NR	✓	M.E.D. Communications, Woodbridge, N.J. (DMB&B)	12.7	14.2	(10.0)	83.6	93.0	100	120
70	64	✓	Towne, Silverstein, Rotter, New York	12.5	12.5	0.0	83.0	83.0	45	45
71	76	✓	QLM Associates, Princeton, N.J.	12.4	10.5	18.0	82.3	69.7	96	87
71	79	✓	Barry Blau & Partners, Fairfield, Conn.	12.4	10.3	20.3	101.2	85.3	128	118
73	78	✓	Carmichael Lynch, Minneapolis	12.1	10.5	15.7	87.9	76.2	190	160
73	83		Martin-Williams, Minneapolis	12.1	9.8	23.5	100.0	83.0	133	115
75	67		Al Paul Lefton Co., New York	11,900.0	11,700.0	1.7	70,000.0	68,000.0	153	149
76	69		Henderson Advertising, Greenville, S.C.	11,858.0	11,272.0	5.2	80,669.0	75,148.0	106	104
77	68		Cole & Weber, Seattle	11,855.9	11,573.5	2.4	89,908.6	93,264.6	145	156
78	81	✓	Valentine Radford, Kansas City, Mo.	11,798.1	10,195.9	15.7	79,381.1	70,286.5	153	147
79	70	✓	Gross Townsend Frank Hoffman, New York	11,755.6	11,267.4	4.3	78,374.9	75,153.3	120	109
80	NA	✓	Lois/GGK Chicago, Chicago	11,400.0	NA	NA	80,000.0	75,000.0	105	91
81	174		Lord Einstein O'Neill & Partners, New York	11,356.0	4,558.7	149.1	78,593.7	32,712.8	89	78
82	97	✓	Deutsch Inc., New York	11,266.3	8,315.9	35.5	75,108.9	54,984.6	105	77
83	77		Russ Reid Co., Pasadena, Calif.	11,100.0	10,500.0	5.7	74,000.0	70,000.0	155	155
84	65	✓	Miller Advertising Agency, New York	11,000.0	12,500.0	(12.0)	73,500.0	83,500.0	160	190
85	80		Noble Communications, Springfield, Mo.	10,993.0	10,294.0	6.8	80,093.9	76,777.2	206	190
86	74	✓	Liggett-Stashower, Cleveland	10,950.0	10,609.0	3.2	72,400.0	70,300.0	140	135
87	99		Bentley, Barnes & Lynn, Chicago	10,747.4	8,221.0	30.7	71,649.2	54,806.9	172	136
88	101		Slater Hanft Martin, New York	10,593.0	8,099.0	30.8	69,935.0	53,274.0	68	56
NR	NR		Poppe Tyson, New York (Bozell)	10,550.0	8,600.0	22.7	75,000.0	64,000.0	116	124
89	91		Mullen Advertising, Wenham, Mass.	10,457.2	8,831.2	18.4	69,714.8	58,904.4	86	79
90	86	✓	Carraliello-Diehl & Associates, Irvington-on-Hudson, N.Y.	10,450.0	9,190.0	13.7	69,413.0	60,993.0	106	94
91	73	✓	William Cook Agency, Jacksonville, Fla.	10,300.4	10,697.0	(3.7)	72,065.3	76,462.7	132	147
NR	NR		Wahlstrom & Co., Stamford, Conn. (FCB)*	10,142.1	8,708.7	16.5	67,614.0	58,058.0	142	128
92	219		Kern/Mathai Direct Mail Advertising, Santa Monica, Calif.	10,100.0	3,160.0	219.6	15,750.0	6,100.0	15	10
93	107		DMCA Direct, St. Louis*	10,035.0	7,758.7	29.3	61,345.0	47,085.0	420	390
NR	NR	✓	Frank J. Corbett, Chicago (BBDO)	9,860.3	9,786.0	0.8	65,768.0	65,272.6	80	78
NR	NR	✓	Brouillard Communications, New York (JWT)	9,738.9	9,951.5	(2.1)	64,958.5	66,376.4	79	85
94	162		Messner Vetere Berger Carey Schmetterer, New York	9,733.2	4,933.8	97.3	72,098.0	49,338.0	52	28
95	127*	✓	Kresser, Craig/D.I.K., Los Angeles	9,621.6	6,471.2	48.7	67,721.6	44,620.6	78	55
96	102	✓	Devon Direct Marketing & Advertising, Malvern, Pa.	9,600.0	8,000.0	20.0	82,000.0	66,200.0	76	46
97	87		Meldrum & Fewsmith, Cleveland	9,500.0	9,031.0	5.2	62,000.0	60,200.0	111	108
98	93	✓	Ackerman, Hood, & McQueen, Oklahoma City	9,103.5	8,679.0	4.9	64,190.0	60,992.0	114	121
99	103	✓	Lawler Ballard, Norfolk, Va.	9,094.0	7,886.0	15.3	60,656.0	52,598.0	159	151
100	88		Burrell Communications Group, Chicago	9,049.6	9,001.8	0.5	60,330.4	60,012.3	110	108

Notes: Dollars are in thousands. NR indicates agency not ranked. Initials in parenthesis indicate the parent company in which the subsidiaries' figures are included. ✓ indicates the agency received signature of an independent accountant verifying figures supplied in *Advertising Age*. * indicates that gross income and/or total volume figures are *Advertising Age* estimates.

Exhibit 3–2.   United States Advertising Agencies Ranked 101 to 500 in 1990—Ranked by Worldwide Gross Income

U.S.-based agencies by domestic gross income

Rank 1989	1988		Agency, headquarters	U.S. gross income 1989	1988	% chg	U.S. billings 1989	1988	U.S. employees 1989	1988
101	128	✓	Hesselbart & Mitten Advertising, Fairlawn, Ohio	9,003.6	6,462.7	39.3	60,251.9	43,127.8	107	88
102	92	✓	Miller Meester Advertising, Minneapolis	9,000.0	8,790.0	2.4	60,030.0	58,629.3	110	99
103	72	✓	Keye/Donna/Pearlstein, Los Angeles	8,751.2	10,834.7	(19.2)	61,370.3	72,267.4	76	100
104	89	✓	Keyes Martin & Co., Springfield, N.J.	8,750.0	9,000.0	(2.8)	58,000.0	58,000.0	90	100
105	84	✓	Dorritie & Lyons, New York*	8,713.4	9,396.4	(7.3)	55,000.0	50,000.0	57	55
106	98	✓	Elkman Advertising, Bala Cynwyd, Pa.	8,671.0	8,300.0	4.5	57,820.0	55,328.0	110	110
107	95		McAdams, Richman & Ong, Bala Cynwyd, Pa.	8,545.0	8,600.0	(0.6)	56,977.0	57,500.0	87	90
NR	NR	✓	Saatchi & Saatchi Direct, Rochester, N.Y. (S&SAW)	8,538.0	8,857.0	(3.6)	54,911.0	59,148.0	115	120
108	96	✓	Marketing Resources, Overland Park, Kan.	8,517.9	8,337.2	2.2	56,900.0	55,700.0	160	178
109	124		Jack Levy & Associates, Chicago	8,474.1	6,530.5	29.8	56,500.6	43,540.5	82	51
110	230	✓	Gearon Hoffman Conlon & Nye, Boston	8,310.0	3,027.4	174.5	40,678.0	20,040.8	34	33
111	122		Berenter Greenhouse & Webster, New York	8,301.0	6,600.0	25.8	60,076.0	48,022.0	52	48
112	109		Martin Marshall Jaccoma Mitchell, New York	8,250.0	7,500.0	10.0	55,000.0	50,000.0	53	50
113	NR		FKB direct, Nashville*	8,208.8	NA	NA	54,504.0	NA	190	NA
114	106	✓	Colle & McVoy, Minneapolis	8,191.3	7,795.2	5.1	58,382.5	57,712.8	118	141
115	94		Richardson, Myers & Donofrio, Baltimore	8,135.0	8,654.0	(6.0)	60,980.0	59,282.0	99	101
116	112	✓	Bader Rutter & Associates, Brookfield, Wis.	8,119.8	7,126.4	13.9	54,142.8	50,309.8	116	111
117	108	✓	Dugan/Farley Communications, Upper Saddle River, N.J.	8,046.4	7,653.3	5.1	52,576.9	50,026.2	164	147
118	120		Goodwin Dannenbaum Littman & Wingfield, Houston	7,982.4	6,606.6	20.8	56,550.0	49,400.0	96	72
119	113		Goodby, Berlin & Silverstein, San Francisco*	7,920.0	7,050.0	12.3	52,800.0	47,000.0	55	55
120	150		Fogarty & Klein, Houston	7,913.9	5,540.1	42.8	51,812.0	36,936.2	68	48
121	36	✓	LGFE Inc., New York	7,722.0	24,590.0	(68.6)	59,290.0	NA	92	129
122	145	✓	Grace & Rothschild, New York	7,717.0	5,754.0	34.1	51,450.0	38,360.0	43	34
123	105		William R. Biggs/Gilmore Associates, Kalamazoo, Mich.	7,705.0	7,820.0	(1.5)	51,162.0	52,300.0	100	110
124	131	✓	North Castle Partners, Stamford, Conn.	7,690.0	6,310.0	21.9	62,110.0	50,404.0	78	65
125	146	✓	Berline Group, Birmingham, Mich.*	7,667.7	5,749.0	33.4	63,389.9	48,593.0	56	42
126	137	✓	Mendoza, Dillon & Asociados, Newport Beach, Calif.	7,632.5	6,006.0	27.1	50,010.0	39,340.0	46	52
127	140	✓	Babbit & Reiman Advertising, Atlanta	7,600.0	5,900.0	28.8	53,901.0	41,850.0	62	41
128	100	✓	MARC Advertising, Pittsburgh	7,542.1	8,220.0	(8.2)	50,306.0	54,811.0	95	105
129	90	✓	Christopher Thomas/Muller Jordan Weiss, New York	7,540.0	8,990.0	(16.1)	50,444.5	71,150.0	104	110
130	110	✓	Eric Mower & Assoc., Syracuse, N.Y.	7,476.3	7,429.2	0.6	49,866.8	50,451.4	103	117
131	123	✓	Yellow Pages Marketing Services, Mequon, Wis.	7,472.0	6,566.0	13.8	49,824.0	43,775.0	140	140
132	116		Ruhr/Paragon, Minneapolis	7,435.8	6,847.0	8.6	55,500.0	51,100.0	80	86
133	130	✓	Robert A. Becker EWDB, New York	7,400.0	6,363.0	16.3	50,000.0	42,422.0	62	65
134	111	✓	Levy, King & White, Buffalo	7,383.0	7,275.0	1.5	47,260.0	48,500.0	124	127
135	149	✓	Saugatuck/FKB, Westport, Conn.*	7,353.6	5,585.8	31.6	47,676.0	40,352.7	41	34
136	178	✓	Sutton Healthcare Group, New York	7,300.0	4,300.0	69.8	52,300.0	28,800.0	96	64
137	125	✓	Borders, Perrin & Norrander, Portland, Ore.	7,261.0	6,518.0	11.4	48,434.0	41,674.0	91	90
NR	NR	✓	Chapman Direct Advertising, New York (Y&R)	7,226.0	7,745.0	(6.7)	48,198.0	51,650.0	62	70
138	114	✓	Mintz & Hoke, Avon, Conn.	7,162.0	7,040.0	1.7	47,750.0	46,933.0	88	98
139	133	✓	Lally, McFarland & Pantello, New York	7,000.0	6,250.0	12.0	54,400.0	50,400.0	80	91
139	132	✓	Malone Advertising, Akron, Ohio	7,000.0	6,300.0	11.1	76,355.5	70,021.0	133	110
NR	NR		Hoffman York & Compton, Milwaukee (S&SAW)	6,838.1	5,948.9	14.9	40,227.1	33,383.6	110	101
141	119	✓	Smith/Greenland, New York	6,800.0	6,712.0	1.3	45,086.8	44,040.0	68	71
142	144	✓	Frankenberry, Laughlin & Constable, Milwaukee	6,780.0	5,775.0	17.4	45,200.0	38,500.0	74	67
143	134	✓	Eisner & Associates, Baltimore	6,760.0	6,113.0	10.6	52,196.7	46,005.0	70	70
144	115	✓	Henry J. Kaufman & Associates, Washington*	6,750.0	6,975.0	(3.2)	45,000.0	46,500.0	70	65
145	121	✓	Grant/Jacoby, Chicago	6,700.0	6,600.0	1.5	66,022.0	65,680.0	95	95
146	164	✓	HutchesonShutze, Atlanta	6,684.4	4,850.0	37.8	44,717.0	33,274.1	72	68
147	117	✓	Waring & LaRosa, New York	6,640.0	6,800.0	(2.4)	53,600.0	50,200.0	60	60
148	138	✓	McFarland & Drier, Miami	6,500.0	6,000.0	8.3	43,000.0	40,000.0	65	62
149	136	✓	Edwin Bird Wilson, New York	6,439.9	6,076.6	6.0	49,326.9	44,876.6	66	82
NR	NR		Anderson & Lembke, Stamford, Conn. (C/D/M)	6,400.0	6,000.0	6.7	45,000.0	40,000.0	50	35
150	143	✓	VanSant, Dugdale & Co., Baltimore	6,390.0	5,810.9	10.0	42,600.0	38,739.3	75	63
151	148	✓	Eric Ericson & Associates, Nashville	6,326.8	5,598.3	13.0	42,199.9	37,340.3	94	86
152	104	✓	J. Richard Smith Ltd., Bethpage, N.Y.	6,319.0	7,840.0	(19.4)	41,257.1	40,150.0	36	36
NR	NR	✓	Albert Frank-Guenther Law, New York (FCB)	6,255.0	8,284.0	(24.5)	41,718.0	55,258.0	57	72
153	129	✓	Arnold Advertising, Boston	6,175.5	6,402.1	(3.5)	41,497.0	42,447.4	110	112
154	160	✓	Paolin & Sweeney Advertising, Cherry Hill, N.J.	6,100.0	5,000.0	22.0	33,700.0	24,200.0	58	49
155	118	✓	Campbell & Wagman, Los Angeles	6,053.0	6,774.0	(10.6)	45,730.0	58,494.0	51	53

Source: *Advertising Age,* March 26, 1990, pp. S 15, 16, 18. Reprinted with permission from *Advertising Age.* © Crain Communications, Inc.

Exhibit 3–2. (Continued)

Rank 1989	Rank 1988		Agency, headquarters	U.S. gross income 1989	1988	% chg	U.S. billings 1989	1988	U.S. employees 1989	1988
156	172	✓	Northlich Stolley LaWarre, Cincinnati	5,924.0	4,642.0	27.6	39,514.0	30,935.0	75	69
157	154	✓	Lord, Sullivan & Yoder, Columbus, Ohio	5,893.5	5,341.0	10.3	45,349.4	43,842.9	83	90
158	142	✓	Abelson-Taylor, Chicago	5,852.3	5,838.4	0.2	44,669.0	43,954.0	75	75
159	139		Buntin Advertising, Nashville	5,834.4	5,989.0	(2.6)	38,896.1	39,926.9	103	100
160	170	✓	Greenstone Rabasca Roberts, Melville, N.Y.	5,827.8	4,676.8	24.6	39,531.8	31,194.0	93	53
161	156	✓	Price McNabb Advertising, Asheville, N.C.	5,739.1	5,269.9	8.9	42,115.6	41,590.6	88	88
162	141	✓	Jayme Organization, Cleveland	5,734.1	5,856.2	(2.1)	45,428.8	46,658.2	91	105
163	147		Ad Team, North Miami Beach, Fla.	5,660.0	5,660.0	0.0	0.0	NA	49	46
164	171	✓	Great Scott Advertising, New York	5,646.8	4,659.1	21.2	35,449.0	29,251.9	49	52
165	155		Jordan Tamraz Caruso Advertising, Chicago	5,604.0	5,338.5	5.0	37,360.0	35,589.8	80	75
166	152		Kolon, Bittker & Desmond, Troy, Mich.	5,500.0	5,400.0	1.9	31,941.0	30,000.0	94	101
NR	NR		Conill Advertising, New York (S&SAW)	5,470.0	5,550.0	(1.4)	36,450.0	37,000.0	57	73
167	163		Hameroff/Milenthal/Spence, Columbus, Ohio	5,373.0	4,900.0	9.7	41,974.3	38,372.0	115	121
168	151		Lauer Markin Gibbs, Maumee, Ohio	5,262.6	5,475.1	(3.9)	34,404.4	35,866.3	97	93
169	157		Cox Landey & Partners, New York	5,250.0	5,250.0	0.0	35,000.0	35,000.0	30	30
170	176	✓	Trahan, Burden & Charles, Baltimore	5,200.0	4,500.0	15.6	47,400.0	40,800.0	65	62
171	153		Newmark Posner & Mitchell, New York	5,111.0	5,369.0	(4.8)	30,093.4	30,873.0	NA	NA
172	159	✓	Winius-Brandon Advertising, Bellaire, Texas	5,092.0	5,019.7	1.4	39,351.2	39,525.1	43	43
173	167		Stone & Simons Advertising, Southfield, Mich.	5,091.9	4,743.2	7.3	32,048.3	31,560.5	48	48
174	NR		Donahoe & Purdhit, Rosemont, Ill.	5,000.0		NA	5,800.8	NA	11	NA
175	181	✓	Doe-Anderson Advertising Agency, Louisville	4,991.7	4,213.3	18.5	37,220.3	31,106.4	77	69
176	168	✓	Leonard Monahan Lubars & Partners, Providence, R.I.	4,849.9	4,820.5	0.6	32,348.8	32,152.6	55	70
177	240		Puskar Gibbon Chapin, Dallas*	4,812.5	2,812.5	71.1	38,500.0	22,500.0	35	30
178	168	✓	Haddon Advertising, Chicago	4,800.0	4,725.0	1.6	43,347.5	43,011.8	47	50
179	192	✓	Gilbert, Whitney & Johns, Whippany, N.J.	4,745.0	3,875.0	22.5	32,600.0	26,000.0	71	56
180	179	✓	Simons Michelson Zieve, Troy, Mich.	4,680.6	4,275.0	9.5	32,800.0	29,000.0	67	74
181	189	✓	Pedone & Partners, New York	4,553.8	3,961.9	14.9	30,361.2	26,412.5	29	25
182	218	✓	Dorland Sweeney Jones, Philadelphia	4,550.2	3,166.9	43.7	31,944.5	22,967.6	57	51
183	161		Taylor Brown Smith & Perrault, Houston	4,528.9	4,952.5	(8.6)	30,203.0	33,028.2	53	55
184	237	✓	Girgenti, Hughes, Butler & McDowell, New York	4,520.0	2,850.0	58.6	30,100.0	19,000.0	42	26
185	276		CHC Advertising, Woodridge, N.J.	4,500.0	2,250.0	100.0	30,000.0	15,000.0	25	14
186	175		Kenneth C. Smith Advertising, La Jolla, Calif.*	4,500.0	4,500.0	0.0	30,000.0	30,000.0	32	32
187	169	✓	Gray Kirk & Evans, Baltimore	4,483.9	4,700.0	(4.6)	40,300.0	39,165.0	70	69
188	182		Stone, August, Baker Communications Cos., Troy, Mich.	4,361.2	4,183.5	4.2	30,878.1	30,373.0	52	55
189	205	✓	Aydlotte & Cartwright, Atlanta	4,356.0	3,485.0	25.0	22,000.0	17,000.0	52	40
190	252		Publicis Inc., New York	4,291.0	2,666.0	61.0	31,683.0	19,040.0	NA	NA
191	264	✓	Bonneville Media Communications, Salt Lake City	4,254.1	2,448.9	73.7	25,327.3	14,355.4	130	120
192	186	✓	Marketing Support, Chicago	4,251.4	4,020.0	5.8	37,348.0	36,891.4	65	62
193	250	✓	Keroff & Rosenberg Advertising, Chicago	4,244.6	2,698.8	57.3	35,133.4	29,863.4	65	57
194	191		Wolf Blumberg Krody, Cincinnati	4,227.0	3,902.0	8.3	28,180.0	26,013.3	55	51
195	216	✓	Larkin, Meeder & Schweidel, Dallas	4,206.4	3,230.4	30.2	28,040.4	21,253.6	45	40
196	195		Harris & Drury Advertising, Ft. Lauderdale	4,202.4	3,750.8	12.0	28,021.0	25,010.0	58	50
197	194		Lohmeyer Simpson Communications, Morristown, N.J.	4,200.0	4,050.0	3.7	28,000.0	27,000.0	37	38
198	241	✓	Zwiren Collins Karo Trusk & Ayer, Chicago	4,200.0	2,800.0	50.0	30,000.0	24,000.0	30	22
199	194		Sawyer Riley Compton, Atlanta	4,176.6	3,761.7	11.0	27,044.0	24,497.8	46	41
200	203	✓	Karsh & Hagan, Englewood, Colo.	4,160.1	3,493.9	19.1	26,845.7	22,592.4	53	55
201	180	✓	Leslie Advertising Agency, Greenville, S.C.	4,123.8	4,267.9	(3.4)	27,944.1	30,110.5	70	61
202	256		Floathe & Associates, Bellevue, Wash.	4,081.5	2,599.4	57.0	28,332.3	18,579.3	64	44
203	196		Stern Advertising, Pepper Pike, Ohio	4,050.0	3,750.0	8.0	27,000.0	25,000.0	50	45
204	197	✓	Reimel Carter Advertising, Philadelphia	4,048.0	3,741.0	8.2	26,181.0	24,212.0	40	38
NR	NR		Baxter, Gurian & Mazzei, Beverly Hills, Calif. (BBDO)	4,000.0	2,650.0	50.9	26,000.0	17,675.5	45	30
205	210	✓	Lowe Tucker Metcalf, New York*	4,000.0	3,400.0	17.6	27,000.0	23,000.0	58	50

Exhibit 3-2. (Continued)

Rank 1989	1988		Agency, headquarters	U.S. gross income 1989	1988	% chg	U.S. billings 1989	1988	U.S. employees 1989	1988
206	177		McKinney Inc., Philadelphia	3,960.0	4,328.0	(8.5)	30,616.0	31,216.0	69	80
207	173	✓	Shelly Berman Communicators, Westerville, Ohio	3,956.9	4,569.4	(13.4)	26,356.6	30,476.9	69	87
208	198		Marquardt & Roche, Stamford, Conn.	3,943.3	3,738.0	5.5	25,996.0	24,656.3	40	45
209	188		Cranford Johnson Robinson Woods, Little Rock, Ark.	3,927.7	3,969.0	(1.0)	26,197.4	26,473.4	72	68
210	190	✓	Juhl Agency, Mishawaka, Ind.	3,908.6	3,905.0	0.1	30,026.5	29,163.0	67	69
NR	NR	✓	Botto, Roessner, Horne & Messinger, New York (Ketchum)*	3,897.9	1,191.6	227.1	25,986.0	7,944.0	38	38
211	204		Sullivan Higdon & Sink, Wichita, Kan.	3,883.6	3,490.1	11.3	33,715.0	27,654.3	55	53
212	193	✓	Tromson Monroe Advertising, New York	3,830.0	3,765.0	1.7	30,200.0	29,500.0	40	40
213	202		Lawrence Butner Advertising, New York	3,816.2	3,649.0	4.6	25,239.6	24,337.8	44	35
214	222	✓	Davidoff White Good, Westport, Conn.	3,800.5	3,070.8	23.8	25,337.0	20,473.0	52	52
215	199		Stan Merritt Inc./Advertising, New York	3,797.5	3,717.0	2.2	28,500.0	28,000.0	20	18
216	166	✓	Lyons Inc., Wilmington, Del.	3,750.7	4,751.8	(21.1)	25,108.3	30,573.9	67	77
217	225		Houston Advertising, Boston	3,742.0	3,057.0	22.4	24,958.0	20,382.0	43	43
218	221	✓	Goldfarb Hoff & Co., Southfield, Mich.	3,713.2	3,108.5	19.5	24,255.8	20,350.0	44	41
219	214	✓	McDougall Associates, Peabody, Mass.	3,705.0	3,255.0	13.8	24,700.0	21,700.0	33	31
220	226	✓	Marcus Advertising, Cleveland	3,704.9	3,055.5	21.3	24,869.1	22,373.4	53	48
221	187		Franklin Spier Inc., New York	3,699.8	3,988.1	(7.2)	24,677.5	26,600.6	43	43
222	255		Food Group, New York	3,611.5	2,616.8	38.0	23,498.0	17,075.8	22	23
223	302	✓	Fessel, Siegfriedt & Moeller Advertising, Louisville	3,602.8	1,908.3	88.8	13,272.2	9,758.8	36	30
224	185	✓	Decker Rickard, Glastonbury, Conn.	3,600.0	4,048.0	(11.1)	24,000.0	27,000.0	47	47
224	279	✓	McConnaughy Barocci Brown, Chicago	3,600.0	2,200.0	63.6	33,000.0	20,250.0	35	23
224	NR		Ted Thomas Associates, Philadelphia*	3,600.0	NA	NA	24,000.0	NA	50	45
227	234	✓	Brady Co., Menomonee Falls, Wis.	3,590.0	2,942.3	22.0	23,945.3	20,575.8	63	61
228	227	✓	Gardner Communications, San Francisco	3,555.0	3,045.0	16.7	23,700.0	20,300.0	32	30
229	206		Dudnyk Co., Horsham, Pa.	3,550.0	3,480.0	2.0	23,700.0	23,200.0	44	45
230	207		Warren/Kremer Advertising, New York	3,550.0	3,475.0	2.2	19,600.0	19,465.0	39	39
231	208	✓	Frank C. Nahser Inc., Chicago	3,539.3	3,446.4	2.7	24,949.5	25,234.7	47	47
232	260		Forsythe Marcelli Johnson Advertising, Newport Beach, Calif.	3,530.4	2,530.8	39.5	23,088.1	16,553.6	40	33
233	215	✓	Rubin Reid Noto & Ehrenthal, New York	3,490.0	3,251.0	7.4	33,470.0	31,867.5	36	34
234	158	✓	Vickers & Benson/FKQ, Buffalo	3,479.9	5,033.3	(30.9)	23,203.6	33,563.3	42	87
235	239	✓	Harris, Baio & McCullough, Philadelphia	3,477.1	2,818.3	23.4	23,181.3	18,795.8	23	21
236	258	✓	Kaufman & Maraffi Advertising, New York	3,461.5	2,544.0	36.1	22,547.4	16,700.0	24	18
237	211	✓	Kolesar & Hartwell, Minneapolis	3,453.4	3,373.4	2.4	23,022.5	22,500.5	45	44
238	213	✓	Salvati Montgomery Sakoda, Costa Mesa, Calif.	3,405.9	3,298.7	3.2	22,717.1	22,002.7	41	37
239	229	✓	Siddall, Matus & Coughter, Richmond, Va.	3,341.0	3,042.2	9.8	33,735.4	30,181.3	39	39
240	232		Hughes Advertising, St. Louis	3,314.0	3,010.2	10.1	21,678.1	19,729.3	43	39
241	267		Advertising Communications, Davenport, Iowa	3,300.0	2,400.0	37.5	22,770.0	16,970.0	63	55
242	261		Berenson, Isham & Partners, Boston	3,279.2	2,504.5	30.9	18,691.5	17,557.6	19	18
243	238		Gerber Advertising Agency, Portland, Ore.*	3,263.3	2,836.2	15.1	19,868.0	18,005.0	51	39
244	224		Potter Hazlehurst, East Greenwich, Conn.*	3,262.5	3,057.0	6.7	21,750.0	20,381.0	46	53
245	257	✓	Hallmark Advertising, Pittsburgh	3,259.0	2,571.0	26.8	17,880.0	17,137.0	49	48
246	242		Gumpertz/Bentley/Fried, Los Angeles	3,258.4	2,780.8	17.2	23,117.3	22,500.0	34	34
247	201		John Malmo Advertising, Memphis*	3,204.7	3,692.9	(13.2)	21,139.0	23,959.0	46	58
248	200		Kerker & Associates, Minneapolis	3,202.3	3,701.2	(13.5)	23,592.1	26,835.0	NA	46
249	235	✓	Clarity Coverdale Rueff Advertising, Minneapolis	3,200.0	2,900.0	10.3	20,845.0	19,700.0	29	23
250	220		Pihas, Schmidt, Westerdahl Co., Portland, Ore.	3,167.7	3,149.0	0.6	22,789.8	23,003.4	56	51
251	245		Stephan & Brady, Madison, Wis.	3,156.9	2,750.0	14.8	23,398.3	21,185.6	48	44
252	233		Advertising Works, Honolulu*	3,150.0	3,000.0	5.0	21,000.0	20,000.0	46	42
252	311	✓	Nash Direct, New York	3,150.0	1,806.0	74.4	21,003.2	12,042.4	35	14
254	271		Finnegan & Agee, Richmond, Va.	3,136.6	2,323.5	35.2	20,911.4	18,005.1	53	55
255	223		Healy-Schutte & Co., Buffalo	3,108.4	3,063.6	1.5	23,995.9	23,346.8	58	56
256	319		Lewis, Browand & Associates, Oakland, Calif.*	3,098.0	1,713.0	80.9	20,653.0	11,418.0	40	25

35

Exhibit 3–2. (Continued)

Rank 1989	Rank 1988		Agency, headquarters	U.S. gross income 1989	U.S. gross income 1988	% chg	U.S. billings 1989	U.S. billings 1988	U.S. employees 1989	U.S. employees 1988
257	236	✓	Sefton Associates, Grand Rapids, Mich.	3,081.5	2,857.0	7.9	20,441.0	19,060.0	49	47
258	246		Silverstone, Adkins & Breit, Stratford, Conn.*	3,072.1	2,746.8	11.8	20,242.8	18,108.5	17	17
259	183		Barnum & Souza, New York	3,070.6	4,115.1	(25.4)	27,370.5	36,493.9	35	38
260	272	✓	Fox MMJM Direct, New York	3,063.0	2,277.0	34.5	20,071.5	15,006.6	30	25
261	274	✓	Lockhart & Pettus, New York	3,057.0	2,261.0	35.2	20,380.0	15,073.0	32	33
NR	NR	✓	Blair Advertising, Rochester, N.Y. (BBDO)	3,025.9	3,756.4	(19.4)	20,173.0	25,042.5	44	52
262	263	✓	Fitzgerald & Co., Atlanta	3,006.7	2,490.7	20.7	21,615.5	16,710.5	29	21
263	278	✓	S.J. Weinstein Associates, New York	3,000.0	2,200.0	36.4	20,000.0	14,667.0	32	24
264	275	✓	Arian, Lowe & Travis Advertising, Chicago	2,924.8	2,260.4	29.4	20,072.7	15,742.2	44	34
265	285	✓	Wilson Sculley Associates, St. Louis	2,890.0	2,150.0	34.4	19,276.3	14,340.5	29	24
266	244	✓	Harris West Blaisdell Advertising, Minneapolis	2,836.3	2,750.0	3.1	17,856.0	20,260.0	28	36
267	251	✓	Hitchcock Fleming & Associates, Akron, Ohio	2,830.3	2,684.5	5.4	18,567.6	17,654.5	49	50
268	421		Creative Alliance, Louisville	2,825.0	750.7	276.3	17,584.8	4,700.9	32	16
269	284	✓	Quest Business Agency, Houston	2,777.5	2,152.1	29.1	18,354.1	14,221.3	45	38
270	294	✓	McFrank & Williams Advertising, New York	2,750.0	2,000.0	37.5	15,750.0	12,000.0	50	45
271	253		Baron & Zaretsky Advertising, New York	2,723.1	2,640.0	3.1	17,500.0	17,050.0	25	25
272	247	✓	Duffy & Shanley, Providence, R.I.	2,704.0	2,702.2	0.1	18,035.5	18,023.9	40	40
273	248		KK&M Advertising, Boston	2,700.0	2,700.0	0.0	26,500.0	28,700.0	35	45
274	243		McKone & Co., Irving, Texas	2,699.4	2,766.9	(2.4)	18,005.3	18,455.5	35	33
275	231		Waldbillig & Besteman, Madison, Wis.	2,687.5	3,014.6	(10.9)	18,075.2	21,409.1	29	34
276	249		John Emmerling Inc., New York	2,654.5	2,699.7	(1.7)	17,697.0	18,000.0	15	16
277	209		Salthouse-Torre-Norton, Rutherford, N.J.	2,650.0	3,410.0	(22.3)	41,175.0	48,744.0	41	37
278	288	✓	Bauerlein, New Orleans	2,633.5	2,077.8	26.7	18,148.2	14,782.9	42	39
NR	NR	✓	Caravetta Allen Kimbrough, Miami (BBDO)	2,614.7	1,647.6	58.7	16,894.8	10,984.0	34	32
279	259	✓	Baker Advertising, Troy, Mich.	2,605.3	2,532.6	2.9	17,377.5	16,892.5	36	40
280	217	✓	Zechman & Associates, Chicago	2,576.5	3,179.7	(19.0)	16,234.1	17,637.6	26	34
281	291	✓	Umphenour Martin Lonsdorf, Atlanta	2,545.7	2,043.5	24.6	19,266.2	15,143.2	28	23
282	212	✓	Soghigian & Macuga Advertising, Washington	2,538.4	3,310.0	(23.3)	17,145.3	20,101.0	16	26
283	282	✓	Chaffee-Bedard, Providence, R.I.	2,505.5	2,173.4	15.1	16,678.6	14,496.8	37	33
284	228	✓	BHN Advertising & PR, St. Louis	2,494.2	3,043.3	(18.1)	17,135.4	19,439.1	54	65
285	289	✓	Lieberman-Appalucci, Allentown, Pa.	2,479.6	2,069.8	19.8	17,014.7	14,225.6	45	40
286	270		Kelley & Wallwork, Boston	2,475.0	2,325.0	6.5	16,500.0	15,500.0	20	16
287	266	✓	Penny/Ohlmann/Neiman, Dayton, Ohio	2,474.6	2,413.3	2.5	23,517.0	22,626.3	46	50
288	254		Lipman, Richmond, Greene Advertising, New York	2,473.8	2,636.0	(6.2)	15,526.8	15,951.9	33	32
289	277	✓	Dudreck Depaul Ficco & Morgan, Pittsburgh	2,440.0	2,250.0	8.4	18,082.5	17,975.0	37	39
290	265		E.H. Brown Advertising, Chicago*	2,374.6	2,448.3	(3.0)	15,830.9	16,321.7	27	28
291	273	✓	Chester Gore Co., New York	2,352.5	2,271.4	3.6	15,442.0	14,888.9	20	21
292	299		Maris, West & Baker, Jackson, Miss.	2,276.7	1,952.5	16.6	14,370.0	13,021.5	35	34
293	262		Spencer Bennett Nowak, Seekonk, Mass.	2,250.0	2,500.0	(10.0)	15,000.0	16,697.0	28	35
294	310	✓	Lohman Organization, New York	2,204.2	1,807.0	22.0	15,397.2	12,105.9	23	22
295	286	✓	Stiegler, Wells & Brunswick, Bethlehem, Pa.	2,201.1	2,140.0	2.9	14,667.3	14,273.8	35	35
296	331	✓	Rainoldi, Kerzner & Radcliffe, San Francisco	2,145.6	1,597.4	34.3	14,262.0	10,622.8	23	20
297	287		Ovation Marketing, La Crosse, Wis.	2,144.1	2,095.8	2.3	14,596.0	12,902.7	28	31
298	327		Loeffler Ketchum Mountjoy, Charlotte, N.C.	2,131.7	1,627.4	31.0	14,218.5	10,855.1	35	29
299	301		Solin Associates, New York	2,117.0	1,942.0	9.0	23,100.0	20,100.0	19	15
300	328	✓	Martcom Inc., Columbus, Ohio	2,102.5	1,620.9	29.7	13,882.9	10,789.0	19	18
301	375	✓	Pagano Schenck & Kay, Providence, R.I.	2,097.5	1,137.3	84.4	19,072.2	11,032.1	35	26
302	NR		Rhea & Kaiser Advertising, Naperville, Ill.	2,085.4	NA	NA	13,909.5	NA	41	37
303	298	✓	Michael & Partners, Dallas	2,062.0	1,974.0	4.5	13,753.0	13,166.0	33	35
304	NR	✓	Van Dine Humphrey Herbert Alber & Manges, Pittsburgh	2,044.2	NA	NA	13,222.0	NA	23	NA
305	292	✓	Rick Johnson & Co., Albuquerque, N.M.	2,038.1	2,027.8	0.5	13,575.7	14,334.5	53	50
306	306	✓	McFarland Group, Elm Grove, Wis.	2,031.3	1,878.8	8.1	10,877.1	9,848.2	20	20
307	296	✓	Letven/Diccicco Advertising & PR, Horsham, Pa.	2,022.0	1,985.0	1.9	13,467.2	13,100.0	28	35
308	344		More Direct, Minneapolis	2,021.0	1,450.0	39.4	13,584.0	9,034.0	22	19
309	295	✓	Associated Advertising Agency, Wichita, Kan.	2,017.5	1,996.3	1.1	13,456.6	13,315.1	46	44
310	305	✓	Aves Advertising, Grand Rapids, Mich.	2,014.0	1,885.0	6.8	13,010.0	11,875.0	38	34

Exhibit 3–2. (Continued)

Rank				U.S. gross income			U.S. billings		U.S. employees	
1989	1988		Agency, headquarters	1989	1988	% chg	1989	1988	1989	1988
311	281	✓	Detrow & Underwood, Ashland, Ohio	2,006.7	2,179.1	(7.9)	5,852.0	6,554.2	15	15
312	318		Harris & Love Advertising, Salt Lake City	2,002.6	1,720.1	16.4	12,035.1	11,730.8	27	27
314	268	✓	Cole Henderson Drake, Atlanta	2,000.0	2,400.0	(16.7)	15,200.0	17,300.0	32	34
313	309	✓	Scharfberg & Associates, Jenkintown, Pa.	2,000.0	1,827.0	9.5	13,363.3	12,659.7	26	26
315	297		Fern/Hanaway, Warwick, R.I.	1,985.7	1,975.6	0.5	13,245.0	13,177.3	39	39
316	308		Bailey Lewis & Associates, Lincoln, Neb.	1,965.7	1,856.8	5.9	13,108.1	12,382.3	39	36
317	333		Lee & Riley, St. Paul, Minn.	1,959.3	1,582.6	23.8	13,045.1	10,540.6	22	20
318	324		Kaprielian/O'Leary Advertising, New York	1,952.5	1,650.4	18.3	13,017.3	12,316.7	24	21
319	365		Sandler Communications, New York*	1,951.5	1,214.1	60.7	12,431.1	7,577.0	30	25
321	NR		Dawson Johns & Black, Chicago*	1,950.0	NA	NA	13,000.0	NA	20	NA
320	303	✓	Ken Schmidt Co., Milwaukee, Wis.	1,950.0	1,900.0	2.6	12,751.5	11,778.3	33	31
322	312		Simms & McIvor, Somerville, N.J.	1,945.5	1,805.0	7.8	13,275.0	12,338.0	28	27
323	293		Barney & Patrick Advertising, Mobile, Ala.	1,943.0	2,017.0	(3.7)	12,640.0	13,018.0	20	22
324	354	✓	J.P. Hogan & Co., Knoxville	1,942.1	1,366.3	42.1	14,347.3	9,108.4	28	22
325	313		Penny & Speier, Houston	1,933.5	1,794.3	7.8	17,960.8	15,428.6	26	27
326	361	✓	Roni Hicks & Associates, San Diego	1,928.7	1,291.3	49.4	12,612.5	8,499.0	28	25
327	340		John Risdall Advertising, New Brighton, Minn.	1,918.5	1,511.8	26.9	13,210.0	10,081.0	15	15
328	369		Hal Langerman Co., Blue Bell, Pa.	1,909.4	1,182.3	61.5	12,656.0	12,287.3	10	10
329	304		Pool Communications, Los Angeles*	1,890.0	1,900.0	(0.5)	12,600.0	10,700.0	16	16
330	320		John Volk Co., Chicago	1,883.6	1,710.3	10.1	13,002.8	15,738.2	29	26
331	336		Sullivan & Brownell, Randolph, Vt.	1,865.0	1,561.2	19.5	10,042.7	8,406.5	8	8
332	300		Meyer Jehs & Wallis, Milwaukee	1,863.4	1,946.4	(4.3)	14,593.0	13,899.4	32	28
333	280	✓	Townsend Agency, Rosemont, Ill.	1,858.9	2,183.6	(14.9)	12,412.9	14,685.5	23	28
334	317		Martiny & Co., Cincinnati	1,848.2	1,724.2	7.2	12,321.4	11,500.5	26	26
335	322		ProClinica Inc., New York	1,830.0	1,680.0	8.9	12,150.0	11,200.0	27	31
336	307	✓	Sturm Communications Group, Chicago	1,805.8	1,861.0	(3.0)	12,547.6	12,282.2	28	28
337	342		Maleson Advertising, Owings Mills, Md.*	1,800.0	1,500.0	20.0	12,000.0	10,000.0	18	15
338	368	✓	Jason Group, Short Hills, N.J.	1,798.0	1,188.8	51.3	16,970.0	12,280.0	18	18
339	290		Buyer Advertising, Newton, Mass.	1,773.3	2,058.6	(13.9)	11,541.6	13,325.4	40	44
340	339	✓	Francioli Richartz Weiman & Fliss, Parisippany, N.J.	1,769.6	1,521.0	16.3	11,500.0	9,800.0	15	12
341	NR		Saunders & Lyons Advertising, Buffalo, N.Y.	1,746.3	NA	NA	10,277.1	NA	17	NA
342	335		Phillips, Miller, Speyer & Frost, Amityville, N.Y.	1,734.7	1,568.2	10.6	11,528.6	10,279.3	26	24
343	341		Advertising, Boelter & Lincoln, Madison, Wis.	1,727.4	1,504.6	14.8	10,872.6	10,032.8	33	28
344	326		Lewis Communications, Mobile, Ala.	1,722.6	1,634.5	5.4	1,115.0	11,847.1	31	30
345	334		Wendt Advertising Agency, Great Falls, Mont.	1,721.5	1,582.3	8.8	11,549.3	10,579.1	31	30
346	330		Semel/Kaye & Co., Northbrook, Ill.	1,717.5	1,612.5	6.5	10,628.5	10,011.8	21	18
347	315		Wardrop Murtaugh Temple, Chicago	1,716.0	1,748.0	(1.8)	10,900.0	11,200.0	21	24
348	359		Jeffrey Nemetz & Associates, Chicago*	1,700.0	1,300.0	30.8	11,339.0	8,671.0	15	15
349	323		NKH&W Marketing Communications, Kansas City, Mo.	1,654.0	1,666.0	(0.7)	11,024.0	11,112.0	40	36
350	329		Rivers Trainor Doyule & Leicht, East Providence, R.I.	1,640.0	1,620.0	1.2	10,920.0	10,800.0	26	23
351	347		Sage Marcom, Syracuse, N.Y.	1,637.9	1,438.0	13.9	10,628.0	9,318.5	38	30
352	371		Harmon Smith, Kansas City, Mo.	1,634.1	1,178.8	38.6	12,527.2	8,924.6	25	22
353	349		Gann-Dawson, Scranton, Pa.	1,620.8	1,417.7	14.3	10,561.8	9,247.9	22	20
354	332	✓	Donald L. Arends Inc., Oak Brook, Ill.	1,617.0	1,584.0	2.1	10,785.4	10,565.3	20	22
355	269		CPA Inc., Key Biscayne, Fla.	1,610.6	2,385.8	(32.5)	10,581.8	15,672.0	19	25
356	353	✓	Furman Roth Advertising, New York	1,603.9	1,372.6	16.8	10,692.4	9,150.7	22	21
357	355		Armando Testa Advertising, New York	1,600.0	1,322.0	21.0	10,500.0	9,915.0	20	20
358	343		Beckman Associates Advertising, Albany, N.Y.	1,592.7	1,490.8	6.8	10,898.0	10,701.2	35	35
359	379	✓	McCormick Advertising, Amarillo, Texas	1,585.7	1,090.2	45.5	10,728.4	9,239.0	23	22
360	387	✓	Strategic Promotions, Dallas	1,577.2	1,028.7	53.3	10,518.3	6,860.4	26	24
361	314	✓	Haselow & Associates, Beachwood, Ohio	1,564.7	1,749.4	(10.6)	10,436.8	11,668.3	23	22
362	405	✓	Capener Co., San Diego	1,560.0	857.0	82.0	10,170.0	5,519.0	26	18
363	352		Sargent & Potratz, Brookfield, Wis.	1,560.0	1,400.0	11.4	7,800.0	7,000.0	17	12
364	337		Marontate & Co., Auburn Hills, Mich.	1,558.0	1,539.0	1.2	10,868.1	10,731.6	20	20
365	362	✓	Esrock Advertising, Orland Park, Ill.	1,540.0	1,280.3	20.3	10,267.0	8,535.0	30	28

Exhibit 3–2. (Continued)

Rank 1989	Rank 1988		Agency, headquarters	U.S. gross income 1989	1988	% chg	U.S. billings 1989	1988	U.S. employees 1989	1988
366	346	✓	Hiebing Group, Madison, Wis.	1,539.5	1,439.0	7.0	11,784.2	10,892.6	30	33
367	350		Beaumont, Heller & Sperling, Reading, Pa.	1,530.5	1,412.5	8.4	10,557.9	9,457.6	40	37
368	366	✓	Blake, Walls & Associates, Los Angeles	1,513.7	1,200.0	26.1	4,900.5	4,137.0	13	10
369	377	✓	Ira Thomas Associates, Youngstown, Ohio	1,492.3	1,108.8	34.6	9,953.0	8,067.5	30	24
370	396	✓	FKQ Advertising, Clearwater, Fla.	1,488.6	939.8	58.4	10,181.2	6,678.9	21	18
371	316	✓	Mitchell & Comer, Toledo, Ohio	1,482.3	1,738.5	(14.7)	10,803.4	12,454.2	22	30
372	283		Schenkein Inc., Denver	1,477.0	2,167.0	(31.8)	9,851.0	14,455.0	25	25
373	345	✓	G. Temple Associates, Southfield, Mich.	1,471.2	1,442.9	2.0	9,243.6	9,329.8	19	18
374	386	✓	Daniel Glassman Advertising, Fairfield, N.J.	1,465.0	1,029.0	42.4	6,622.0	5,129.0	120	110
375	395	✓	Cascino & Purcell, Atlanta	1,463.2	951.8	53.7	9,363.4	6,348.5	13	12
376	394		Significs Inc., Rochester, N.Y.*	1,461.2	963.0	51.7	9,745.6	6,422.5	20	18
377	363	✓	Grant Marketing Communications, Lafayette Hill, Pa.	1,450.5	1,275.0	13.8	9,670.3	8,503.0	22	20
378	382	✓	Adams Colway & Associates, Rochester, N.Y.	1,426.8	1,065.3	33.9	9,219.3	7,490.9	37	26
379	360	✓	Martz & Wadas, Scottsdale, Ariz.	1,411.6	1,296.8	8.9	9,000.0	8,500.0	28	22
380	376	✓	San Jose & Associates, Chicago	1,406.2	1,121.3	25.4	8,813.8	7,476.8	17	14
381	398	✓	Fletcher, Gampper & Wirth, Kansas City, Mo.	1,403.4	936.0	49.9	10,243.3	7,662.4	23	11
382	383	✓	Kingswood Advertising, Ardmore, Pa.	1,338.4	1,050.8	27.4	8,927.3	6,945.0	20	20
383	356	✓	Wolkcas Advertising, Albany, N.Y.	1,323.6	1,317.0	0.5	8,304.4	8,169.3	19	18
384	373	✓	Nordensson Lynn Advertising, Tucson, Ariz.	1,300.5	1,156.8	12.4	8,740.2	7,837.1	30	30
385	348	✓	Thielen & Associates, Fresno, Calif.	1,295.0	1,426.1	(9.2)	8,543.5	9,289.9	16	18
386	NR	✓	Sisti, Zinbarg & Howard, Paramus, N.J.	1,279.7	NA	NA	4,615.9	NA	18	NA
387	358	✓	Topline Design, Islandia, N.Y.	1,277.0	1,312.6	(2.7)	8,161.2	8,387.6	24	26
388	364	✓	McLaughlin, Del Vecchio & Casey, New Haven, Conn.*	1,275.0	1,245.0	2.4	8,500.0	8,300.0	16	16
389	414	✓	Pierson & Flynn, Chicago	1,266.1	792.9	59.7	8,126.4	5,168.6	12	10
390	399	✓	Dugan, Valva Associates, Fairfield, N.J.*	1,255.9	933.9	34.5	8,323.7	6,189.4	19	14
391	338		Estey-Hoover, Newport Beach, Calif.	1,237.6	1,526.7	(18.9)	8,243.6	10,124.3	16	18
392	351		Emery Advertising, El Paso, Texas	1,213.0	1,400.0	(13.4)	7,291.9	8,204.1	24	24
393	367	✓	Nemer, Fieger & Associates, Minneapolis	1,209.2	1,197.9	0.9	8,062.0	7,987.0	18	16
394	380	✓	Sanna, Mattson, MacLeod & Macri, Smithtown, N.Y.	1,202.8	1,083.0	11.1	6,380.2	6,060.3	16	14
395	357	✓	Brett Associates Advertising, Little Falls, N.J.	1,200.0	1,313.8	(8.7)	1,880.4	2,058.8	11	7
395	381	✓	Qually & Co., Chicago	1,200.0	1,080.5	11.1	8,000.0	7,500.0	17	17
397	NR	✓	Goldberg Fossa Seid Advertising, New York	1,195.6	NA	NA	7,750.0	NA	8	NA
398	321	✓	Gregory Inc., Cleveland	1,179.3	1,684.3	(30.0)	7,750.6	11,733.3	19	25
399	404		Phelps Group, Los Angeles	1,162.5	870.0	33.6	7,750.0	5,800.0	16	11
400	389	✓	Tri-State Advertising Co., Warsaw, Ind.	1,157.0	1,023.5	13.0	6,441.3	6,661.4	19	17
401	390	✓	McKee Advertising, Elk Grove Village, Ill.	1,102.5	1,021.1	8.0	9,469.3	9,023.0	18	20
402	403	✓	Lortz Direct Marketing, Omaha	1,098.0	897.5	22.3	8,651.0	7,083.5	11	10
403	409		Haller Schwarz Meade Ullman, Agoura Hills, Calif.	1,093.6	833.0	31.3	8,445.2	5,556.0	19	11
404	378	✓	George P. Clarke Advertising, New York	1,075.6	1,097.7	(2.0)	7,105.3	7,253.2	16	16
405	393	✓	Landers & Partners, St. Petersburg, Fla.*	1,068.6	976.7	9.4	7,026.0	6,424.6	18	15
406	384	✓	Tepe, Hensler & Westerkamp, Cincinnati	1,066.7	1,038.3	2.7	8,684.0	8,209.0	20	19
407	374		Hickman & Associates, Indianapolis	1,059.5	1,140.1	(7.1)	7,152.0	7,405.8	26	24
408	325	✓	Communication & Design Agency, Latham, N.Y.	1,058.0	1,642.5	(35.6)	13,012.0	11,756.0	25	25
409	400	✓	Delfino Marketing Communications, Valhalla, N.Y.	1,049.3	930.5	12.8	6,898.8	6,155.0	13	13
410	410	✓	Carter Callahan Advertising & PR, San Jose, Calif.	1,026.6	830.1	23.7	7,558.8	6,229.6	12	12
411	388	✓	Harold Warner Advertising, Buffalo, N.Y.	1,024.5	1,023.9	0.1	6,800.4	6,724.4	9	9
412	397		Coakley Heagerty Cos., Santa Clara, Calif.*	1,020.9	938.2	8.8	6,805.9	6,254.4	15	13
413	NR	✓	Katsin/Loeb & Partners, San Francisco	1,013.0	NA	NA	8,998.7	NA	13	NA
414	391	✓	Smith & Yehle, Kansas City, Mo.	1,011.0	1,001.0	1.0	6,737.4	6,676.9	18	19
415	402	✓	Kopf Zimmermann Schultheis, Melville, N.Y.	1,004.3	906.3	10.8	6,185.2	5,593.5	16	15
416	385	✓	TCI Advertising, Stamford, Conn.	1,002.5	1,032.4	(2.9)	7,430.4	7,582.8	16	16
417	425	✓	Duke Unlimited, Metairie, La.	996.0	721.0	38.1	6,109.0	5,108.0	13	15
418	408	✓	Haynes & Pittenger Direct, Indianapolis	993.2	853.3	16.4	6,653.3	5,889.5	22	20
419	416	✓	Stevens Kirkland Kreer, Chicago	991.5	775.0	27.9	6,612.5	5,166.5	11	9
420	429	✓	Bruce Novograd Advertising, New York*	975.0	675.0	44.4	6,500.0	4,500.0	10	6
421	370	✓	Laven Fuller & Perkins Advertising, Chicago	973.5	1,182.2	(17.7)	6,490.0	7,841.2	20	23

Exhibit 3–2. (Continued)

Rank 1989	1988	Agency, headquarters	U.S. gross income 1989	1988	% chg	U.S. billings 1989	1988	U.S. employees 1989	1988
422	392	Richardson, Thomas & Bushman, Plymouth Meeting, Pa.	953.7	986.5	(3.3)	6,095.0	6,327.9	14	14
423	413 ✓	Richard Yeager Associates, Morristown, N.J.	946.7	806.6	17.4	7,635.4	6,654.4	14	15
424	417	Noble Arnold & Associates, Schaumburg, Ill.	944.0	765.0	23.4	6,083.3	4,916.1	14	12
425	444 ✓	Halbleib & Moll Associates, Louisville	934.5	594.0	57.3	5,617.6	4,351.9	18	15
426	401	Adelante Advertising, New York	923.6	923.6	0.0	6,034.0	6,034.0	15	15
427	436 ✓	Hively Agency, Houston	914.8	633.6	44.4	5,943.7	4,148.8	20	10
428	372 ✓	MacDonald Boyd White, Boston	909.4	1,169.1	(22.2)	5,846.9	7,639.9	14	16
429	407	New-Venture Advertising, Los Angeles	880.0	854.0	3.0	5,795.5	5,625.4	7	7
430	424 ✓	DPL Advertising, Battle Creek, Mich.	879.1	721.6	21.8	5,639.1	4,577.4	16	14
431	419 ✓	Fischbein & Partners, Minneapolis*	856.0	759.0	12.8	5,434.4	4,601.0	18	14
432	415 ✓	Praco Ltd., Colorado Springs, Colo.	834.8	787.7	6.0	5,566.9	5,164.6	19	19
433	435 ✓	Lardis, McCurdy & Co., Meriden, Conn.	831.0	635.0	30.9	4,753.0	4,494.0	16	15
434	426	Poindexter Associates, Roanoke, Va.	829.9	720.4	15.2	6,425.2	4,723.6	11	13
435	422 ✓	Perry Ballard/advertising, St. Joseph, Mo.	823.0	732.6	12.3	5,656.0	4,696.1	19	21
436	423 ✓	Saxton Communications Group, New York	820.0	730.0	12.3	5,469.4	4,869.1	5	5
437	412	Gardiner-A Marketing Co., Salt Lake City	805.5	813.7	(1.0)	5,372.5	5,427.3	18	17
438	NR	Jules Rabin Associates, Valley Stream, N.Y.*	805.3	NA	NA	5,303.8	NA	22	1
439	445 ✓	K.I. Lipton Inc., Doylestown, Pa.	803.0	588.1	36.5	4,685.2	4,565.8	14	15
440	433	FitzSimons Advertising & Public Relations, Cleveland	779.5	645.2	20.8	5,199.5	4,208.8	19	15
441	411 ✓	Sheldon Fredericks Advertising, New York	776.1	829.3	(6.4)	4,988.0	5,373.0	15	16
442	448	Graff Advertising, Palo Alto, Calif.	771.0	579.2	33.1	4,587.4	3,511.4	10	6
443	459 ✓	Maged & Behar, New York*	750.0	450.0	66.7	5,000.0	3,000.0	7	4
444	420 ✓	Smith Advertising & Associates, Fayetteville, N.C.	741.5	750.7	(1.2)	4,852.6	4,850.5	19	18
445	441 ✓	Dusenbury & Alban, Atlanta	738.5	604.3	22.2	5,669.9	4,875.4	7	8
446	476	Rutkin Costello McCullam Whitley, New York	725.0	325.0	123.1	4,700.0	2,000.0	6	4
447	462 ✓	Shepler/CoDA & Co., Hickory, N.C.	722.7	427.7	69.0	4,345.8	2,930.4	13	6
448	434	Smith & Associates, Charlotte, N.C.	710.9	644.0	10.4	4,421.3	4,000.0	10	10
449	443	Keating Magee Long, New Orleans	697.0	598.0	16.6	4,280.9	3,667.5	12	10
450	NR	Hollingsworth Inc., Rockford, Ill.	695.0	NA	NA	4,524.0	NA	12	11
451	427 ✓	Kocs, Wesson & Associates, Brookfield, Wis.	690.0	712.5	(3.2)	4,600.0	4,750.0	9	9
453	451	Langworth Taylor Co., White Plains, N.Y.*	675.0	540.0	25.0	4,500.0	3,600.0	20	14
452	430	Don Wise & Co., New York	675.0	675.0	0.0	4,500.0	4,500.0	8	8
454	438	Human Resources Advertising, Santa Clara, Calif.	673.8	616.0	9.4	3,500.0	3,200.0	13	13
455	449 ✓	Sader & Associates, New York	671.0	570.0	17.7	4,473.0	3,800.0	6	6
456	NR	William Jenkins Advertising, Philadelphia*	658.9	NA	NA	4,240.9	NA	15	NA
457	442 ✓	Ferrell-Cleary, Exton, Pa.	635.3	599.4	6.0	4,253.4	4,010.6	10	10
458	440 ✓	Advertising & Promotional Services, Sycamore, Ill.	633.1	612.9	3.3	4,223.5	4,144.8	12	13
459	446	Peter Vane Advertising, New York	632.5	584.0	8.3	4,188.0	3,808.6	8	10
460	428 ✓	Hull & Signorile, Florham Park, N.J.	631.4	689.4	(8.4)	4,260.2	4,658.8	6	6
461	468	Kert Advertising, Ft. Lauderdale, Fla.	614.5	381.4	61.1	7,392.2	4,027.1	14	9
462	477	Severance & Associates, Nashville*	613.3	320.9	91.1	4,001.0	2,934.0	5	5
463	437	Exclamation Point, Billings, Mont.	608.1	630.6	(3.6)	4,054.8	4,216.8	15	15
464	406 ✓	Patterson Advertising Agency, Topeka, Kan.	595.0	854.6	(30.4)	3,661.2	5,585.2	25	31
465	452 ✓	AIM Inc., Foster City, Calif.	593.2	509.8	16.4	3,900.1	3,362.0	7	7
466	458 ✓	Marken Communications, Sunnyvale, Calif.	592.5	452.5	30.9	3,951.0	3,017.4	10	10
467	456 ✓	Gurley Associates, Rogers, Ark.	588.7	481.9	22.2	3,924.2	3,641.3	13	11
468	NR ✓	Guthrie & Associates, Greenville, S.C.	579.1	NA	NA	5,390.8	NA	16	NA
469	NR ✓	Tate's Co., Malvern, Pa.	572.1	NA	NA	3,363.6	NA	6	NA
470	432 ✓	MarketAide Inc., Salina, Kan.	569.9	647.4	(12.0)	3,803.7	4,318.0	12	16
471	455 ✓	Smith Group, Syracuse, N.Y.	566.6	486.5	16.5	3,959.2	3,399.8	6	5
472	479 ✓	Geoghegan/Griffiths, Cincinnati	565.4	310.0	82.4	3,769.0	2,063.9	14	9

Exhibit 3–2. (Continued)

Rank			U.S. gross income			U.S. billings		U.S. employees	
1989	1988	Agency, headquarters	1989	1988	% chg	1989	1988	1989	1988
473	450 ✓	**DFK Advertising**, New York*	555.0	555.0	0.0	3,700.3	3,700.3	12	12
474	439	**Martin Thomas**, Providence, R.I.	523.7	615.5	(14.9)	3,277.9	4,103.0	9	6
475	431	**Jiloty Communications Inc.**, Holly Hill, Fla.	518.2	663.2	(21.9)	3,370.3	4,308.5	10	10
476	457	**Bryan/Donald Advertising**, Kansas City, Mo.*	504.0	480.0	5.0	3,360.0	3,200.0	6	5
477	453 ✓	**James & Thomas**, Chicago	497.0	508.8	(2.3)	3,263.2	3,340.8	9	9
478	463	**Lubicom**, New York*	495.0	420.0	17.9	3,300.0	2,800.0	26	26
478	NR	**Tortami Metro P.R.omotions**, Long Island, N.Y.*	495.0	NA	NA	3,300.0	NA	9	8
480	NR ✓	**Neiman Group**, Harrisburg, Pa.	488.8	NA	NA	6,950.7	NA	17	NA
481	461 ✓	**Kinzie & Green**, Wausau, Wis.	480.7	440.5	9.1	3,075.6	2,805.2	12	12
482	NR ✓	**Kobs Gregory & Passavant**, Chicago	462.3	NA	NA	3,151.6	NA	11	NA
483	465 ✓	**Metro Marketing Group**, Indianapolis	460.9	394.9	16.7	2,953.9	2,070.1	14	7
484	474	**Stein Killpatrick & Rogan Advertising**, New York	460.5	339.5	35.6	3,846.1	2,193.8	9	9
485	494 ✓	**Integrated Target Marketing**, Chicago	426.5	196.0	117.6	2,838.1	1,387.4	10	5
486	467 ✓	**Goff Communications**, Corning, N.Y.	412.0	384.2	7.2	2,747.7	2,562.5	9	8
487	460	**Brewster Advertising**, Cambridge, Mass.	409.0	443.0	(7.7)	2,977.0	3,188.0	5	6
488	478 ✓	**MWA Direct**, Minneapolis	408.6	317.7	28.6	2,725.0	2,119.1	4	5
489	NR ✓	**Opus Group**, Ridgewood, N.J.	404.6	NA	NA	2,690.5	NA	8	8
490	466 ✓	**Hautigan Advertising**, Chicago	403.7	386.9	4.3	2,692.7	2,523.9	5	5
491	490 ✓	**DK Group**, Hillsdale, N.J.	401.2	220.6	81.8	2,128.5	1,471.3	8	8
492	447 ✓	**CTS Associates**, Detroit	399.9	581.7	(31.3)	2,426.5	4,767.7	7	9
493	454 ✓	**Hinton & Steel**, Seattle	393.3	492.5	(20.1)	2,622.9	3,284.6	10	10
494	NR	**NPC & Associates**, Landover, Md.	386.5	NA	NA	2,457.5	NA	10	9
495	471	**MSA Advertising**, Philadelphia	379.4	360.2	5.3	3,238.8	3,267.0	7	7
496	464	**Ruhe & Co.**, Reading, Pa.	356.4	401.6	(11.3)	1,670.6	1,814.0	6	6
497	486 ✓	**Burgess, Brewer, Stanyon & Payne**, Portland, Maine	355.2	245.0	45.0	2,277.6	1,632.1	12	8
498	481 ✓	**G. Duff Associates**, Somerville, N.J.	339.2	309.0	9.8	2,307.4	2,029.2	4	4
499	473 ✓	**Creel Associates**, Oak Brook, Ill.	334.0	339.9	(1.7)	2,328.6	2,371.4	9	10
500	475 ✓	**Cross Keys Advertising**, Doylestown, Pa.	325.1	338.9	(4.1)	3,269.3	4,090.8	7	6

Notes: Dollars are in thousands. NR indicates agency not ranked. Initials in parenthesis indicate the parent company in which the subsidiaries' figures are included. ✓ indicates the agency received signature of an independent accountant verifying figures supplied in *Advertising Age*. * indicates that gross income and/or total volume figures are *Advertising Age* estimates.

Identifying the Agency Search Group

The advertiser's first task is to identify the person or persons in its own organization who will be responsible for finding a qualified advertising agency. Occasionally, a single employee will undertake this task, especially for advertisers with limited advertising budgets or with programs in which only one person in the company deals with the agency. Usually, however, several persons in a company will deal with the agency that is ultimately selected. These people should participate in the search process. Just what positions they hold varies from company to company and reflects the way in which each advertiser chooses to deal with its agency. In general, however, the search group will consist of a senior marketing executive, plus one or more of the following: line marketing executives (product managers and/or group product managers) directly responsible for the product or service that the new agency will be assigned; a director of marketing or advertising services; and specialists from research and development, marketing research, and/or the financial department. The search group will also include an outside consultant specializing in agency selection, if the company has decided to employ one to help in the agency search. Typically, the senior marketing executive serves as the chairperson of this group. No matter how widespread agency contact is within the advertiser organization, the search group rarely exceeds five persons and often is limited to two or three.

This search group is usually responsible for screening agencies and identifying the final group or "short list" of agencies that will make a final presentation to the advertiser. These final presentations are usually made to a wider group of company executives, including its top management. But the search group almost always has the final responsibility, after the formal agency presentation, of making the final agency selection, which will be subject to review and approval by senior advertiser management.

Using an Outside Consultant

An increasing number of companies now use an outside consultant to help with the advertising agency search and selection. The ideal consultant has considerable experience in finding solutions to advertising problems, a very broad knowledge in the advertising agency business, a wide acquaintance among advertising agency chief executives, and a reputation for integrity within the agency community.

A well-qualified consultant can make at least six substantive contributions to the agency search and selection.

1. An experienced consultant can direct the total search and selection process in a way that will assure the advertiser that it has been exposed to the very best agencies available to work on its advertising account.
2. The consultant can assure the objectivity of the search process.
3. The consultant will know a lot more about many advertising agencies than even the most knowledgeable advertisers.
4. The consultant can act as an intermediary between the advertiser and the advertising agency community, thus protecting the advertiser from much time-consuming contact with a host of candidate agencies during the search process.
5. The consultant can handle all of the detailed work and contact with prospective agencies that an agency search entails.
6. The consultant knows how to make the candidate agencies show the advertiser what it should see to make a knowledgeable appraisal of the candidates instead of an appraisal based only upon what the agencies want the advertiser to see.

It is easy to describe the broad outlines of the process that the agency search group should follow in identifying the best agency for the advertising account. It involves five steps.

1. Prepare a profile of the advertising account for which an agency is sought.
2. Develop a list of minimum criteria that agencies must meet in order to be considered.
3. Develop a "long list" of qualified agencies.
4. Develop a "short list" of qualified agencies.
5. Select the best agency for the advertising account.

The first two steps involve a good deal of internal work on the part of the advertiser or its outside consultant. This is the "homework" phase of finding an advertising agency, the subject of this chapter. The development of a "long list" of candidate agencies is discussed in Chapter 4. The development of a "short list" of qualified agencies is discussed in Chapters 5 and 6. The final selection of the advertising agency is discussed in Chapters 7 and 8.

The Advertising Account Profile

Once the agency search group has been established, its first task is to organize its thinking so that all members agree both on the exact definition of the advertising account for which an agency is sought, and the basic, required characteristics of the agency candidates. Thus, the first tasks of the search group are to prepare the Advertising Account Profile and the Minimum Criteria for Candidate Agencies.

The Advertising Account Profile provides a clear description of the exact nature of the account in need of an agency. In due course, this Advertising Account Profile will be distributed or described to potential agency candidates to apprise them of the work they will be expected to do. For this reason, the formal profile should include not only information about the account, but also facts about the advertiser and its expectations. The following kinds of information are contained in the profile.

• What does the account consist of? Is it advertising a product, a service, or an institution? Is the product or service new or established? Will the assignment include all of the advertising for the brand?

• What have the billings, if any, been on the advertising account in the last year or two? What billings are anticipated in the next calendar year?

• What are the distinctive features of the product or service to be advertised? Is the product comparable to those already marketed, or does it have distinctive characteristics that have important potential implications for advertising?

• Does the account have unusual service requirements? Will the agency be expected to supply all marketing research for the brand or service? Will agency personnel be expected to maintain extensive and continuing contact with client field sales representatives or franchisee or dealer organizations? Will the agency be expected to devise, design, and produce client sales presentations?

• What are the seasonal, regional, or other peculiarities of the typical advertising program for the brand or service to be advertised?

• On what basis, and to what extent, will the advertising agency be compensated? Does the advertiser intend to compensate the agency for any work it is asked to do in soliciting the account? How does the advertiser intend to compensate the advertising agency that is finally appointed to handle the advertising account?

• Finally, the Advertising Account Profile should include the exact name of the advertiser company, the address from which the agency search

43

is being conducted, and the name and title of the search group member or consultant coordinating the agency search and serving as contact for interested agencies.

Of course, in providing this information, the advertiser need not bare his soul to the advertising community. Brief summaries of data already in the public record will suffice. If it is necessary to reveal information that is not publicly known, it can be limited to what an advertising agency must know to decide whether it wishes to solicit the account, and what it must know to present intelligently the agency's basic qualifying characteristics. It is almost impossible to invite agency solicitations for an advertising account without releasing a minimum amount of basic information about the account. Of course, the advertiser can control how those basic facts are perceived by the advertising agency community. However, if it does not release the facts in a consistent and relatively comprehensive form, the agency rumor mills are likely to substitute their own fantasies for reality. The farther these fantasies deviate from reality, the more the advertising agency search may be compromised in a way that damages the advertiser.

One advertising agency was asked to solicit a line of new dessert products for a medium-sized manufacturer of packaged foods. Individual members of the agency search committee contacted agencies they believed to be well-qualified to handle the assignment. One agency was told that the exact size of billings was not finally determined, but was likely to be in the range of $2.5 to $3 million. The president of this agency mentioned this figure to the president of a competing agency in their weekly golf game and was startled when he was told that the billings were estimated to exceed $10 million. A subsequent trade press report mentioned an eventual billing level of $5 million with a two-year or longer interim developmental period, and with agency compensation by fee. The first agency concluded that the divergence of billing estimates implied that the advertiser was disorganized, and seriously considered withdrawing from the solicitation. When the advertiser realized that different versions of the account were being spread by search committee members, a formal written description was quickly prepared and distributed.

The formal Advertising Account Profile accomplishes a variety of worthwhile purposes.

• First, it clarifies the advertiser's thinking about its account. Personnel in an advertiser organization may perceive an advertising account and its salient characteristics in an amazing number of different ways. Some of this variation in perspective comes from differences in exposure to the basic facts of the matter. In many companies, for example, the *exact* size of an advertising appropriation for a particular brand or service may be kept secret. This may be because of company policy, or it may be because of an organizational structure that limits the number of people who are privy to the advertising budget. So a straight factual statement of past appropriations (if feasible from a security standpoint) and a factual statement of the anticipated appropriation for the year ahead can reduce much potential misinformation in the advertiser's organization.

• Second, the Advertising Account Profile guarantees that all the agencies that express interest in the account or who are subsequently approached by the advertiser start from a common base of knowledge about the account. This is only fair to the agencies, some of which, left to their own devices, may develop a bizarre understanding of the characteristics of the account. In addition, the Advertising Account Profile saves the advertiser or its outside consultant time and frustration in briefing different agencies and in responding to their requests for further information. If no formal description of the account exists, no explicit limitation will be imposed on the amount and kind of information that will be divulged to soliciting agencies.

When all agencies receive the same information, they have a common basis for agency solicitation that is controlled by the advertiser. The common information base created by the Advertising Account Profile tends to regularize subsequent agency responses—whether answers to advertiser questionnaires, formal personal presentations, or informal meetings and telephone conversations.

• Finally, and most important, the Advertising Account Profile provides a basis for agencies to assess their own qualifications for servicing the account. Much of the circuslike atmosphere that often surrounds the solicitation of advertising accounts is a result of the activities of advertising agencies that yearn for new business, yet simply do not have enough information about the account to know that they are not qualified to solicit it.

A soundly constructed and candid Advertising Account Profile becomes a useful tool in helping such unqualified agencies to eliminate themselves from the competition. It saves them from pressing themselves on a client whom they cannot adequately serve, no matter how much they might like to try.

When a major airline asked agencies to solicit their account, they pointed out in the Account Profile that it would be necessary for the winning agency to establish a service office in their headquarters city if the agency did not have an office there already. (The headquarters city had virtually no advertising agencies.) This office would be used to produce and place the large volume of destination/schedule/fare advertisements routinely developed by the airline and accounting for about 75 percent of its advertising expenditures.

Several agencies immediately withdrew from the solicitation, apparently because they did not wish to establish a local service office or because they had not previously understood the disproportionate amount of local advertising required by the account.

The Minimum Criteria for Candidate Agencies

The next job of the agency search group is to define the minimum criteria that any candidate agency must meet. This first set of criteria is likely to have a negative rather than positive character. It will set out the minimum characteristics that qualified agencies must have before they can be considered as candidates for the account. If an agency has the minimum qualifications, it may be subject to further consideration, but if it does not meet the minimum criteria, it is dropped from the competition.

If the primary objective of the list of minimum criteria is to eliminate as many unsuitable agencies as possible, a secondary objective is to ensure that these criteria do not eliminate any qualified contenders. The minimum criteria tend, therefore, to be objective and overt rather than subjective and subtle. The criteria include obvious agency characteristics that the search group unanimously believes a contending agency must possess. Such a list includes criteria such as the following.

Size

An important criterion for the selection of advertising agencies is size: either according to "billings"—that is, the media dollars that the agency places—or according to agency gross income. Advertising agencies can be classified by size only arbitrarily. A very large agency may have domestic billings in excess of $1.5 billion. A medium-sized agency may have domestic billings between $200 million and $1 billion. A small agency may have domestic billings between $25 and $200 million. A very small advertising agency may have domestic billings of less than $25 million.

Such classifications are totally arbitrary, however. Perhaps a better way to gain a perspective on the relative size of advertising agencies is to study the array of agencies that report their income and/or billings on an annual basis to *Advertising Age*. These data are shown in Exhibits 3–1 and 3–2.

Some advertisers may have very large accounts that they believe can only be handled by the very largest advertising agencies. Also, some advertisers may have an account that they believe will require particularly sophisticated agency service, which, in turn, the search group may believe can only be provided by a large advertising agency. For example, an advertiser may have a new product that has a variety of potential appeals to the ultimate consumer; thus it may require sophisticated advertising research and advertising positioning work to guarantee success. The advertiser may believe that only the largest agencies are likely to be able to supply such expertise, and it may be willing to pay a substantial fee to receive the benefits of such experience if the initial commissions will not support such agency work.

Other advertisers have no interest in getting lost in the immensity of a large advertising agency. While acknowledging the relative excellence of the work of the larger agencies, they believe that only the largest accounts receive full benefit from the resources of such agencies and that smaller accounts tend to get lost in the hustle and bustle of ongoing activities. So advertisers with accounts in the average range (perhaps between $10 and $20 million in 1990 dollars) often prefer to find an agency of smaller size. They believe that they are likely, in such agencies, to receive some professional attention from *the* senior marketing, creative, media, and research specialists, simply because such specialists in smaller agencies tend to be closer to the strategic issues involved in all of the agency's accounts than do such specialists in very large agencies. In addition, advertisers who choose medium-sized agencies may believe that they will have greater leverage in using *all* the agency's resources to solve their marketing and advertising problems.

Smaller advertisers have an even more difficult problem because, as Exhibit 3–2 indicates, there are so many small advertising agencies from which to choose. Other criteria will, of course, help the smaller advertiser sort out the available agencies, but it is almost inevitable that such advertisers, because of the small size of the account, will end up with a smaller advertising agency. Small accounts often do not generate enough revenue to interest moderate- to large-sized agencies, and the astute smaller advertiser realizes that it is more likely to receive superior service in a smaller agency.

Specialization

An obvious criterion for the selection of an advertising agency is whether some particular specialization is required. If the advertiser is a pharmaceutical manufacturer, and is seeking an advertising agency that specializes in the development of advertising copy for pharmaceutical drugs and specialized media expertise in this category, then the agency search will be limited to such agencies.

Similarly, if the advertiser wishes to mount a cooperative yellow pages advertising program, it will likely limit the search to agencies that specialize in yellow pages advertising—especially those with experience in cooperative yellow pages advertising programs.

Surely, most advertisers who are seeking an agency will not want just any advertising agency. They will almost certainly prefer one that has some sort of prior experience in the particular product category. The experience may be direct or analogous, but allied experience should be there, and it will provide a crucial minimal criterion in the first stage of the agency selection process.

A second consideration for many advertisers is whether a full-service advertising agency is required, or whether a limited-service advertising agency will suffice. As discussed in Chapter 1, most advertisers find it in their best interest to deal with some sort of full-service advertising agency, but this need not always be the case. If some advertisers need only creative service, media planning and placement service, or strategic planning service, then that requirement clearly becomes an important first minimum selection criterion.

Account Conflicts

An obvious minimum criterion is account conflict. As we have discussed, consumer goods advertisers are likely to be rather conservative about account conflict. They are likely to impose strict rules on the kinds of account conflict they will countenance when considering new advertising agencies. Industrial, business, and technical advertisers seem, on the other hand, to be considerably more liberal in dealing with actual and potential account conflicts.

Certainly, the advertiser who is seeking a new agency should be explicit about whether—and to what extent—it will permit conflicting accounts among potential agencies. The search group must address the following questions.

Directly Conflicting Accounts. Will the advertiser consider an advertising agency that now has a directly conflicting account? If, for example, the advertiser is looking for an agency to handle an aspirin brand, will it place this brand of aspirin with an agency that already handles another brand of aspirin?

On the face of it, the answer to this question, or comparable questions for other advertisers, must be no. Such direct product conflicts should always eliminate the agency from any list of potential agencies for the new assignment. It is not unknown, however, for agencies with a small account in a product category to be available for a much larger account in that same category.

Indirectly Conflicting Accounts. Where does the advertiser draw the line in matters of indirect product conflict? Is tea in conflict with coffee? Is a canned fruit drink in conflict with a soft drink? Is a cake mix in conflict with a gelatin dessert? Is an analgesic in conflict with a cold remedy? Is an airline that flies predominantly in the East in conflict with a western regional airline with one or two overlapping routes? Is a line of stereo receivers in conflict with a line of portable television sets?

There are, of course, no unequivocal answers to product conflict questions of this kind. In each instance, the advertiser must make its own decisions as to what constitutes product conflict for its company. What may seem ludicrous in matters of product conflict to one advertiser may seem no more than routine business practice to another. In any event, the advertiser search group will make its own product conflict rules explicit.

The president, executive vice president, and advertising vice president of a cola soft-drink manufacturer visited about six advertising agencies hand-picked by the advertising vice president. He had selected the candidate agencies quite hurriedly because of his president's insistence that the incumbent agency be fired and that a new agency quickly be found to replace it. The advertising vice president had screened potential candidate agencies on the basis of several criteria, including competitive conflict, and several agencies were dropped from consideration because they handled soft-drink accounts. As this august and serious group of officers was ushered into the conference room of one of the six surviving agencies, the president's glance fell upon an exhibit case that displayed many of the packaged goods products advertised by the agency. The president turned to his advertising vice president and said, "I didn't realize these people handled _____ [a line of canned fruit drinks], did you?" The advertising vice president responded that he didn't consider the fruit drinks a conflict. The president thought for a moment and then turned to the agency chairman, saying, "I'm sorry, but we're not going to have a meeting here today. That fruit drink is in direct competition with our product, and no matter how good you folks are, or what arguments you come up with, we're not going to be able to do business with you." With that statement and some apologies, the soft-drink delegation withdrew, to seek noncompetitive help elsewhere.

Formulating a Conflict Policy. Finally, the advertiser must formulate a corporate conflict policy as it searches for a new advertising agency. If there are companies in such close competition with the advertiser that it does not wish to patronize their advertising agencies, then it should make this fact clear at the beginning.

If it is true that General Motors does not use the same advertising agencies as Ford does, it is also true that other companies' competitive relationships are no less sharply drawn, and they will also refuse to do business with competitors' agencies.

Once again, there is nothing wrong with such policies: They are the prerogative of the advertiser and its alone to make. But, from the standpoint of the agency search, such policies must be made explicit by the search group if it is to be fully effective in weeding out inappropriate advertising agencies. If such corporate policies do not exist, the search group must make this explicit, too, lest well-qualified agencies be overlooked.

Location

Many advertisers believe that they can receive optimal advertising agency service only if their agency or agencies are physically close to them, as in the airline example mentioned earlier.

This condition can take one of two forms. In the first place, some advertisers want either the principal office or a major, full-service branch office of the agency to be near the advertiser's home office. Thus, advertisers whose main offices are in Los Angeles may only wish to do business with agencies having headquarters or major service offices in Los Angeles.

Such proximity is, of course, not always possible. If an advertiser's central office is, for example, in Amarillo, Texas, or Fort Lauderdale, Florida, or Gadsden, Alabama, it may be unrealistic to insist that the account be serviced from the main office of an agency or from a full-service branch, since full-blown, full-service advertising agencies simply do not exist in every place that advertisers have chosen to run their businesses.

In such cases, if the advertiser's billings and/or determination support it, the agency can create a *service office* specifically for the advertiser in its headquarters' city. Such dedicated service offices are especially im-

portant for those accounts that involve a hefty volume of individual advertisements, especially if such advertisements are subject to continuous
change. Physical proximity of agency and client may be, in such circumstances, not only desirable, but imperative.

Some advertising agencies seem to be opposed to the establishment of
any kind of ancillary or branch service offices. They object on at least two
grounds. First, it is impossible to guarantee, they believe, the quality of
service and depth of personnel that can be routinely offered in their headquarters' office. Standards fall in branch offices, they feel; and it is almost
impossible to impose management controls, from a distance, to overcome
this deterioration in performance. Second, agencies feel that it is often impossible to make reasonable profits in a branch office operation. Furthermore, these agencies claim that modern transportation and communication provide ready access to the agency headquarters personnel and service
by client offices, *wherever* they may be.

One story, perhaps apocryphal, illustrates this point. Advertising
agency Papert Koenig & Lois had been in competition for a major food
account headquartered in Chicago. The PKL agency won the competition
on merit, but the advertiser's marketing director was reluctant to give PKL
the business because it had only a New York office, while other finalists
had Chicago offices. A telephone conversation between the advertiser and
PKL president, Frederick Papert, focused on this point. Papert, apparently
at a loss for words upon hearing this objection, said that he would respond
in an hour or two. He then left immediately for LaGuardia Airport,
boarded a Chicago-bound airplane, and appeared in his prospective client's office, ready to work, in less than four hours. The Papert agency won
the account.

Other agencies believe that they can run branch offices with a standard of service quality and personnel depth that approaches that of their
headquarters office and that undoubtedly exceeds the quality of local
agencies. An important argument is that the branch office is never dependent *only* on its own resources. The resources of the headquarters' office
are always available to the branch, and thus to its clients. Agencies that are
firmly committed to branch office networks apparently are satisfied that
branch offices can be collectively, even if not individually, profitable
enough to justify their existence.

There are clearly two sides to this branch office question. The important point is that the advertiser should know exactly what kind of service it
will need and whether or not this service will require a nearby agency office. Once this is known, the agency search group should establish a criterion about the source of agency service for their account.

International Service

Just as some advertisers require that their accounts be serviced in a particular domestic geographic location, some also insist that agency service be available in specific overseas locations.

This may be the case, for example, with an airline account with many overseas destinations. Such an airline insists that all of its destination-fare-schedule advertising be coordinated in all of its service markets, locally and internationally.

Similarly, the advertiser of a product or service may have extended or may intend to extend its distribution to a foreign country. The advertiser may wish to have a consistent advertising campaign in each country, or may want the same strategic information and planning base developed for each country. In either instance, overseas agency service offices may be required.

When international sales and marketing are important for a product or service, the availability of agency service outside the United States may be an important criterion in agency selection. If so, it should be included by the search group in the list of minimum criteria.

Media Competence

Advertisers often seek an agency that does especially outstanding work in one or another advertising medium, and/or with particular kinds of advertising target groups. For example, an advertiser may spend the bulk of its money in network television or spot radio or magazines, and may want an agency with demonstrated competence in these specific media. Or, an advertiser may want to reach well-to-do male audiences, younger children, or people over sixty years of age, and seeks an agency that has special experience in using media to reach these target groups.

Such advertisers will usually want to place their account with a full-service advertising agency that has general competence in all media as well as experience with a wide variety of advertising audiences. Nevertheless, such advertisers will want to assure themselves that prospective agencies have a significant level of billings and a wide range of experience with the media or the audiences that are of particular interest.

Of course, some advertising agencies specialize in work that appears in *only* a particular medium, or in work that deals *only* with a particular kind of audience. Frequently, in such specialist agencies, the particular characteristics of media are interwoven with the idiosyncracies of particular target audiences. Thus, there are agencies that specialize in recruitment, help wanted, medical, classified, industrial, business-to-business, financial, direct response, retail, yellow pages, theatrical-entertainment, investment, and other such advertising activities.

The media competence criterion emphasizes experience in a particular medium and/or competence in using media to reach certain specialized audiences.

Agency Ownership

Sometimes, advertisers establish criteria that deal with the ownership of advertising agencies.

Some advertisers, for example, believe that public ownership diverts the attention of agency managers from advertising issues and concerns to a preoccupation with the satisfaction of shareholder concerns. If an advertiser feels this way, it is likely to seek an advertising agency that is privately rather than publicly owned.

Similarly, some advertisers believe that absentee ownership is not a positive factor in the creation of superior advertising, since an agency that is owned by a nonadvertising person or company will be concerned with satisfying its outside owner as well as its advertising clients. Thus, some advertisers prefer not to do business with advertising agencies that are owned, as an investment, by disinterested outsiders—domestic or foreign.

The Account Solicitation Fact Sheet

At this point, the search group has accomplished two basic tasks. It has developed a description of the account that is to be solicited, and it has established minimum criteria for those agencies qualified to solicit the account. This information should be summarized in an Account Solicitation Fact Sheet, as indicated in Exhibit 3–3. This fact sheet can serve two purposes. As an internal document, it is an early progress report on the work of the agency search group. As an external document, it can be used with identified or self-nominated agency candidates to indicate both the characteristics of the account and the criteria for candidate agencies.

Now the advertiser is prepared to search actively for its new advertising agency. The advertiser, in the creation of Minimum Criteria for Agency Selection and the Advertising Account Profile, has made a statement of the facts about its account and the criteria by which it will begin to eliminate agencies. However, although these documents provide a basis for eliminating agencies that are not interested in the account or can't do

Exhibit 3–3.   Account Solicitation Fact Sheet

A. Advertising Account Profile

1. Company name, address, zip code. Company contact in the agency selection process.
2. Exact description of the advertising account or assignment that is available for solicitation.
3. Billings, if any, in the past calendar year.
4. Anticipated billings in the current calendar year.
5. Anticipated billings in the next calendar year.
6. A brief description of the distinctive characteristics of the product/service/institution to be advertised.
7. A brief statement of the particular needs in servicing the account: marketing, creative, media, research, promotional, and other special needs.
8. Seasonal, regional, and other peculiarities of the advertising program.
9. A general statement of how the advertiser intends to compensate the advertising agency for work done while soliciting the account and how the winning agency will be compensated for handling the account.

B. Minimum Agency Selection Criteria

1. Minimum/maximum size of advertising agencies that will be considered for the assignment of the account.
2. Advertising agency specialization required to service the account.
3. Advertiser conflict policy:
   - Advertiser will not accept conflict.
   - Advertiser will not accept indirect conflict (define).
   - Advertiser will not accept corporate conflict.
4. Required location of advertiser main and/or branch offices.
5. Required international service capabilities.
6. Media competence or competences required.
7. Ownership characteristics required.

the job, they do not provide an effective basis for identifying agencies that *are* qualified.

The first step in this process of positive identification is the development of the "long list" of potentially qualified advertising agencies. Chapter 4 deals with the development of the long list of agencies.

The Long List of Advertising Agencies

The next step in the selection of an advertising agency is the development of the so-called long list of potential agencies to handle the advertising account. The creation of the long list is a positive step: It is the first time in the agency selection process that attention is focused on the actual selection of potential candidate agencies. Heretofore, the advertiser has been concerned with developing an explicit description of the advertising account and minimum criteria for the elimination of advertising agencies to service it. Although in the development of the long list, the advertiser is presumably not yet in direct contact with potential agency candidates, its perspective is now positive: It is actively seeking potential advertising agency candidates.

Developing Positive Criteria for Agency Selection

In the Account Solicitation Fact Sheet (Exhibit 3–3), a list of negative criteria was developed to eliminate agencies that were unsatisfactory, for one or more reasons, for the advertising account in question. As the perspective shifts from the negative to the positive, it is necessary to develop additional criteria to apply to those advertising agencies that have survived the original negative screening. The advertiser knows that it wants an agency of a particular size, located in a particular geographic area, with or without certain specializations, free of particular conflict situations, and, perhaps, with an international service capability, a particular media competence, or a particular ownership structure. But this is not all the advertiser

55

wants. It also wants specific, positive, professional characteristics in the advertising agencies it considers.

It should be noted that as the first cut at the long list of agency candidates is developed, the advertiser is still working from publicly available information. Its objective is to do as much screening and eliminating of agencies as possible before the time- and resource-consuming process of actually meeting with and appraising advertising agencies commences.

So the question remains: What kind of positive selection criteria should now be developed to add to the negative screening criteria that have already been incorporated in the Account Solicitation Fact Sheet? Following are some additional criteria to be considered in developing the long list of candidate agencies.

Industry Reputation

Both as a result of their work and their client lists, most advertising agencies develop a distinct reputation within the industry. For example, John O'Toole, in his book, *The Trouble with Advertising*, described the reputations of several leading advertising agencies in the early 1980s. O'Toole commented that although Young & Rubicam is the "biggest American advertising agency," it "is regarded less for its size than its ability to produce very high quality advertising."[1] McCann-Erickson, O'Toole says, is known for its success in international advertising markets: "Its overseas business is so dominant that it shapes the agency's identity. Within the business, we think of McCann-Erickson primarily as the agency upon which the sun never sets."[2] O'Toole believes that the Ogilvy & Mather agency, influenced by its dynamic founder, David Ogilvy, avoids patronizing the consumer: "David and his agency have demonstrated an unusual respect for the consumer's intelligence in their work."[3] Grey Advertising, on the other hand, seems to lack a distinguishing character: "Grey is another one that is hard to get a handle on even though it's been in business since 1917. . . . Its client list now, however, includes many major brands from such marketing giants as Procter & Gamble, General Foods, Gillette and Revlon. Yet few campaigns spring to mind when the name Grey is mentioned."[4] The Leo Burnett agency reflects the legacy of its founder: "A determination to base every campaign

---

[1] John O'Toole, *The Trouble with Advertising* (New York: Chelsea House, 1981, pp. 175–76.
[2] *Ibid.*, p. 177.
[3] *Ibid.*, p. 178.
[4] *Ibid.*, p. 184.

on the 'inherent drama' that is to be found in every product. The campaigns of this agency are, to an unusual degree, admired by those of us in the business and liked by those without."[5]

Although knowledgeable advertising people do not agree completely about the characteristics of every agency, most agencies have a reputation at any point in time that is not unlike the description developed by O'Toole in the early eighties. These reputations change and evolve with the passage of time, to be sure, as the nature of the advertising agency industry itself changes and evolves. Clear and distinct or blurred and vague, these consensus reputations tend, in general, to reflect both the nature of the advertising the agencies produce and their basic attitude toward conducting business.

It is naïve to think that any advertising agency will be so clearly distinguished from its immediate competitors that it can be chosen on this basis alone. Yet one factor in the selection process will usually be the contemporary reputation of the candidate agency. In any event, the advertiser will tend to shy away from agencies whose reputations are distinctly incompatible with its attitudes and business practices.

If, for example, the company perceives itself to be conservative, it will probably not want an agency whose business style is flamboyant or whose creative work is unconventional or avant garde. Such a company will feel more comfortable with an agency that has a low profile; an agency that is not known for its controversial public statements and views about advertising; an agency with low-key, professional principals who are perhaps just a little bit dull.

Quality of Creative Work

Advertising agencies have one dominant characteristic: It is not hard to be aware of their work because it is on continuous public display. The work of various agencies can therefore be collected and analyzed. Printed advertisements can be clipped from the media in which they appear, and commercial services are happy to provide "photo board" reproductions of television commercials, as well as off-the-air recordings of radio and television commercials.

Thus, the advertiser has it well within its power to make a subjective appraisal of the general quality of the creative work of individual advertising agencies. It is almost certain to do this in an informal way, identifying

---

[5]*Ibid.*, p. 181.

advertisements that it particularly "likes" or "dislikes" and identifying the agency responsible for them.

Also, while assembling its long list of advertising agencies, the advertiser can systematically inform itself about the general quality of the work produced by prospective advertising agencies. It can determine which agencies consistently produce advertising that seems to contain elements that are clearly related to sales success. Also, it can find out which agencies consistently produce advertising that seems to be irrelevant to commercial gain, obscure, or self-conscious.

Kinds of Problems Solved

While reviewing the advertising created by a variety of prospective advertising agencies, the advertiser can also apply another criterion. Has the agency had success in developing solutions to advertising problems that seem, at least on their surface, to be analogous to those faced by the advertiser's brands? Is the agency good at differentiating, through advertising, brands or services that seem to differ little from their competitors? Is the agency good at finding ways to extend the sales base for retail establishments that might otherwise fall into a sales rut? Is the agency especially good at finding ways of presenting products of self-indulgence (such as fine fragrances, cigarettes, or alcoholic beverages) in a way that sharply and compellingly differentiates them from their competitors?

More than a little imagination is required here on the part of the advertiser. If the advertiser's products are directly competitive, it is quite likely that the agency will be unavailable to the advertiser for reasons of product conflict. The trick is to find an agency or agencies with advertising successes in product categories that are close enough to the advertiser's category to suggest that the agency's skills and insights may be readily transferable to the advertiser's problem.

This is not merely a matter of finding advertising that the advertiser admires. It is rather a matter of identifying a way of thinking about advertising problems and a way of converting that thinking into effective advertising solutions that parallel the exact kinds of advertising issues that are routinely faced by the advertiser.

Recent Business History

There is much to be said for doing business with advertising agencies that have demonstrated a certain stability in their business affairs. Accordingly, the advertiser should find out about the recent account gains and losses of candidate agencies. It should also try to determine the degree to which long-term clients have continuously increased their commitment to the advertising agency.

How many new accounts has the agency gained in the last two years? Has the agency consistently failed in its new business solicitations? If so, what is the reason? Is the agency doing a good job for its current clients, but a bad job in selling itself to prospective clients?

Or, has the agency been spectacularly successful in acquiring new accounts in recent months—has it been "hot," in the patois of the trade? In this case, is the agency large enough to absorb its successes, or does the agency seem to be having trouble servicing its new accounts, as well as maintaining a strong level of service for its long-term clients?

The other side of the coin is, of course, the agency's record of account losses in recent months and years. Has there been a steady drain of accounts out of the agency? Has this drain been offset by an influx of new accounts? As we have seen, advertising agencies lose accounts for a variety of reasons. Sometimes the agency has done a good job and loses the account in spite of it. On the other hand, advertising agencies can also lose their professional sharpness over a period of time. In any event, the advertiser should know if the agency is beginning to show signs of competitive weakness. If this is the case, the advertiser should decide whether it is willing to take a chance on a renaissance in agency fortunes that may benefit the advertiser's account.

Many advertising agencies believe that the strongest statement they can make about their growth is that it has continuously been enhanced by new assignments from existing clients. The argument—and it is a powerful one—is that if the accounts assigned to the agency consistently increase in size, and if existing clients increase the number of assignments to an incumbent agency, it is the best possible endorsement of the quality of that agency's work.

Although this argument is generally true, especially when the billings of existing accounts burgeon, it must also be recognized that many advertisers often prefer to add assignments to existing agencies, even if their work is merely competent, for no other reason than because it is easy to do so. This is particularly the case when relatively small, new accounts are to be awarded. Why go through the potential trauma of a search for a new agency when it is as simple as assigning the brand to the agency in place, conflict-free as it is, competent, and easily able to absorb the business in a manner that is comfortable and convenient, even if undistinguished, for both sides?

There is no question that an important indicator of agency vitality is the current state of its business. Ideally, the advertiser would like to identify agencies that are not losing an excessive number of accounts; that are gaining new business, but at an easily absorbable rate; and that are gaining substantial new account assignments from existing clients on the basis of solid accomplishment on previous assignments from those clients.

Personnel Turnover

Finally, there is the question of the stability of the advertising agency organization. Advertising agencies are, after all, nothing more than a collection of people. The strength of an advertising agency is the strength of its employees. And, if an advertising agency's work is strong or weak, that strength or weakness must ultimately be traced to them.

At the preliminary stage of developing a long list of advertising agency candidates, it is impossible to make anything more than a superficial appraisal of advertising agency talent. However, one key indicator of stability and internal harmony is the degree of turnover among the senior people (directors, presidents, executive vice presidents, even senior vice presidents) in the agency. In every agency, there is a small cadre of talented senior people who bear the primary responsibility for the work of the agency. Good agencies usually manage to maintain a stability of employment among the members of this group. If an agency cannot hold its key personnel together, it should give the advertiser pause. Usually this means that either these people are not compensated adequately and competitively or that there is a lack of mutual respect among the principals of the agency and their senior employees. It could also mean that the professional attention of the senior people in the agency is being corroded by the blight of politics and political maneuvering and infighting.

So, if trade press reports indicate more than ordinary movement of senior personnel in an agency, it may be a solid clue that the agency is having trouble keeping its professional commitments.

Identifying Potential Candidates

It is now time to begin to identify specific agencies that may qualify for the long agency list. As individual agencies are identified, they will be evaluated against the positive and negative criteria that have been outlined earlier. If they pass, they will then be added to the long list of advertising agencies to be considered for account assignment.

Of course, it is one thing to say that the time has come for the development of a long list of advertising agencies, and it is another thing to determine exactly how potential candidates for this long list will be identified. In fact, there are a variety of sources of advertising agency lists, and each of these may be used in developing a first cut at the long list. Once the names of agencies have been identified, the positive and negative criteria can be used as a basis for the final decision to place the agency on the long list. The following pages describe several common sources of candidate agencies for the long list of advertising agencies. It is not unusual for each of these sources to provide different kinds of information about each of the potential agency candidates.

Agency Letters of Solicitation

An obvious source of agency candidates is file correspondence that has accumulated over a period of time. Various agencies have made contact with the advertiser, describing their characteristics and capabilities, and asking the advertiser to keep them in mind in the event it seeks professional advertising agency help at some time in the future. A substantial volume of such mildly speculative letters are written by advertising agencies. If nothing else, these letters indicate agencies that have taken the trouble to identify the advertiser as a prospective client, that believe their capabilities will be of interest and potential service to the advertiser, and that have taken the initiative to write a thoughtful letter in order to inform and interest the advertiser in their work.

Many advertisers believe that they would rather do business, other things being equal, with supplier companies that have shown at least minimum prior interest in their company. One large airline, when seeking a new agency several years ago, started its long list of agencies by simply placing on it every advertising agency that had sent the airline a soliciting letter within the past year. Incidentally, it was a year in which there had been no indication of any kind that the airline had any intention of changing its agency affiliation. Other agencies were subsequently added to the agency long list for a variety of reasons, but all of the agencies that had written soliciting letters were automatically included.

General Knowledge

Perhaps the most important source of names for the long list of advertising agencies is the agency search group's general knowledge. These men and women, regardless of their job responsibilities and titles, do not live in an information vacuum. They read about advertising agencies in the trade press; they are exposed to agency representatives at meetings of professional organizations and local advertising clubs. In fact, they are continuously exposed to the work of agencies in the various media. They may become acquainted with the new business representatives of agencies in ordinary social situations, or at trade conventions. And they discuss the work of the individual agencies in meetings, business and social, with their peers. So these people routinely hold a significant amount of knowledge about advertising agencies in their mental files, and this knowledge becomes one basis for identifying a long list of potential agencies when the need arises.

References

Another prime source of names for the long list of advertising agencies is agency references solicited by members of the agency search group. Search group members know people who work with or have worked with particular advertising agencies. Nothing is simpler than telephoning these people and asking them to express their candid views about the agencies.

Such contacts tend to produce a mixed bag of responses that is hard to systematize because the individual informants may not use the same criteria of evaluation. Nevertheless, reference contacts inevitably produce a kind of gross evaluation—positive or negative—that is valuable in developing the preliminary long list of advertising agencies.

Friendships

Perhaps one of the most important sources of knowledge about advertising agencies stems from friendships between agency and advertiser personnel—either principals or senior officers. Time and again an agency is placed on the long list for no other reason than the mutual friendship and respect of two important individuals: one in the advertiser and the other in the agency. In fact, it is not unusual for the strength of such friendships to shortcut the rest of the agency selection process, leading directly to the appointment of the agency. Such agency selection scenarios tend to infuriate many advertising agency principals (though rarely the beneficiaries of such friendships) because they believe that such agency appointments ignore the professional issues and appraisals that should provide the basis of the selection of any advertising agency.

There is no record of the relative success or failure of advertising agencies that have been chosen only on the basis of friendship, as opposed to agencies chosen as a result of rational evaluations and comparisons. Certainly, diligence and objectivity in the search for an advertising agency will eventually pay substantial benefits. But there is no reason why agencies that are known to the advertiser solely on the basis of friendship should not be added to the long list of candidates. Likewise, there is no reason why such candidates should receive any special treatment; they should be evaluated on the basis of the same criteria that are applied to other agencies.

Consultants

Advertising agency search consultants are a particularly fertile source of identification of advertising agencies for the long list. Such consultants deal with a wide variety of marketing and advertising situations, companies, and personalities. As a result, they may be well informed about the current performance of a large number of advertising agencies in actual on-line marketing or advertising situations.

In addition, the consultants may have insight into the way individual agencies work, both with their employees and with their clients—the kind of insight that can almost never be achieved by a third party advertiser who is on the outside looking in. Perhaps the strongest contribution a consultant can make is to identify agencies that he or she knows are well-suited to a particular advertiser's advertising problems—especially agencies that hitherto have been totally unknown to the advertiser.

A major fast-food chain was looking for a new advertising agency in 1987. At the same time that executives of the chain retained an outside consultant to help them with their search, a long list of advertising agencies had already been developed. This long list reflected the industry reputation of agencies, known agency conflicts, and executive friendships with agency counterparts.

The consultant suggested that three additional agencies be added to the long list. There was some resistance to this suggestion since none of the advertiser executives had personal knowledge of or contacts with any of the three agencies. In the end, however, the three agencies were added to the long list. After all of the long list agencies had made a credentials presentation to the search committee, three of the long-list agencies were selected as finalists. Two of the three finalist agencies came from the three agencies that had originally been recommended by the consultant.

There are a variety of other contributions that responsible and competent consultants can make to the advertising agency selection process, as we will see in the following pages.

Standard Directory of Advertising Agencies

If an advertiser wants to be absolutely certain that it has left no stone unturned in the search for an advertising agency, it can always review the 3,588 advertising agencies that have listed themselves in the *Standard Directory of Advertising Agencies*, or, as it is known in the trade, "The Red Book."

As with any comprehensive directory, there is no easy way to review its alphabetical listings. There is, in fact, no alternative but to move through the pages of the register and evaluate each listed agency on the basis of the objective criteria set up in the agency selection process. Most of the listed agencies will be quickly eliminated because of size, location, specialization, or product conflict. And there is no guarantee that, even after the comprehensive (and tedious) review has been completed, any new candidates of potential merit will have been identified.

Yet if the advertiser wants to be absolutely certain that it has exhausted every alternative in its search for an advertising agency, the only way is to review rigorously the listings in the *Standard Directory of Advertising Agencies*. One way to accomplish this without using senior employee time is to give the job to an outside consultant.

Finalizing the Long List

The advertiser is now at a point where it has a list of advertising agency names that may qualify as candidates for its advertising account assignment. As we have just seen, these names may have come from a variety of sources and been subjected to varying degrees of critical evaluation.

The first crucial step, after the first draft of the long list has been completed, is to resubmit every name on the list to the negative and positive criteria that have previously been developed. Typically, some of the agencies on the first draft will have been thoroughly screened according to the preestablished criteria, while others will not have been. For example, names derived from a review of the *Standard Directory* are very likely to have been screened according to the predetermined list of criteria, because such screening is usually organized and efficient. Yet it is quite likely that agency names that have been added to the first draft of the long list on the basis of friendships have not been subjected to an evaluation based on established positive and negative selection criteria.

Every advertising agency on the final long list should meet all the criteria set by the search group. Every agency on this list should be the appropriate size, possess whatever specialization is needed, have the regional and/or international offices that are required, be free of overt conflicts, and have the media competence and ownership structure that has been specified. Every agency on the long list should have a satisfactory reputation, have a creative product that appears to be generally acceptable to the advertiser, and appear to have solved advertising problems that are similar or analogous to those of the advertiser. It should have a vital but not turbulent recent business history and a reasonable senior personnel turnover rate.

After all the screening work is done, the advertiser is presumably left with a list of advertising agencies that seem to be potentially acceptable. The number of candidates remaining on this preliminary list of agencies is important. If only two or three agencies remain, the search may have to be prolonged. Such a result may mean that the agency screening process has not been far-reaching enough. Of course, there is always the possibility that only two or three agencies will, in fact, satisfy *all* of the advertiser's criteria and that an honest appraisal will yield only two or three realistic alternatives. However, the number and variety of advertising agencies listed in exhibits 3–1 and 3–2 strongly suggest that in most cases there should be more than a few realistic alternative agency candidates.

It is more likely that the preliminary screening will yield too many candidates. If we assume that the advertiser will ultimately be making both written and personal contact with all of the agencies on the long list, then there must be a practical limit on the number of agencies on that list. A list of 30 or 40 agencies will certainly seem too long to most advertisers, unless they are a government office that is required by law to give equal attention to all candidates, qualified or not.

What then is a reasonable number of candidates on the long list of agency candidates? Clearly the number is arbitrary, and clearly the number will depend on the number of agencies that the advertiser wants to screen. *There is no magic number.* Many advertisers seem to believe that a long list, rigorously developed, of eight to ten agencies is ideal. A few work with long lists of as many as 12 to 15.

What happens when the developed list of qualified agencies must be pared down? If all the agencies are equally qualified, this poses a problem. But, realistically, it is unlikely that all agencies will be equally qualified on subjective criteria such as industry reputation, quality of creative work, experience on similar advertising problems, and the like. A more rigorous application of these criteria almost inevitably eases the chore of paring the long list of qualified agencies down to a reasonable and practical number.

The harder the advertiser works to develop a sound long list of advertising agencies, the more likely it is to guarantee a superior agency selection. Certainly, it is usually impossible to expand the advertiser's agency horizon *after* the long list of agencies has finally been determined.

Advertising agencies have an intense interest in advertisers' long lists. Many agencies shape their own promotional strategies with the primary objective of making sure that they will end up on the long lists of advertisers whom they wish to serve.

As one advertising agency president recently remarked:

We *know* who we want as clients. We have developed a list of 100 companies, large and small, on an industry-by-industry basis that we would like to serve. And we are updating that list constantly. We communicate with key executives in those companies constantly. Every one of them receives a letter from me every 18 months saying we don't think he's looking for a new agency, but when he does, he should consider us, and I tell him why. And we send them direct-mail pieces about us and our work every three or four months. If our media guy makes a speech somewhere that I think is good, we send the speech to all these prospects, with a brief covering note from me, telling why the speech is good and what it has to do with how good our agency is. We send out a reel of our ten best commercials every year. We look for interesting things that reflect favorably upon us, and when we find them, we circulate them. We do this with only one thought in mind: We want to be *considered* when those advertisers decide they need a new agency. We can't solicit the business if we don't make the long list. And you're a hell of a lot more likely to make the long list if they *know who you are*.

Making Contact with Prospective Advertising Agencies: The Agency Questionnaire

The advertiser is now prepared to begin to make direct contact with prospective advertising agencies. Up to this point, the advertiser has been collecting information about agencies from secondary sources, from informal conversations with friends and contacts in the industry, from a consultant, and so forth. This kind of information is adequate as the basis for the long list of advertising agencies to be considered, but it cannot be used as a basis for a final choice or even to narrow the field of contenders. Direct contact between advertiser and agencies is now required.

Some advertisers send a formal questionnaire to the long-list agencies to acquire the information they will need in order to discriminate further among them. Other advertisers find the formal questionnaire too impersonal and inflexible at this stage of their search and prefer to have informal meetings with the long-list agencies. Most advertisers send questionnaires *and* hold informal meetings. This procedure works best, as we shall see, because of the shortcomings in both the questionnaires and the informal meetings.

In any event, at the end of this information-gathering process, the advertiser should have accumulated enough new information about the long-list agencies to be able to reduce the list to three to five finalists.

Using a Questionnaire

When the advertiser decides to use a questionnaire, informal meetings, or both, it must carefully define the purpose of these activities. It is axiomatic that contacts with the advertising agencies should be designed to find out *what the advertiser wants to know* about the agency, rather than to let the agency tell the advertiser only *what the agency wants it to know*. Therefore, the advertiser needs a well-thought-out information plan to serve as a basis for these first direct contacts with the advertising agency. At the end of the initial contact, the advertiser should have all of the elements contained in its information plan for every agency on the long list. With this information, the short list of agencies can then be developed. The agency questionnaire is emphasized in this chapter with the understanding that the advertiser's information objectives at this stage are identical for both the questionnaire and the informal meetings.

The more thought that goes into the preparation of the questionnaire, the more likely it is to yield pertinent new information that will help the advertiser in its selection process. Writing effective questionnaires, of any kind, is not just a matter of writing a long list of questions. Rather, it is a matter of writing a list of questions that are specifically related to the purpose of the questionnaire writer—questions that one can reasonably expect the prospective respondents to be *able* and *willing* to answer.

Many advertising agency executives regard advertiser-initiated questionnaires with mixed emotions. On the one hand, they are delighted to be included among a group of peers being considered for new business. On the other hand, they often find the questionnaires to be too long, redundant, impertinent, unrelated to the relative excellence of the agency's service, and so loosely thought-out that they are difficult to answer. The agency executives especially resent questionnaires with such defects because they must spend their own time—and often a substantial amount— in preparing the answers, since a formal response to a formal questionnaire must portray the agency as favorably as possible.

Such agency truculence about questionnaires may not concern many advertisers. After all, if an agency wants the business, at least it can hustle a little to get it, even if the hustling requires filling in a questionnaire. Yet, if the questionnaires require too much work, advertising agencies may simply refuse to answer them. Usually, the very agencies that are likely to be most attractive to advertisers are those that are successful enough to refuse to answer questionnaires.

For example, David Ogilvy, the legendary advertising agency leader, has long been outspoken in his annoyance with advertising questionnaires: "Now it so happens that I deplore the practice of selecting agencies by questionnaire, and I have consigned dozens of them to garbage cans."[1] However, Ogilvy's antipathy for filling in agency questionnaires appar-

---

[1] David Ogilvy, *Confessions of An Advertising Man* (New York: Atheneum, 1963), p. 37.

ently varies with the magnitude of the prize that the sponsor of the questionnaire represents: "But I stayed up all night drafting answers to the Shell questionnaire."[2]

In any event, there are good reasons for the advertiser to make the questionnaire as easy to answer as possible. At least, this endeavor will produce a less grudging response from those agencies that are not enchanted with questionnaires. Furthermore, well-thought-out questionnaires are likely to elicit more complete answers with more relevant information from agencies.

Specifying Information Needs

In general, agency questionnaires tend to reflect the specific companies that prepare them and the companies' particular concerns about their advertising programs. No one questionnaire will be well-suited, therefore, to all companies. Yet most advertisers will be concerned with the same general kinds of information.

The agency questionnaire should be designed to yield five general types of information.

Basic Facts

The first category of information includes the agency's billings, current accounts, recent account gains and losses, branch offices, financial references, examples of its current campaigns, its organization, descriptions of the professional backgrounds of its senior people, and the like.

Most, if not all, of such information is available in the public record—in the *Standard Directory of Advertising Agencies*, in the annual *Advertising Age* issue devoted to advertising agencies, and often, too, in the agency's standard introductory brochures.

The advertiser should have accumulated most of this kind of information while producing the long list of advertising agencies. There is certainly no need in the questionnaire to ask the agency to repeat information that the advertiser already has, or should have, from a standard, credible source. At least, this should be the rule—*unless* the advertiser wants to confirm that the agency gives the same information about itself to public sources as it does in responses to agency questionnaires.

---

[2]*Ibid.*

Ordinarily, then, there should be no need for the advertiser to load up its questionnaire with facts that are (or *should* be) already available.

There is, however, one class of important facts about the agency that may not be reliably gleaned from the public record. This has to do with recent account losses. One area of concern for the potential advertiser is whether the agency is a vital, productive concern. An agency that is consistently satisfying and keeping its current clients is more likely to satisfy a prospective new client. It is reasonable, therefore, to ask the agency to list those clients that it has lost within a relatively recent period—two or three years, for example. It is also reasonable to ask the agency to comment on these account losses, if it wishes to do so. Some agency executives may feel that it is no one's business why a particular account was lost. Most agency executives, on the other hand, are anxious to give their side of account-loss stories, and the candor with which they describe these situations may give the advertiser important insight into the agency that it can gain in no other way.

Many questionnaires go a step further and ask the agency to describe the accounts that it has *acquired* in the past two or three years. At least for those agencies with account gains that have offset account losses, this permits the respondent the opportunity to square up the record. Agency executives may also be asked to comment on why they believe they were awarded these new account assignments. Once again, the advertiser is given an opportunity to gain some insight into the apparent candor with which the agency handles such questions. In addition, the advertiser can assess these answers to determine whether the agency has gained new business for reasons that appear relevant to the advertiser's needs.

A good way to determine the account stability of an agency—at least for agencies that have existed for some time—is to compare client lists of today with those of five and ten years earlier. If many of the same clients are on each of these lists, a substantial agency stability is clearly demonstrated. If, on the other hand, there is a substantial difference between the lists, this finding speaks for itself. Without the questionnaire, an advertiser might have difficulty determining exactly what clients a particular agency had as long ago as five or ten years. If this is the case, it is reasonable to ask the agency to provide this information in the questionnaire.

Operation

A second general category of questioning has to do with how the agency actually operates in certain key areas that will specifically and predictably affect how it services its existing and prospective clients. Here are some examples of the kinds of agency behavior that will affect client–agency relationships directly.

Cost Accounting System.   Does the agency have an internal cost accounting system? The advertiser is not interested in immersing itself in the internal financial affairs of the agency, especially at this early stage in the agency evaluation process. Nor is it likely that any agency will have much enthusiasm for questionnaire inquiries about the details of its internal financial processes and procedures. But the existence of an internal cost accounting system and a description of its general outline are important to most advertiser-agency relationships, since it produces agency cost data that are essential to agency compensation conversations.

If the advertiser wishes to discuss a labor-based fee basis of compensation with the agency, it must know about the existence of an internal agency time-cost accounting system. This knowledge is essential because in the typical agency more than 60 percent of all costs are for personnel time. If these are not closely accounted, there is no way to itemize and specify the bulk of agency costs as a basis for determining an adequate fee.

However, even if the advertiser contemplates compensating its agency by a commission arrangement, it is still reasonable for it to ask about the existence of an internal time-cost accounting system. The existence of such a system suggests a mature and businesslike handling of agency financial affairs and business practices. An advertiser should be reassured about the cost-account system regardless of the method of compensation it intends to use.

In addition, presuming the existence of a time-cost accounting system, it is not inappropriate for the advertiser to ask how the system works, how long it has been in existence, and even how the agency's experience with the system has led to modifications. Answers to such questions will give the advertiser further insight into the solidity of the internal time-cost accounting system that the agency has adopted and also further insight into the agency's business practices.

Financial History.   Most advertisers want to know whether they are dealing with financially successful agencies. The agency has, of course, a legal responsibility to make media payments in the advertiser's behalf. Certainly, the advertiser wants to know if the agency has a history of prompt payment and the financial stability and strong credit rating that this implies. Beyond this, however, most advertisers believe that the agencies they deal with should be profitable enterprises. They believe they should be profitable for two reasons. First, profitable business organizations demonstrate that their principals have learned to manage the complexities of running a business successfully. Second, agency profitability frees the agency managers to concentrate on planning and developing superior advertising ideas and campaigns, which is precisely why the advertiser hires the advertising agency in the first place.

Financial performance information is readily available for the publicly owned agencies, but these are a small minority of all advertising agencies. It is inappropriate for advertisers to expect to see balance sheets and operating statements from privately owned agencies at this preliminary stage in agency screening. Many privately owned agencies feel that it is inappropriate for advertisers to see their detailed financial results at any time. This is a matter for discussion between advertisers and agencies that have an ongoing relationship. When advertisers are screening prospective agencies, the advertiser should simply inquire into the historic financial results of the agency and invite the prospective agency to make any statement it wishes about its financial prosperity or lack of it. Some agencies will answer such inquiries quite fully, while others will be more reticent. Yet the answers that are given, in conjunction with discreet inquiries through other sources in the financial community, should produce a general picture for the advertiser of the relative prosperity of the agency.

Organization.   Another crucial, nonfinancial aspect of agency behavior is how the agency organizes itself to go to work. This is really two questions. First, how does the agency organize itself as a whole to serve its clients? Second, how does the agency organize itself specifically to handle the typical client? There should be direct and clear answers to both of these questions. Overall agency organization will suggest overall emphasis on various phases of agency work, such as media, creative, account management, research, sales promotion, etc. A study of the organization of the candidate agencies should provide an interesting basis for comparison.

The typical agency organization chart for an individual client will show how the agency believes it should staff an account and perhaps will show how it would respond to the advertiser's specific needs.

These questions should yield answers that will suggest what kind of general staffing to expect from each prospective agency. Again, a comparison of agency answers will provide a firm preliminary basis for discriminating among agencies on this crucial matter of account staffing.

Top Management Involvement.   Another matter of some importance is how the top management makes contact with client top management. Some agency managers may have no plan at all, while others may have developed practices to involve themselves with client management.

Another aspect to consider is how much the agency top management participates in the development of advertising plans and programs for their clients. It's obvious, for example, that the typical agency president cannot be expected to spend a great deal of time on every client. More likely, the agency top manager will become professionally involved with only a few of the agency's accounts, and these will usually be the largest and most important ones.

However, if the agency is properly organized and managed, the agency top manager will have a general awareness of issues and problems of all accounts, by means of formal or informal internal agency meetings and status report documents. The actual professional responsibility for handling most accounts is then delegated to senior account managers, who report directly to agency top management.

The advertiser should expect at this point in the agency search to learn through the questionnaire about this pattern of professional involvement by agency top managers. It should also know how the agency's top management intends to maintain continuing contact with the advertiser.

Personnel Development. Finally, the advertiser will want to know whether the agency has formal plans for internal personnel development, and, if so, what they are. The assignment of an advertising account presumes a long-term relationship, and the implication is that the agency should be able to continuously staff itself to perpetuate that relationship in the same way as when the account is first assigned.

Some agencies go to rather elaborate lengths to recruit and train outstanding graduates of colleges and business schools. Other agencies maintain elaborate internal training and seminar programs to make sure that their employees not only are professionally current but are constantly acquiring skills so they can move upward in the agency if they have the talent. Other agencies prosper without either formal personnel recruitment or training programs.

No matter how the agency approaches this subject, it is both reasonable and in the advertiser's interest to obtain information about how the agency intends to maintain the continuity of its professional service.

Advertising Philosophy

What attitudes does the agency hold about advertising, the advertising process, and the creation of successful advertising programs? Advertising is the product of the advertising agency. An advertising program reflects the work of an amalgam of people with skills in marketing, creative, me-

73

dia, research, and other areas. The way in which these people are trained, organized, and directed will determine the character and quality of the advertising product of every advertising agency. Each advertising agency presumably performs its work with specific attitudes about advertising. Presumably, also, the agency has defined effective advertising and organized itself so that it will continuously produce such advertising.

It is reasonable to pursue such matters in the agency questionnaire. The agency may be asked its definition of effective advertising. It may be asked what it does to assure that its organization produces effective advertising. It may be asked to describe the internal controls and procedures it uses to assure that its clients' advertising meets its self-imposed definitions of effective advertising.

This line of questioning will reveal the agency's philosophy about advertising, if indeed it can make its philosophy explicit. In addition, it will also reveal how the agency has organized itself to implement its advertising philosophy.

Note well that many successful agencies seem to produce highly effective advertising continuously without a stated advertising philosophy, and without attempting to control the work in concert with any philosophy. Advertising is a creative process, after all, and some of its most successful practitioners feel strongly that it requires the continuous application of specialized advertising *talents* to produce great advertising, rather than the continuous application of a particular *philosophy* or set of rules.

The point of this discussion, from the standpoint of the advertising agency questionnaire (and subsequent meetings with prospective agencies), is not that one approach is good or bad. It is that the philosophy or attitude the agency follows in developing its advertising product is at the heart of the relationship between an advertiser and its agency, especially since it will ultimately determine the nature of the agency's advertising product. It is appropriate for the advertiser to know about the prospective agency's philosophies about advertising—because such philosophies are so closely tied to the final product *and* because if the advertiser disagrees with the agency's philosophy, it is unlikely that the relationship will ever be comfortable.

Pertinent Agency Experience

What does the agency know about the advertiser's business? Another matter that the agency questionnaire should cover is the agency's experience in the advertiser's line of business.

The advertiser's preliminary investigation will have ascertained that the agency at present has no conflicting account. In addition, this investigation may have also provided information about prior agency experience in the product category. It is now appropriate, through the agency questionnaire, to obtain further information about agency experience that is directly related to the advertiser account assignment.

Thus, the agency should be asked to describe experience that *it* believes to be most directly pertinent. It should be emphasized that this is *agency* experience rather than *employee* experience in previous jobs. The objective is to identify recent, relevant agency experience that reflects the collective work of the organization—from chief executive officer to art bullpen.

Perhaps the agency has no experience that is directly related to the advertiser. It is important that the advertiser know this now, if this information is important. On the other hand, perhaps the agency will describe experience that is at least sufficiently related in some way to suggest that it would give the agency a real advantage in approaching the advertiser's account. Whatever the exact situation, it is best to air the issue of agency experience at the questionnaire stage. The question should be phrased so that the agency can decide which portion of its experience is pertinent. This gives the agency license to bring whatever it believes to be relevant to the advertiser's attention, thus giving the advertiser another insight into the way the agency thinks and presents itself.

Current Agency Clients

Finally, many advertisers want to know what current agency clients may think about the agency and its work. A standard question, then, is about current agency clients whom the advertiser may contact for references.

Of course, the advertiser may already know responsible persons in companies that are serviced by the agency and may contact them for reference, regardless of the agency's wishes.

Asking for references in the questionnaire provides the advertiser with sources to check if the search group members do not personally know any of the agency's clients. In addition, a list of references may reveal something about the strength of existing agency–client relationships. Does the agency supply as references its leading or most important clients, or does it limit its references to seemingly secondary or minor accounts?

Preparing the Questionnaire

All of the information outlined above can now be combined into a formal questionnaire, an example of which is given in Exhibit 5–1. The order of

Exhibit 5–1.   Comprehensive Advertising Agency Questionnaire

Agency _____

Address _____

Telephone _____

Name and Title of Agency Contact _____

A. Agency Ownership and Key Employees

1. When was your agency founded?

2. Who owns your agency?

3. Who controls the management of your agency?

4. Please identify the ten most important executives in your agency, and provide a short one-paragraph description of each of their careers. Also tell exactly what they now do in your agency.

5. Is there anything else you would like to tell us about the ownership of your agency or its key employees?

B. Agency Organization and Service

1. Provide a functional organization chart for your agency. (It is not necessary to indicate names.)

2. Please describe how your agency provides agency service to a typical client. Is it possible to provide a functional account organization chart indicating contact points between agency and client?

3. Please describe the function of your account management. How does it interact with a typical client? What are its specific responsibilities within the agency? What fraction of your full-time employees are in account management?

4. Please describe your creative department. How would you characterize its strengths? To what extent and under what circumstances are representatives of the creative department in direct contact with your clients?

5. Please describe your media department. How would you characterize its strengths? To what extent and under what circumstances are representatives of your media department in direct contact with your clients?

6. Please describe your research department. How would you characterize its strengths? To what extent and under what circumstances are representatives of your research department in direct contact with your clients?

7. When your agency is awarded a new account, does it typically staff it from within, or do you also augment internal staffing with professional people newly hired from outside the agency?

8. Is there anything else you would like to tell us about your agency's organization and how it serves its clients?

C. Top Management Participation in Account Service

1. How does the chief executive officer maintain contact with your clients?

2. Does the chief executive officer participate directly in the professional conduct of any client advertising programs? Would you mind telling us which ones these are?

Exhibit 5–1. (Continued)

3. Who—by title—is the senior agency executive responsible for the professional conduct of other agency accounts?

4. Is there anything else you would like to tell us about the participation of your top management in account service?

D. **Agency Personnel Recruitment and Development Policies**

1. Do you maintain a formal program to recruit particular types of recent college or graduate school students into the employ of your agency? If you do, please describe these programs.

2. Do you maintain a training program or programs for young people entering your agency? If you do, please describe the program(s).

3. Do you maintain any internal training programs for long-term employees of your agency? If you do, please describe these programs.

4. Is there anything else you would like to tell us about your personnel recruitment and development policies?

E. **Account Gain and Loss History**

1. What accounts has your agency lost in the past two years?

2. If you have lost accounts within the past two years, would you care to comment on why they were lost?

3. What accounts has your agency gained in the past two years?

4. If you have gained accounts within the past two years, would you care to comment on why your agency was chosen to service these new accounts?

5. Would you give us your list of accounts as of January 1, 19__ (five years prior to date of questionnaire)?

6. Would you give us your list of accounts as of January 1, 19__ (ten years prior to date of questionnaire)?

7. Is there anything else you would like to tell us about your account gain and loss history?

F. **Agency Financial Standing and Policies**

1. Is your agency profitable?

2. We are not interested in financial details that you do not wish to provide, but we would be interested in any comments on your history of profitability you care to make, as well as any supporting data you wish to supply.

3. How would you characterize your balance sheet?

4. Again, we would be interested in any additional comments you might wish to make about your balance sheet.

5. Do you have any preference between the fee and commission methods of compensation? If you do, please tell us why.

6. Do you have an internal time-cost accounting system? If you do, when was it put in place? If you do, what has been your experience with the system?

7. If you would like to tell us, we would like to know approximately what proportion of agency internal time is charged against client accounts and what proportion is charged against general management, general overhead, and/or unallocated direct salary expense.

8. We would be interested in any comments that you wish to make about your credit rating, your media payment policies, whether you consistently earn cash discounts, etc.

Exhibit 5–1. (Continued)

9. What is the distribution of your billing by media?

10. Is there anything else you would like to tell us about your agency's financial standing and policies?

G. **Agency Views about Effective Advertising**

1. How would you describe effective advertising?

2. Does your agency have any specific philosophy or practices that you believe consistently produce effective advertising?

3. Does your agency follow any procedures to maintain the effectiveness of the advertising you produce on an account-by-account basis?

4. Is there anything else you would like to tell us about your agency's views about effective advertising and how it may best be obtained?

H. **Agency Experience**

1. In general, how would you characterize the experience of your agency? With what kinds of accounts do you believe yourself to have special strength?

2. What agency experience, if any, is directly related to the product(s)/service(s) for which we now seek an advertising agency?

3. What other agency experience, although not directly relevant, do you believe might provide useful background if you were to be awarded the advertising account for this product(s)/service(s)?

4. Is there anything else about your agency experience that you believe would be helpful for us to know?

I. **References**

1. Would you object if we were to talk with some of your current clients about the effectiveness of your creative product and the excellence of your account service?

2. If you would not object, please list three or four of your current clients whom we might contact.

the questions does not follow the preceding outline exactly, having been arranged, instead, to provide an orderly flow of information. The more difficult or controversial questions are placed toward the end of the questionnaire.

This questionnaire is designed to be comprehensive, including all of the subjects discussed. Because of its comprehensiveness, the questionnaire is unlikely to suit exactly any individual advertiser; there are bound to be one or more topics in which it has little or no interest. These topics may be omitted.

In addition, the advertiser may have topics arising from the particular nature of its business that should be added to the questionnaire. This is certainly reasonable as long as the topics reflect some peculiarity of the advertiser's business that is truly related to the search for an advertising agency. Every additional question should be evaluated in terms of its ability to add to the advertiser's basic knowledge of the agency and how it can serve the advertiser. In addition, every extra question should be evaluated in terms of its ability to provide the desired information. Sometimes a questionnaire is simply ill-suited to obtaining particular kinds of information; such questions may be better answered in an informal meeting with the agency personnel.

Exhibit 5–2 is designed to evaluate the questionnaire as a source of information for the advertiser. The basic premise of Exhibit 5–2 (like the basic premise of our approach to the whole question of advertising agency questionnaires) is that it is sometimes difficult to find out everything one wants and needs to know from a written question. The questionnaire is inherently limited—primarily to matters of record or fact—and it should not be expected to deliver more information than it can.

Transmitting the Questionnaire

Once the questionnaire has been developed, it must be delivered to the agencies on the advertiser's long list. The fact that the advertiser has included all these agencies on its long list may come as a surprise to the agencies that receive the questionnaire. Therefore, a cover letter should be sent, as well.

Basically, the transmittal letter should make these four points:

1. That the advertiser is searching for an agency to handle a specific advertising assignment.
2. That the assignment is described in detail in the attached Advertising Account Profile.
3. That a number of other agencies are included in this search.
4. That, once the completed questionnaire is received, the advertiser would like to make an informal visit to the advertising agency premises to become more fully informed about the agency's past work, etc.

If the advertiser has not previously publicly stated that it is searching for an agency, the release of the questionnaire and the Advertising Account Profile to the long list of agencies will almost certainly make the search publicly known. This, in turn, will lead to a deluge of requests for consideration from agencies not included on the long list. How these requests are handled is entirely up to the advertiser. The whole agency search process that has been described is designed to assure the advertiser

Exhibit 5–2. An Evaluation of the Questionnaire as a Source of Information about Agencies

1. General Character of the Agency	Evaluation of Questionnaire*
Date agency founded?	Excellent
Management young and vigorous or seasoned and sedentary?	Fair
Who owns agency and who controls its management?	Excellent
Agency an integrated whole or separate fiefdoms?	Good
Management style—heavy-handed and military or light and purposeful?	Fair
Agency zest for advertising and its creation?	Fair
Agency professionalism versus hucksterism?	Fair
Agency practice in staffing accounts?	Good
Agency practice in maintaining top management contact with accounts?	Good
Agency dependence on training programs versus outside recruitment?	Fair
Agency media billing mix?	Excellent

2. General Experience of the Agency	
How does agency describe its own expertise?	Excellent
In what kinds of advertising assignments does agency excel?	Fair
What kinds of advertising assignments does agency acknowledge that it is unprepared to handle?	Poor
How does agency describe its particular experience in advertiser product category?	Excellent
Does agency have experience in other product categories that it believes to be especially pertinent?	Excellent

3. The Stability of the Agency as a Business Entity	
What is the financial history of agency?	Good
Is agency profitable?	Good
	(continued)

*Based on a four-position subjective scale: Excellent, Good, Fair, Poor.

Exhibit 5–2.   (Continued)

	Evaluation of Questionnaire*
Does agency pay its bills promptly?	Good
Does agency have an internal time accounting system?	Excellent
How does agency's internal time accounting system work?	Good
How long has this system been in place?	Excellent
What fraction of agency internal time is applied directly against accounts?	Good
What fraction of agency internal time is applied to general management, to general overhead, and/or to unallocated direct salary expense?	Good
Does agency have any preference between fee and commission compensation methods?	Excellent
What accounts has agency lost in the past two years and why?	Excellent
What accounts has agency gained in the past two years and why?	Excellent
What accounts did agency have five years ago?	Excellent
What accounts did agency have ten years ago?	Excellent

4. **The Advertising Philosophy of the Agency**

Does agency have a viewpoint about what constitutes effective advertising?	Good
How does agency demonstrate the application of its philosophy to the creative work developed for specific client accounts?	Poor
How is agency organized to produce advertising of high caliber?	Excellent
How does agency determine that each of its clients receives advertising of high caliber?	Excellent
How does this agency philosophy relate to the specific advertising assignment for which an agency is now sought?	Fair

*Based on a four-position subjective scale: Excellent, Good, Fair, Poor.

that it has screened out, in advance, all those agencies that are least likely to be able to handle the assignment. Yet it is possible that one or two qualified agencies have been overlooked and that they will now be able to convince the advertiser that they, too, should be included in the long list of agencies. Yet again, just as there is no law that says the long list of agencies may not be extended, it also must be recognized that the long list was developed as a result of a professional process designed to produce the optimal list of agency candidates.

As the questionnaires begin to come back, it will become clear that they are most useful for comparing agencies rather than for making absolute judgments about agencies. Since all advertising agencies, in a group selected for comparability, do approximately the same things, the most important issue to consider is how these agencies differ. The questionnaire responses will begin to reveal these differences. Informal meetings with the agencies that respond to the questionnaire are likely to reveal and clarify these differences even more.

Developing the Short List of Advertising Agencies

It now remains to reduce the long list of advertising agencies to a shorter, more manageable number. It is time to narrow the selection process to the three, four, or five agencies that seem, on the basis of all the prior information-gathering, to be the most qualified to handle the advertiser's account.

Companies that have used a questionnaire as a part of the agency search will now have the results in hand. Other companies may have chosen not to use an agency questionnaire. In either event, it is now time to arrange first-hand meetings with the long list of candidate agencies in order to get a look at them in the flesh. In this chapter, it is assumed that the advertiser has used a questionnaire like the one described in Chapter 5. However, whether or not a questionnaire has been used, the informal agency meetings constitute the last step in the process of selecting finalist agencies.

Get-Acquainted Meetings

The advertiser should explain to the agencies that the purpose of the first meeting is to allow the two parties to get acquainted in a relatively relaxed and informal manner. This is not a final meeting in which a choice is to be made. Later, a formal presentation meeting will accomplish that purpose. The get-acquainted meeting is one in which the advertiser intends to become acquainted with the agency executives and managers. It is a meeting in which the agency describes itself, its people, and its work.

The advertiser is represented in this informal meeting by the agency search group, as described in Chapter 3. The chairperson of that group or the outside consultant will contact the agency by telephone or by letter. He or she addresses either the person specified by the agency in its response to the questionnaire or the agency's chief executive officer. The request for the informal meeting works best if it is a little vague. One of the purposes of the get-acquainted meeting is to see how the agency handles itself and how it presents itself when little specific direction is given. The advertiser wants to understand the agency's self-perception because this is a strong indicator of the agency's general character. So the proposal for a get-acquainted meeting is best composed in a rather nondirective way. Perhaps the advertiser will say or write something like this:

We'd like to visit your agency, on an informal basis, just to get acquainted. In such a meeting, we would like to get to know your key people and, if you wish, some of the people who might be assigned to the account for which we now seek an agency. We do not seek a formal presentation at this time. We would like to talk about your agency and how it works for its clients (and clarify and discuss in more detail some of the responses to the questionnaire that you recently completed). You may also wish to show us some of your current creative work, and tell us anything else that you think we ought to know about your agency.

Such an approach leaves the structure of the meeting almost entirely in the hands of the agency. Some agencies, in response to such a request, will limit agency participation to two or three top executives. They will each discuss those aspects of agency service for which they are particularly responsible and will do their best to portray the agency and its activities in the most favorable light. Current advertising and recent innovations in media, research, promotion, or whatever will also be described. When agencies handle the informal meeting in this way, the advertiser learns a great deal about the top executives of the agency, but usually gets little insight into the agency as a vital client service organization.

At the other extreme, some agencies will respond by meeting the prospective client with one or two top executives, plus five or six people who would actually work on the account if it were awarded to the agency. When an agency does this, one of the top executives, frequently the chief executive officer, serves as a kind of ringmaster in the meeting. Each of the employees who would work on the new account—a group typically including account, creative, media, and research representatives—is asked to speak about his or her responsibility within the agency and how each one works with clients. If these individuals have backgrounds in the area of business of the new account, they will be asked to describe their background. In addition, as in the agency-executive-only type meetings, current creative work will be described, as well as recent agency professional innovations.

Between these extremes, there are all kinds of agency responses to the advertiser request for an informal get-acquainted meeting. How the agency chooses to respond will tell the advertiser an immense amount—both about the character, quality, and forthrightness of the agency and its people and about its ability to respond to a relatively unstructured situation in which it must portray itself as favorably as possible.

Specific Meeting Objectives

In the informal meeting, the agency tries to put its best foot forward, while modifying its standard approach on the basis of what it knows or speculates about the advertiser's needs. The agency usually has a well-thought-out strategy for presenting itself in these informal meetings.

Some agencies develop a low-key approach, attempting to project an image of professional competence without giving the appearance of frenetic high pressure. Other agencies prefer to come on strong, hard selling all the way, in order to create the impression of intense, high-strung excellence. Other agencies fall somewhere between these extremes in their approach to the informal meetings. The approach depends on the personalities of the agency and its principals.

Once the informal get-acquainted meeting actually starts, however, the agency's responses, regardless of its overall approach, must be more or less instinctive, because the agency cannot control the entire exchange. The advertiser has called the meeting to get acquainted with the agency and directs some portions of the meeting with its questions and comments. These advertiser-directed parts of the meeting constitute uncharted water for the agency and are most likely to yield the most valuable information for the advertiser.

What, then, are the advertiser's objectives in the informal get-acquainted meeting? Obviously, one objective is to get a feel for the agency and its people, but the advertiser should intend to accomplish considerably more than this. In general, it should first find out the information that a questionaire cannot provide.

Second, the advertiser should begin to sense whether or not this agency is suitable—whether its character, enthusiasm, and approach show an organization that the advertiser's people could work with effectively—and whether it is an organization that would do a superior advertising job. In the end, the best advertiser–agency relationships are char-

85

acterized by a mutual enthusiasm and respect, especially from the agency side. One of the most important things that an advertiser can do in the informal meetings, therefore, is to begin to determine whether the candidate agency, because of a mixture of aggressiveness, knowledge of the advertiser's business, and zest for the advertising business, is likely to bring an added dimension to the advertiser–agency relationship that other agencies, no matter how competent, simply cannot offer.

Thus, the advertiser should enter the informal meeting with a set of specific objectives to be accomplished in the meeting, almost in spite of what the agency attempts, strategically, on its own account. The informal meeting will have been successful for the advertiser if it comes away knowing exactly what it wants to know about the agency, rather than what the agency wants it to know.

The Meeting Agenda

The purpose of the informal get-acquainted meeting is to add to what the advertiser already knows about the agency, either through the agency questionnaire, previous information-gathering activities, or both. Typically, the advertiser's agenda for the meeting will cover the elements discussed in the following paragraphs.

The first objective of the informal get-acquainted meeting is to make up, insofar as possible, for the inherent shortcomings of the agency questionnaires. Five issues of agency management need clarification.

Quality

The informal meeting must, first of all, be used as an opportunity to assess the quality of the agency's management.

Are these executives apparently intelligent? Are they well-informed about their own agency and its strengths, or do they, in some instances, contradict each other about basic facts?

In one recent agency search, for example, an agency was dropped from consideration because the principals seemed not to share a common awareness of the strengths and weaknesses of their agency.

Do the agency representatives seem to have a good general knowledge of advertising and marketing, or are they vague at the mention of standard advertising and marketing terms or concepts? Do they seem well-informed about the advertiser company?

Do these executives make realistic claims about the prowess of their agency, its creative work, its professional innovations, etc.? Or do they oversell the basic capabilities of their agency? Do they assert that all of their accounts are equally successful? Or are they candid about advertising created by their agency that has been unsuccessful? Are they candid and straightforward in discussing past account losses and the reasons why, or do they claim that their losses are *always* the result of their former client's shortcomings?

Does the management of the agency control all of the agency resources, or are the agency and its resources split into individual fiefdoms, based on individual relations with specific accounts?

Are these executives young in spirit and aggressive, or are they seasoned to the point of staleness, regardless of their age? Do these executives have a zest for advertising and for advertising's ability to affect favorably the sales and profits of products? Or are they silent about advertising as an effective business tool that if properly used can positively direct the fortunes of many products and services?

Versatility

Do these executives speak candidly about the kinds of advertising work at which their agency excels, admitting a lack of aptitude for certain kinds of advertising? Or do they assert that their agency excels in all kinds of advertising assignments, including consumer packaged goods, direct-response, institutional, yellow pages, business advertising, entertainment advertising, and all other advertising specialties? If the agency management claims such versatility, can it demonstrate it?

Style

What is the management style of those who run the agency? Is the agency highly organized, with well-defined areas of responsibility and authority? If so, is it an unwieldy bureaucracy or a well-organized business with quick and positive routes of agency response to client requests? Or is the agency organized in a relatively looser way with a lighter management hand on the controls? Is there evidence that senior people have considerable latitude in the way they do their jobs and respond to clients? Are these senior people also given considerable latitude in organizing their personnel and distributing responsibilities among them? Or is an overall agency organization scheme imposed on all of the workers regardless of their personal styles?

This issue of the nature of agency organization has important implications for the agency selection process. In the first place, obviously, there is no right or wrong agency organization. An agency's organization will depend upon how the senior people in the agency like to work and how much they participate personally in the professional work on individual accounts. It *is* important, however, for the prospective client to get some sense of how the agency works. If the client is tightly organized, a loosely organized agency will almost certainly pose problems in the future, unless the account service can be arranged to mirror and respond to the advertiser's organization and its expectations and demands. Similarly, a loosely organized client may find a strictly organized, bureaucratic agency too inflexible to work with effectively.

An agency's organization is closely related to the way it delivers its advertising work. Advertisers should develop insight into agency work habits to protect themselves from selecting an agency that will not mesh well with the advertiser's work habits and practices.

Advertising Philosophy

Agency management has been given ample opportunity to state its philosophy of advertising in the agency questionnaire. If this philosophy is more than window dressing, agency executives should be able to relate it specifically to the advertisements that have been produced by the agency. The informal get-acquainted meeting offers an excellent opportunity to probe into this matter.

While the current creative work of the agency is being shown, it is appropriate for one or more of the advertiser executives to ask how this work is related to the agency's philosophy of advertising. Or the advertiser may ask how this philosophy led directly to the advertising that is being presented.

The agency should also be able to tell how it guarantees that its philosophy is applied to the work of all clients, as well as how it would be applied to a prospective client's account. The agency may, for example, describe management-supervised strategy reviews or creative reviews or other mechanisms the agency has developed.

Credibility

Of course, advertisers should hire agencies that have distinguished themselves for the quality of their work—not for the polish of their presentation. Thus, advertisers should prefer agencies that are run and staffed by professional advertising people rather than professional salespeople—that is, dedicated advertising men and women rather than hucksters.

Certainly, every advertiser has the right to hire whatever advertising agency it wishes. If the advertiser is interested in finding agencies with professional advertising people, then the informal meeting is an ideal place to do it. Although the advertiser probably cannot assess an agency's professionalism completely until the formal agency presentation, it should be able to detect the hucksters (those who talk beguilingly but don't know very much about advertising) fairly early in the game—almost certainly in the first informal meeting with the principals.

Other Issues

Finally, in the informal get-acquainted meeting, there will be several specific issues that the advertiser will wish to clarify. They may be issues that have been sparked by an agency's answer to a questionnaire question, or they may be matters of particular import to the advertiser.

For example, an advertiser may wish to know more about an agency's attitude toward compensation methods or variants. It may want to know if there are any particular compensation methods (see Chapter 9 through 13) that the agency especially likes or dislikes. The advertiser may also want to explore whether the agency has an aversion to the particular kind of compensation arrangement that the advertiser is contemplating.

The advertiser may want to know what current proportion of the agency's clients or client billings are on fee compensation and what proportion are on commission compensation.

An advertiser may want to know more about the agency's media-buying capabilities. It may want evidence of the agency's ability in negotiating media rates or concessions, or evidence of the agency's resourcefulness at finding ways to accommodate media proprietors that will benefit the advertiser.

Some advertisers, as a further example, are interested in knowing how the agency prefers to test advertising copy and the agency's general views on this topic. Unless the agency has developed a proprietary copy-testing procedure that it wants all its clients to use, it will very likely point out the great number of existing copy-testing procedures. The agency will then probably state a mild preference for one or two of these methods and indicate the preference of its clients and its range of acquiescence in testing methods. In the end, the advertiser usually determines the means by which advertising copy will be tested, and most agencies will not debate the matter vigorously.

There may be many other matters that the advertiser wants to discuss, and, of course, this informal meeting is the ideal forum in which to have such discussions. One of the great strengths of the informal meeting, especially compared to the formal questionnaire, is its flexibility.

The overall strengths and weaknesses of the informal get-acquainted meeting are evaluated in Exhibit 6–1.

Making the Short List

When the informal get-acquainted meetings with the long-list agencies are concluded, the advertiser will have completed the search for finalist agencies. It should now be able to select the three, four, or five agencies that for documented reasons seem most likely to provide the desired advertising programs and service. These make up the final short list of agencies.

There is no magic procedure by which the advertiser eliminates agencies from the long list. And, no matter how objective an advertiser's selection committee tries to be, a great deal of subjectivity creeps into the process. If the advertiser's selection committee is unimpressed by the creative work an agency shows as its best, the agency will not be likely to make the short list. And if an agency gives the impression of being relatively disinterested in working for the advertiser, the agency will usually not end up on the short list.

Some agencies may disqualify themselves early in the selection process for equally obvious reasons. For example, an agency that has recently acquired a number of new accounts may appear to be unable to give the prospective account sufficient professional attention. If the chemistry between agency top executives and members of the advertiser agency screening committee appears to be unpromising, the agency will almost certainly be eliminated, regardless of its other strengths. Advertisers rarely choose agencies whose top executives make them uncomfortable.

In other instances, there may be little differentiation among the agencies on the long list. The long-list selection process may have been so rigid that there was little variety in the agencies selected. In such situations, agencies are likely to be eliminated for less obvious and less important reasons. Chemistry may still be a factor, of course, when relatively similar agencies are being evaluated. And other, relatively subjective judgments about the nature of agency service or the strength of agency departments may also be decisive.

Exhibit 6-1. An Evaluation of the Informal Get-Acquainted Meeting as a Source of Information about Agencies

1. General Character of the Agency	Evaluation of Get-Acquainted Meeting*
Date agency founded?	Poor
Management young and vigorous or seasoned and sedentary?	Excellent
Who owns agency and who controls its management?	Good
Agency an integrated whole or separate fiefdoms?	Good
Management style—heavy-handed and military or light and purposeful?	Excellent
Agency zest for advertising and its creation?	Excellent
Agency professionalism versus hucksterism?	Excellent
Agency practice in staffing accounts?	Good
Agency practice in maintaining top management contact with accounts?	Good
Agency dependence on training programs versus outside recruitment?	Fair
Agency media billing mix?	Poor
2. General Experience of the Agency	
How does agency describe its own expertise?	Excellent
In what kinds of advertising assignments does agency excel?	Excellent
What kinds of advertising assignments does agency acknowledge that it is unprepared to handle?	Good
How does agency describe its particular experience in advertiser product category?	Good
Does agency have experience in other product categories that it believes to be especially pertinent?	Excellent
3. The Stability of the Agency as a Business Entity	
What is the financial history of agency?	Poor
Is agency profitable?	Poor
	(continued)

*Based on a four-position subjective scale: Excellent, Good, Fair, Poor.

Exhibit 6-1. (Continued)

	Evaluation of Get-Acquainted Meeting*
Date agency pay its bills promptly?	Poor
Does agency have an internal time accounting system?	Poor
How does agency's internal time accounting system work?	Poor
How long has this system been in place?	Poor
What fraction of agency internal time is applied directly against accounts?	Fair
What fraction of agency internal time is applied to general management, to general overhead, and/or to unallocated direct salary expense?	Poor
Does agency have any preference between fee and commission compensation methods?	Good
What accounts has agency lost in the past two years and why?	Good
What accounts has agency gained in the past two years and why?	Good
What accounts did agency have five years ago?	Poor
What accounts did agency have ten years ago?	Poor
4. The Advertising Philosophy of the Agency	
Does agency have a viewpoint about what constitutes effective advertising?	Excellent
How does agency demonstrate the application of its philosophy to the creative work developed for specific client accounts?	Excellent
How is agency organized to produce advertising of high caliber?	Excellent
How does agency determine that each of its clients receives advertising of high caliber?	Excellent
How does this agency philosophy relate to the specific advertising assignment for which an agency is now sought?	Excellent

*Based on a four-position subjective scale: Excellent, Good, Fair, Poor.

Why Agencies Don't Make
the Short List

There are many reasons why agencies may be dropped from the long list of candidates. The following are thirty of the most common.

1. Agency management is not compatible with client management. To the advertiser, the agency people seem to be too young, too aggressive, too insensitive, too flashy, too "New York," too old, too anxious to please, too contemplative, too uninformed about advertising, or too sedentary.

2. The individuals who run the agency and make client advertising recommendations are not in financial control of the agency. Some advertisers prefer their agencies to respond to a single master—the advertiser—rather than to two or more masters—the advertiser and, for example, financial imperatives or profit goals imposed by outsiders with financial control. Such advertisers believe that the agency's independence of thought and fullness of service may be contaminated by such outside influences.

3. Some agencies are little more than a group of separate accounts managed independently from the agency's central management. When such fiefdoms exist in an agency, some may have greater access to the agency's key personnel in the creative, media, and research areas. If this situation exists, the new advertiser and its account may receive scant service from the most gifted people in the agency.

4. The agency is too tightly organized; it is too bureaucratic.

5. The agency is too loosely organized to fully and promptly respond to client requests.

6. The agency seems interested, not in advertising *per se,* but in business policy, corporate marketing strategy, etc.

7. The agency is preoccupied with advertising and the advertising process. It is not interested in the overall thrust of its client's business, nor in fundamental marketing strategy.

8. The agency is top-heavy with salespeople.

9. The agency understaffs accounts or staffs them with fewer people than the advertiser believes necessary.

10. The agency top management has no plan for or interest in maintaining contact with advertiser top management, viewing such contact as primarily social.

93

11. The agency has no plan to perpetuate itself and its management skills.

12. The agency is not experienced in the product category represented by the advertiser's account nor in the type of advertising required by the account. Institutional advertisers, for example, like to find agencies with specific experience in their industry or at least with general experience in institutional advertising.

13. The agency is financially unstable.

14. The agency is not profitable.

15. The agency refuses or is reluctant to consider the client's preferred method of compensation.

16. The agency applies too much time to non-client, service-directed activities.

17. The agency has a recent history of excessive or unexplained account losses.

18. The agency has a recent history of extensive account gains and seems overwhelmed with servicing its new business.

19. The agency shows signs of instability; it has retained few or none of its accounts of five or ten years ago.

20. The agency's viewpoint on the creation of successful advertising is excessively rigid or does not jibe with the advertiser's.

21. The agency talks well about effective advertising but has no organizational means to implement its viewpoint for individual accounts.

22. The agency has no viewpoint about successful advertising.

23. The agency media department is inadequate—either thinly staffed or not staffed with truly experienced and professional media people. The department has a weak record in negotiating favorable prices with the media.

24. The agency research department is inadequate—either thinly staffed or not staffed with truly experienced and professional researchers. The department has a weak record in developing truly innovative research approaches.

25. The agency lacks sales promotion or merchandising skills and/or a sales promotion or merchandising department.

26. The agency creative department is inadequate, and its creative product appears substandard. The department is either thinly staffed or not staffed with truly experienced and professional creative people.

27. The advertiser dislikes the agency's creative work.

28. The agency arrogantly applies its viewpoint on advertising to all of its clients. It is arrogant in presenting its advertising campaigns.

29. The agency seems uninterested in getting the account.

30. The agency is too much like all the other competing agencies.

The final selection of agency short list candidates is sure to contain some subjective elements. Two advertisers with the same long list who are given the same information about each of the candidate agencies will almost always end up with a different short list. One man's meat is another man's poison, and one man's preferred advertising agency is another man's anathema.

An advertiser is almost certain to make mistakes in its assessment of agencies, and an agency is almost certain to make mistakes in its presentations to advertisers. But, finally, the advertiser will end up with a short list of advertising agencies, as perfect as can be made, that reflects the agency search group's best judgment of which agencies are most likely to do a superior job for the account.

The Formal Agency Presentation

The climax of the advertising agency selection process is the formal presentation by each finalist agency. This is the agencies' last opportunity to win the account, and they can be expected to go all out to accomplish this.

Organizing the Agency Presentation

The Advertiser Audience

The formal presentation is the agency's opportunity to present itself in the most favorable light. It is also the occasion on which all interested persons in the advertiser organization will be exposed to the agency selection process. So far, only the agency search group has been involved in the agency hunt. Now the search group has completed its preliminary work by identifying three, four, or five finalist agencies. The formal presentation of these finalist agencies gives all of the concerned executives an opportunity to review the candidate agencies and then to participate in the deliberations leading to the final agency choice.

The size of the advertiser audience for the final agency presentation varies. It always includes the senior marketing executive or executives. It usually includes representatives from top corporate management—typically, the chief executive officer and one or more senior officers. Perhaps the chief financial officer, an associate, or the head of public relations will attend the presentation. Possibly, some other senior officials who are particularly involved with the corporation's advertising will attend. Of course, the search group will also attend. Thus, the audience typically consists of four or five corporate officials, plus the search group, although sometimes only the chief executive officer and the head of the search group are in attendance.

At the other extreme, the basic audience group may include some or all of the marketing personnel that will ultimately have any contact with the agency. Whether a large or small group attends, each advertiser will decide who should attend the final agency presentation. This group, regardless of size, ultimately constitutes the audience when the agencies present their case.

Whatever the final composition of the group that will review the presentations of the finalist agencies, it is important that each member of the group see every presentation. Members that attend only some of the final presentations will not be prepared or qualified to judge the finalist advertising agencies.

Briefing Books

The final presentations are almost always made to an audience that includes executives that were not members of the agency search group. It is customary that these executives "be brought up to speed" on the work that has been accomplished by the agency search group. They will need to know how the agency search has proceeded up to this point and exactly why the finalist agencies were selected.

Probably the best way to inform these executives is to provide them with a briefing book that contains the basic documents that the agency search group has generated in the search process, as well as other documents that summarize the reasons for judgments made by the agency search group. This would include:

- A listing of the members of the agency search group
- Advertising Account Profile
- Minimum Criteria for Candidate Agencies
- Positive Criteria for Agency Selection
- A listing of long-list agencies
- Reasons why apparently qualified agencies were not included on the long list
- Long-list agency credentials:
  Factual—based on questionnaire responses
  Subjective—based on written summaries of informal meetings with agencies
- Reasons for selecting finalist agencies
- Reasons why other long-list agencies were not selected as finalists

The Site of the Presentations

Next, the advertiser must decide where the final presentations will be made—at the advertiser's offices or at the agency's. The larger the advertiser's audience, the more likely that the presentations will be made in the advertiser's offices. Moving large groups of the advertiser's people to the agency's offices involves a great deal of lost time and some expense, depending on the location of the corporate advertiser's headquarters.

Many advertisers, however, believe that it is important to get a feeling for the atmosphere in the agency offices and thus insist that formal presentations take place on the agency's premises. This is usually the case when the advertiser audience is small. Often, larger advertiser audiences visit agency headquarters when senior members of the advertiser's audience strongly believe that they can judge an agency only if they actually see its working premises and the agency's staff.

The Presentation Content

Each finalist agency will decide exactly what its formal presentation will contain. Most agencies will cover certain topics: the agency history; its client list; a summary of new assignments from long-term clients; a statement of how the agency works for its clients, with examples of current creative work and an explanation of how it evolves from the agency's system of working; case histories of successful campaigns; and a formal request for the business. Nevertheless, the prospective client can and should have something to say about how the presentation will relate to the prospective account assignment.

Some advertisers are nondirective about the content of the presentation and simply ask the agencies to include as much specifically pertinent material as possible.

Other advertisers are more specific, asking the agency to demonstrate in detail exactly how it would handle the prospective account. These advertisers usually ask that the people who would work on the account take part in the presentation and demonstrate their specific roles. In addition, these advertisers will want to know how agency philosophies and work procedures would apply to their account. They may ask the agency to provide a work timetable so they can learn exactly when the agency can be expected to deliver preliminary and final advertising strategies, plans, and recommendations. Finally, these advertisers may ask for specific examples of how the agency has worked for other advertisers in situations comparable to the prospective account assignment. In short, such advertisers ask the agency to tell them exactly what they would do if awarded the account but do not ask for any speculative advertising work for the account.

Some advertisers ask the agency to tell them not only how they would proceed if awarded the account, but to demonstrate their ability to develop advertising strategies to address specific advertising problems of the advertiser and/or to produce speculative advertising campaigns. In addition, such advertisers may request specific media, merchandising, or research proposals that would be appropriate to the advertising account.

The specific presentation content requested by the advertiser will depend on a variety of considerations. These four will probably be the most important:

1. First, how can the advertiser best assess the potential performance of the agency? Some advertisers believe that the true measure of an agency is how well it responds to ambiguous and uncertain direction. Such advertisers favor the nondirective approach in specifying the content of agency presentations. At the other extreme, other advertisers believe that the only valid test of an agency's capability is to have the agency either produce strategic solutions to specific advertising problems of the advertiser or create speculative advertising solutions for these problems and/or make specific media, promotion, or research proposals. Such advertisers usually require that such speculative work be presented in considerable detail.

2. Second, how much additional information about the account does the advertiser wish to reveal to the finalist agency? If the advertiser expects an agency to create specific advertising strategies and executions, it must expect to divulge considerable additional information about the product or service to be advertised. Some advertisers do this; others do not.

3. An advertiser may feel that an agency cannot create professional advertising strategies and executions on the basis of one or two briefings, minimal client exposure, and a limited amount of time. Such an advertiser feels that superior creative work results only from substantial exposure to all the available information, as well as from lengthy contact with knowledgeable advertiser personnel. Then the advertiser will not ask an agency to prepare speculative advertising work, but attempt to determine whether agency working methods will mesh neatly with its organization's.

4. Finally, if an advertiser believes that it is very important to see exactly how the individuals who will work on the account perform, it will certainly want to see specific advertising strategies and materials. If an advertiser assesses a person's capabilities by other criteria than specific work performance, it will be less interested in specific advertising.

In the end, only the advertiser can decide how it will assess the potential of the finalist agencies. The important point is that someone in the advertiser's organization—presumably the agency search group—pay attention to this question before instructing agency candidates about specific requirements for the presentation.

One of the problems with formal agency presentations is that often the presenting agencies are indistinguishable. One reason for this is that the agency search group may have narrowed down to a short list of similar agencies. Experience shows, however, that when the advertiser pays too little attention to specifying the presentation content, all the presentations tend to be bland. When the agencies are not sure what is wanted, they tend to play it safe, and safe presentations tend to resemble each other. Therefore, the advertiser will be more able to distinguish among the finalist agencies if specific content requirements (up to and including speculative advertising) are established for the formal agency presentation.

Often agencies develop a standard presentation format that adapts to the client's specific content requests. These standard formats tend to make the agency look professional and slick. They are fascinating to watch, yet they may make the advertiser question the agency's ability to respond to the advertiser's particular needs. One way to gain insight into the agency's flexibility and responsiveness is to ask simple, fundamental questions during the presentation that had not previously been asked, and to see how the agency handles the unexpected.

For example, a jeans manufacturer was screening agency presentations, and, as the president of the company later remarked:

Those presentations were so slick and canned, I couldn't tell whether they were being given by real people or machines. So I asked the agency people, out of the blue, to tell me whether they thought we were in the jeans business, or if it was just a fad, and that we were really in the low-cost fashion business. [The advertiser concluded:] It was fascinating to hear the answers. In two or three of the agencies, no one—not even the senior executive—seemed to understand the question. But in others, one in particular, the people moved right out of their presentation mold and answered my question completely and easily. In this agency, not just one person answered, but the whole team went to work on the question, right before our eyes. Then we knew that was what we wanted from an agency, and those fellows got the business. They were good in the presentation, and they haven't disappointed us yet.

Advertiser Payments for Speculative Work

The use of speculative advertising presentations has undergone a gradual increase. At one time, many advertising agencies, including many of the biggest and most respected shops, flatly refused to make speculative advertising presentations. And most of the advertisers who wanted to see speculative work flatly refused to pay for it. In this situation, advertisers who wanted to see speculative work often had to deal with agencies that were willing to provide it, although they might not otherwise have qualified for the advertiser's short list.

Both sides seem to have mellowed somewhat as the years have passed. Most agencies are now willing to provide speculative presentations, at least for advertising accounts of significant size. Furthermore, most advertisers are now willing to pay for such speculative presentations.

Such payments tend to be token ($25,000 or $50,000 are typical amounts), and advertisers and agencies agree that token payments rarely cover the costs of the presentations. But at least the agencies are now paid something for their efforts, and the advertiser can be assured that it has settled the issue of who owns the contents of the formal presentation.

Briefing the Agencies

The next step is to brief the finalist agencies. The briefing serves two purposes. The first purpose is to convey the information the agency will need to make the final presentation. This will include a description of the advertiser's preference for presentation content, plus enough additional information about the account to provide a basis for the presentation content. Usually, each finalist agency is briefed separately, although mass briefings with provision for private, follow-up questioning by individual agencies are sometimes used. Whatever the format of the briefing, it is important to give all agencies the same basic information initially. By asking questions, individual agencies may obtain information that later may give them an edge in the presentation. There is no reason to guard against this; in fact, this is one way that superior agencies begin to distinguish themselves. However, the basic information upon which the briefing is based should be the same for all candidates.

The second purpose of the briefing is to begin the process of final agency evaluation. How many people does the agency send to the briefing session? Are they the same people who will make the final presentation? Are they also the same people who have been designated by the agency to work on the account if it is awarded? What is the demeanor of the agency representatives? Are they bright and eager to acquire information, or are they merely going through the paces of being briefed? Do they seem to want the business, or do they seem indifferent and uninterested?

One agency made a very determined effort to land an automobile tire account. When they learned that they had not won the competition, they were very disappointed and somewhat surprised because they believed that their presentation had been outstanding. When the dust settled, the agency president decided to find out what had gone wrong in order to make sure that the agency would not make the same mistake again.

The agency president arranged to have dinner with the tire manufacturer's advertising director. After a while, the conversation moved around to the selection of the new advertising agency. The advertising director spoke fully about the selection process: "Did you guys really want our account?" he asked. The agency president, nonplussed, affirmed that the agency really wanted the account, had devoted much time and money to making the presentation, and had done everything possible to convince the potential client that the agency was eager for the assignment. The advertising director responded:

Oh, you guys make a great presentation, no doubt about it, but by the time you got to the presentation you were pretty well out of it. You made a bad impression at the briefing. You sent three people out here with their yellow pads and all their inquiries, but they didn't seem very enthusiastic or really interested in our business. Then we didn't hear from you until the final presentation itself. That's not the way we like to work. Your competition, the guys that won, sent 14 people to be briefed, and they were bright and enthusiastic, and did they want to find out all about tires! Then they were on the phone, two, three times a day, every day until the presentation. We got to know them and the way they worked, and we liked it. I think they had the business pretty well sewed up before they spoke one word in that final presentation.

Such contacts can be very important, as the tire advertising director's remarks indicate. Of course, it is important that the agency make these contacts substantive and not just call and visit for the sake of making a good impression.

The briefing is usually given by one or more members of the search group (plus technical personnel, if needed to deliver product design and performance information), who will make an appraisal of agency performance at this meeting. After all, members of the search group have been engaged in evaluating the finalist agencies in informal meetings and other contacts prior to the briefing meeting, and there is no reason for them to stop now.

Receiving the Agency Presentations

After the agencies have been briefed, little more remains for the advertiser than to wait. This is not a quiet period, however. Most agencies want to have continuing, intense contact throughout the period from the briefing to the final presentation. Thus, members of the search group can expect to hear from representatives of the finalist agencies on an almost daily basis.

But, aside from such contact, the day will finally arrive when the finalist agencies make their presentations. How should the advertiser prepare to maximize the value of these presentations in the selection process?

There are a variety of things that the advertiser should expect to learn about the agencies from their final presentations. Here are the most important kinds of information.

1. What kind of people represent the agency?
   - Will they work on the account, or are they essentially a new-business team, seen only in the formal presentation?
   - Do they seem like the kind of people that could work well and productively with the advertiser organization—by both temperament and professional competence?
2. What role does agency management play in the presentation?
   - Are top agency executives professional advertising participants in the presentation, or do they only make generalizations about the agency and its history?

   The prospective client should expect agency top management to understand the advertiser's basic business problems and opportunities. There is a story, perhaps apocryphal, about an advertising agency that was soliciting a massive soft-drink account, not Coca-Cola. The agency was on the short list of candidates. The day for the formal agency presentation arrived, and various advertiser managers and search team members assembled in the agency's main conference room. The agency presentation proceeded according to plan and seemed to be going extraordinarily well. After about an hour, the agency president suggested that it was time for a break and asked if anyone would like coffee or a Coke. The agency was immediately dropped from further consideration.
   - What professional role will agency top management play in servicing the account?
3. Does the agency welcome questions during the presentation, or does it almost resent them as interruptions in the smooth flow of their "show"?
4. How well does the agency respond to questions?
   - Do members of the team understand the questions?
   - Does the agency answer directly and honestly, or is it unresponsive or evasive?

M. Foster

- Does the agency address questions as a group, working out answers together, or do the agency people defer to the senior agency executive present?

5. Does the presentation deal with the advertiser's business and the problems of that business, or does the presentation seem preoccupied with the agency's concerns?

6. Has the agency made intelligent use of the materials that the advertiser has provided? Are its assumptions about this material realistic or naïve?

7. Has the agency attempted to obtain additional information about the advertiser's business and the issues that are inherent in the account?
   Has the agency done homework, or has it merely accepted what the advertiser briefing told them as an information base? Has the agency done original research? Is the research credible?

8. Is the agency's description of its problem-solving methods:
   - realistic?
   - an approach that the advertiser organization is comfortable with?
   - likely, in the advertiser's judgment, to produce superior advertising?

9. What is the quality of the speculative advertising, strategies and / or programs, if any, that have been presented?
   - Is one or more of the strategies and / or programs a reasonable solution to the advertising problems of the account?
   - Is one or more of the strategies and / or programs an outstanding, break-through solution to the advertising problems of the account?
   - Would any of the advertising strategies and / or programs be used without modification?

10. In general, what is the quality of the agency's thinking as reflected in the presentation? Is it:
    - sound and safe but not outstanding?
    - pedestrian?
    - superficial?
    - genuinely creative?

11. Overall, how good is the performance of the agency? Is it:
    - excellent?
    - very good?
    - medium?
    - poor?

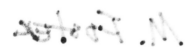

Exhibit 7–1. Agency Evaluation Rating Sheet

	Agree Strongly +5	Agree +2	Not Sure 0	Disagree −2	Disagree Strongly −5
Agency People					
1. Seem easy to work with					
2. Seem intelligent.					
3. Seem knowledgeable about our business.					
Agency Management					
4. Seem to be advertising professionals.					
5. Seem to have good business judgment.					
Agency Presentation					
6. Was related to our business.					
7. Revealed a good way of working.					
8. Reflected all the facts in the briefing.					
9. Agency has done their homework.					
Agency Creative Work					
10. Agency can produce good advertising for us.					
11. Agency advertising is too conservative.					
12. Agency advertising is too flashy.					
13. Agency can explain how its advertising has worked.					
Agency Speculative Work					
(if presented)					
14. Work presented is better than current strategies and/or programs.					
15. One program could be used immediately.					
Overall Rating of Agency					
16. This is the agency for us.					

Evaluating the Agency Presentation

The Evaluation Rating Sheet

Many advertisers feel that it is important to devise an evaluation rating sheet based on questions like those listed above, plus any others that apply to their particular agency selection situation. (See Exhibit 7–1.)

Experience indicates that rating sheets can be useful in making sure that every member of the advertiser audience is given a formal opportunity to appraise the agency. This appraisal should be based upon a comprehensive list of issues that affect the choice of an agency. At least, the rating sheet can focus attention on areas where each agency seems to be strong or weak. They also assure that all evaluators use the same criteria to assess the performance of the agencies.

In addition, however, the rating sheet can be used to produce a numerical score for each agency's performance. In Exhibit 7–1, each "strongly agree" rating receives a score of + 5; each "agree", + 2; each "not sure", zero; each "disagree", − 2; and each "strongly disagree", − 5. Thus, a perfect agency, if rated "strongly agree" on each of the 16 items, would score + 80. The use of positive and negative scores tends to differentiate quite sharply among the agencies and can produce a negative score for an agency that is clearly ill-suited to the advertiser.

Many advertisers feel that some rating items are more important than others and therefore assign them different weights. One advertiser, for example, believes that the overall rating is very important and weights it three times. He also believes the creative factors should have extra weight and weights items 10 through 15 two times. Under this plan, a perfect score would be 120—(9 × 5) + (6 × 10) + (1 × 15).

Although the rating sheet shown in Exhibit 7–1 is a good all-purpose approach, each advertiser will probably want to develop its own version with items that are most appropriate to its own search weighted in the way that is best for it.

The agency presentation is not an end in itself. It is a calculated exercise in agency salesmanship—nothing more and nothing less. As such, it should not be the final basis for selecting an advertising agency, but only one piece of evidence to be weighed in this process, although an important piece. The evaluation rating sheet summarizes the good and bad aspects of the agency's presentation and may be handy for calculating the impact of the presentations in the final decision process, along with all the other pertinent elements.

Debriefing Final Presentation Audiences

After each final agency presentation, the audience to that presentation should be debriefed. The entire group should gather in an isolated location, away from telephones and other interruptions, to discuss its collective reaction to the agency's presentation.

There should be a set and standard agenda for these debriefing sessions that is used in evaluating each agency presentation. The presentation Agency Evaluating Rating Sheet is often used as the topic outline for the debriefing sessions.

The debriefing should not be limited to the agency final presentation. It should also provide an opportunity for the agency search group to introduce additional information about each agency that has not come to light in the final presentation, as well as to make evaluative comments based on the search group's experience with the agency in its contacts during the entire search process.

Outside agency search consultants can also make a contribution to the debriefing sessions by providing a general perspective about advertising agency new business presentations and how certain elements in such presentations may distort expectations of actual performance that the agency will provide the advertiser, if selected.

The debriefing sessions should provide the following insights to each advertiser member:

- A sense of how the group as a whole has reacted to and evaluated each agency's final presentation.

- An understanding of those issues ignored by the agency in its final presentation that are important in evaluating the agency as a potential winner in the competition.

- A feeling of whether the advertiser group has reached a consensus about the potential of each agency. If a consensus has not been reached, the areas of disagreement about the agency and its potential performance as an advertising agency should be isolated.

Selecting the Advertising Agency

Once all the final presentations have been made, the advertiser can make a selection among the finalist agencies. Sometimes this is not really a problem. All the people involved in the agency search and evaluation may unanimously agree. Usually, however, the final selection is more complicated. One of the finalist agencies will appeal to some of the evaluators; other finalists will appeal to other evaluators. How, then, is the final selection made?

What the Advertiser Wants

Throughout the selection process, the agency search group has been guided by a general idea about the kind of agency needed for the new account assignment. It formed a basis for determining the selection criteria for the long list of advertising agencies, and it was an important influence in selecting the short list of finalists.

The first step in making the final selection is to remind all participants in the selection process exactly what kind of an agency the company is looking for. Members of the group that have been exposed to final agency presentations will be familiar with both the minimum and positive criteria for selecting the new agency, either because they have been members of the agency search group, or because they have been briefed prior to the final agency presentations.

In any event, at the moment of final agency selection, it is important that all evaluators know exactly the criteria and procedures that the agency search group has used in selecting the finalist agencies.

Who Chooses?

The final decision about a new advertising agency is made by different people in different companies. Sometimes it is a decision of the chief executive officer alone. In other instances it is the responsibility of the senior marketing executive. In some companies the final decision is the responsibility of another corporate executive, or a group of corporate executives.

Whoever has the final authority, however, he or she or they will almost certainly want to make sure that the decision reflects a consensus among the employees who will work with the new agency. Even if the final decision does not satisfy everyone, there should at least be agreement that the new agency has no serious flaw or shortcoming. The selection of an agency is, after all, the very beginning of what may be a long working relationship. It is therefore important that positive prospects for a long and harmonious interaction appear at the outset.

Certainly, the final decision-maker or makers will lean heavily on the recommendation of the agency search group. In many instances, this group's recommendation is decisive, and the approval of the responsible corporate officer or officers is little more than a formal acceptance of the group's conclusions. In other instances, the decision-making process will be more extensive, and other persons, beyond the agency search group staff, will be asked to participate.

No matter who makes the final formal decision and who participates in the decision-making process, there are certain basic questions that must be resolved.

Questions to Be Resolved

The agency selection will be based on answers to several basic questions pertaining to agency attitude, competence, organization, experience, and performance.

Attitude

Which agency most appears to want the business? The performance of an advertising agency often depends as much on its motivation to do well and succeed as upon its overt capabilities and experience. Many practitioners feel strongly that an agency must demonstrate intense desire to win an account to qualify for the assignment.

Competence

Which agency has the best qualified people? The performance of the agency will depend finally on the people who will serve the account. Therefore, the agency should state whether the people who are on display in the final presentation will actually work for the advertiser.

If this is the case, then the advertiser must assess their qualifications in detail. It is appropriate for the advertiser to ask to see résumés of key personnel and to talk with people for whom they have worked in the past. Key agency personnel will be as important to the advertising account as key marketing employees in the advertiser's organization. The advertiser should be satisfied about their qualifications.

Chemistry

Which agency team appears to offer the best chemistry as co-workers with the advertiser's organization? Assessments of potential chemistry are subjective. Perhaps it is easier to identify those agencies whose chemistry seems poor than to pick the agency with people who are most certain to work harmoniously with the advertiser. At best, a decision on chemistry will be intuitive rather than rational, but it is important to identify such intuitions and act on them.

Organization

Which agency is best organized to work easily and surely with the advertiser organization? This may not be a decisive question in many agency selections. Most agencies have account executives handling the bulk of client contact and coordinating and supervising the work of various internal specialist departments. But agency organization may be an issue if the advertiser wants extensive or direct contact with the specialist department personnel that will work directly on its account. If, for example, the advertiser is eager to have direct access to agency creative or media people, it should be sure that this is consistent with the agency's organization and policies.

Experience

Which agency has the best background to work on the assignment? The best agency is not always the agency with the most direct experience on the type of product or service category represented by the advertiser's account. If an agency has vast experience in the advertiser's product or service, it has probably worked on a competitive account and is now available for the proposed assignment only because it has been dismissed by the competitor. Although the agency may have been dropped for any number of reasons, the main reason might well have been incompetence. Therefore, the nature of past direct experience should be closely evaluated.

Analogous experience is probably as good a criterion for selection as direct experience. If the agency can convince the advertiser that, although it lacks much direct experience, it has extensive knowledge and experience in solving similar types of advertising problems, it is probably capable of handling the assignment.

Presentation

Of course, a crucial question is: Which agency made the best presentation? Many of the preceding questions will have been answered on the basis of impressions formed in the presentation because it is the only time that the advertiser and the search group have been able to see the agency professionally address the specific issues of interest to the advertiser. But besides revealing agency enthusiasm, ability, compatibility, organization, and background, the presentation should indicate how well the agency as a whole can address advertising problems and provide solutions.

Product

Which agency showed the best advertising? Agencies show examples of their work in formal presentations—either work for present clients that they believe to be analogous to that required for the prospective account, or speculative work done expressly for this account.

Advertisers can learn a great deal about how an agency works by studying the advertising presented to them. Does the agency, for example, discuss the creative strategy underlying the work and show how that strategy has been put into action? Does the work contain important new ideas, or does it seem to be unoriginal and dull? Does the advertising seem to be understandable and believable? Is the advertising an integrated whole—without irrelevant ideas? Would the advertising lend itself to a comprehensive campaign, or is it merely a one-shot idea?

In the end, an advertising agency stands or falls on the quality of its creative work. The advertiser should be satisfied that the agency, on the basis of the work shown, understands how to make effective advertising.

Weaknesses

What weaknesses does each finalist agency seem to have? As the advertising people consider the finalist agencies, they tend to emphasize their strengths and minimize or even ignore their weaknesses. Thus, it is important in the final selection process to consider the weaknesses of each agency and to assess how they would affect the performance of the agency.

It seems clear that any agency failing on any of the seven questions just mentioned would be considered to have a fatal weakness, serious enough to eliminate it from further consideration. In addition, there may be minor weaknesses or flaws in the perceived performance of any agency, which should be assessed to make sure that they are not critical. The question is: In what areas of performance could the agency fail, and will these failings be important?

Overview

Finally, to sum up the answers to all the preceding questions, the advertiser should ask, Which finalist agency is best fitted to handle the account? Now the advertiser must decide. Perhaps a consensus will have developed among those who will work with the agency, as a result of the deliberation sketched above. This group will make a unanimous recommendation to the company officer or officers responsible for the final decision. Or, the group may thrash out conflicting opinions about two or more agencies that appear to be well-qualified. Whatever the usual decision-making process used in the advertiser company, a decision about a new advertising agency *will be made*. The responsible officer or officers will make it, with the assumption that most of the contradictory opinions have been resolved and that most of the participants in the decision-making process, if not completely satisfied, will at least cheerfully live with the final decision.

Can't Decide?

Occasionally, the advertiser, no matter how hard it tries, simply cannot choose between two or more of the finalist agencies. Usually, this is not a matter of trying to decide which of two marginal candidates might be able to do the job. Rather, the question is more likely to be which of two equally qualified and potentially excellent candidate agencies will do the *best* job.

In such circumstances, the advertiser may ask the agencies to make a second formal presentation. The advertiser tells each candidate exactly what areas cause doubts or questions, and will ask them to address these questions in the new presentation. Most likely, doubts will be relatively minor, and they will be expressed in the same way to all the surviving agencies, simply to give them a uniform basis for a new presentation. The advertiser then has another opportunity to review these agencies. Or, perhaps, all surviving agencies may have more serious potential problems. They will be asked to address these problem areas in order to clarify the advertiser's appraisal of their work.

When the new presentations are made, the decision process must begin yet again, and, finally, one agency must be chosen over the others.

Even if the winner has now been chosen, two other matters remain to be attended to, before the formal account award and public announcement are made. First, the advertiser and its new agency must agree upon the method of compensation. Second, the advertiser and the agency should agree on a contract that will cover their new relationship.

PART 3

Advertising Agency Compensation

Agency Compensation

Most advertisers seem to agree that advertising agencies should receive a fair, but not exorbitant, profit for their services. This consensus is not easy to implement, however.

An advertising agency provides services to its client—and expects to be compensated for these services. However, there is a certain ambiguity in the services that an advertising agency is required to provide to its clients, and this ambiguity affects the way in which they are compensated.

Neither agency nor client knows in advance *exactly* what the agency will have to do to provide the client with acceptable and effective advertising. The agency services required by an advertiser will depend upon its organization and the sophistication of its employees. It will vary with the competence and creativity of the agency personnel assigned to the account. And, it will depend on how quickly the agency can find superior solutions to the advertising problems that face the advertiser. The question of agency compensation is further complicated by the fact that agency "service" consists of two quite different kinds of agency activities.

In the first place, the agency is supposed to create advertising ideas that will help the advertiser's business grow and prosper. It is virtually impossible to predict how long it will take a given number of people to produce a successful advertising idea. It may take weeks or months of painstaking analytic and exploratory work as ideas are developed and refined. Alternatively, and, at least as often, the successful advertising idea comes to its creator in a flash of insight that takes little or no formal worktime at all.

The second kind of agency service involves the nuturance of advertising ideas once created and their management in continuing advertising programs. This management of advertising ideas is a day-by-day service that requires a stable agency organization that interacts continuously with the advertiser's employees.

Because of these factors it is not easy to determine just how much an agency should be paid for its work, nor what method should be used to assure both advertiser and agency that the agency is fairly compensated for its efforts.

At the least, advertisers and agencies agree that the obligation of the agency to its client involves the four basic services that were identified in Chapter 1:

1. Strategic advertising planning
2. Creation of advertisements
3. Placement of advertisements in advertising media
4. Billing advertisers for placed advertisements and paying the advertising media

As we shall now see, advertisers have developed a variety of ways to compensate agencies for these basic services.

Methods of Compensating Advertising Agencies

Media Commissions

The traditional solution to the problem of agency compensation has been the 15 percent media commission. Under this system, advertising media allow advertising agencies to deduct a 15 percent commission on the gross cost of time or space purchased from the medium by the agency on behalf of the agency's client. Thus, the medium becomes the agency's paymaster, channeling a portion of the advertiser's advertising expenditure back to the agency as compensation for its service to the advertiser. For example, if an advertisement costs $1,000, the agency bills the advertiser $1,000, remits $850 to the medium as payment in full for the purchased space or time, and retains $150 in commission as its compensation.

In the broader world of business, it is not unusual to pay a commission for professional activities that generate sales. What _is_ unusual in the case of advertising agencies is that the commission is based not on the sales, if any, generated by the work of the advertising agency, but rather on the cost of the media purchased to help in the generation of those sales.

This anomaly reflects the historic emergence of the advertising agency during the second half of the nineteenth century. Agencies first appeared as sales agents for newspapers and magazines. The agencies were compensated and encouraged by the media because they were efficient middlemen serving the space-buying advertiser. Later, agencies evolved into media-space brokers. By the 1890s, the agencies were taking on the additional activity of providing the advertising ideas that filled the space that they had sold to advertisers. Again, this activity was encouraged by the media because they realized that the provision of such service was essential in increasing the sales of media space.

Around the turn of the century, the original advertising agency functions associated with the sale of advertising space gradually disappeared, and the agencies concentrated on providing the service that was once only incidental to their existence—that is, the development of creative advertising ideas. Throughout this evolution, agencies were compensated by media commissions on the value of advertising space used by advertisers.

In due course, in the early 1920s, the agency commission granted by the media settled at 15 percent, although in earlier years it had ranged from 10 to 25 percent. This final level of commission reflected neither economic calculus nor certainty. It was, rather, merely an accommodation between the media and the agencies for the creative service provided by the agencies to the advertisers. This commission was allowed only to agencies. If advertisers bought space (and, later, time) directly from the media, they were charged the gross or non-discounted rate.

This accommodation between advertiser and agency had nothing whatever to do with the worth of the advertising ideas created by an agency. As the role of the advertising agency evolved, the 15 percent level of commission proved to be no more, but, no less, than an inspired, if inadvertant, compromise that satisfied not only its original architects but also the advertiser who, from the start, had been only an uninvolved third party to the scheme.

The 15 percent commission system served as a basis of agency compensation until 1956. In that year, the United States Department of Justice promulgated a consent decree that effectively abolished this system. Under this decree the media were required to sell space and time at *net* price to all buyers, rather than only to agencies.

This fundamental change meant that anyone could buy media time and space at net rates. Advertisers were now free to buy media at net rates and negotiate agency compensation from scratch. The result has been the growth of alternative systems of agency compensation, including labor-based fees and modified commissions.

Labor-Based Fees

An alternative way to pay for the services of an advertising agency is the labor-based fee. In this approach, the advertiser pays for the time that agency personnel spend working on the advertising account. Markups for overhead and profit are added, by the agency, to direct labor cost, as they calculate the total amount due them from the advertiser.

Proponents of the labor-based fee point out that lawyers and accountants are usually compensated through some type of labor-based fee, as are other outsiders who are required to produce a relatively continuous flow of ideas, at least some of which are expected to be creative. Advertising agencies are required, on the other hand, to produce an occasional or spasmodic creative idea of great inherent merit. The price for the sustained flow of a lawyer's or accountant's ideas may be high, but it has, traditionally, been considered a direct function of the time that individuals spend working on them. Labor-based fees have been used to compensate advertising agencies, especially since the early 1960s, when David Ogilvy proposed that his agency preferred, or would at least be willing, to work on the basis of such fees.

A major difference between the traditional 15 percent commission and labor-based fee methods of agency compensation is in the degree of advertiser participation in the determination of agency service levels that each implies.

The labor-based fee system virtually forces the advertiser to specify what services it wishes to receive from the agency. There can be no fee without a computation of agency work units, and the advertiser is required to state generally the kind of personnel required by the account and to work out with the agency how much of each kind of skill is needed. One of the benefits of the labor-based fee is that it focuses advertiser and agency attention squarely on advertiser service needs.

Under the traditional 15 percent commission system, the advertising agency is expected to provide as much service as necessary to satisfy the needs of the advertising account. If the advertiser is not satisfied with agency service, it will complain and the agency will make whatever adjustments it can afford within commission revenue. There is probably less incentive for the advertiser to state explicitly its service needs under the commission system, since payment to the agency is automatic and there is no need for a specific negotiation to determine what the agency will be paid for the service that it has agreed to supply.

Modified Commissions

The final major category of advertising agency compensation is modified commissions. This method is similar to the traditional approach in that compensation is based on a percentage of media billings. It differs from the traditional system in that the percentage is not 15 percent and is, in fact, almost always lower than 15 percent.

There are two common variants of the modified commission system of agency compensation. In the first variant, the commission earned by the agency varies with the level of the advertiser's media billings. In the typical case, the higher the advertiser's billings, the less the commission rate paid. Thus, for example, an advertiser might pay 15 percent commission on the first $10 million of media billings, 13 percent on the next $10 million, and 11 percent on all billings in excess of $20 million.

In the second variant, the advertiser pays a flat commission on all media billings, but at a rate that is different, and almost always lower, than 15 percent. Thus, the advertiser might pay the reduced rate of 12 percent on all media billings.

Trends in Methods Used in Compensating Advertising Agencies

The Association of National Advertising has, since the mid-1970s, conducted a triennial study of the practices of its members in compensating their advertising agencies. The three most recent iterations of this study— those conducted in 1983, 1986, and 1989 [1]—reveal very significant changes in the way in which advertising agencies are compensated.

The 15 Percent Commission System Is Declining in Importance

In the first place, the traditional 15 percent commission is declining in importance as a method of compensating advertising agencies. As Exhibit 9–1 shows, 52 percent of all advertisers used the traditional 15 percent commission system to compensate their agencies in 1983; this had fallen to 43 percent in 1986; and it further declined to 35 percent in 1989.

---

[1]Association of National Advertisers, *Current Advertiser Practices in Compensating Their Advertising Agencies* (prepared by William M. Weilbacher), New York, 1983, 1986, and 1989.

Modified Commission Arrangements Are Increasing in Popularity

Meanwhile, modified commission arrangements are gaining in popularity. As Exhibit 9–1 shows, the use of the modified commission arrangement has grown from 19 percent of all advertisers in 1983 to 29 percent in 1989. In 1989, 18 percent of all advertisers used a sliding scale in their modified commission arrangements and the remaining 11 percent used a flat rate of less than 15 percent. In addition, there is some evidence that the sliding-scale approach is gaining in popularity (12 percent in 1986, 18 percent in 1989) and that the flat rate below 15 percent is not (12 percent in 1986, 11 percent in 1989).

Labor-Based Fees Appear to Be Declining in Popularity

Labor-based fees were used by 29 percent of all advertisers in 1983; by 30 percent in 1986; and by 24 percent in 1989, as Exhibit 9–1 reveals. Although the labor-based fee was second in popularity to the traditional 15 percent commission system in both 1983 and 1986, it is now third in popularity, following modified commissions. Thus, the evidence suggests that labor-based fees are now declining in popularity.

Markups on Advertising Production

In commission arrangements it is customary for the agency to charge a markup on production bills. This is analogous to the commission on media space and time, and reflects an extension of the commission principle to other non-media expenditures made by the agency in the client's behalf.

The "traditional" production markup is 17.65 percent. This exactly parallels the traditional 15 percent commission. The 15 percent media commission is *included* in the total price quoted to the advertiser by the media. The 17.65 percent markup yields the same amount of agency revenue when *added* to a production charge that does not include an agency commission.

Just as the use of the traditional media commission has declined in recent years, there has been an erosion in the use of the "traditional" 17.65 percent markup on production bills. According to the 1989 ANA study, [2] almost all commission advertisers (95 percent) continue to permit their

---

[2] *Ibid.,* p. 9.

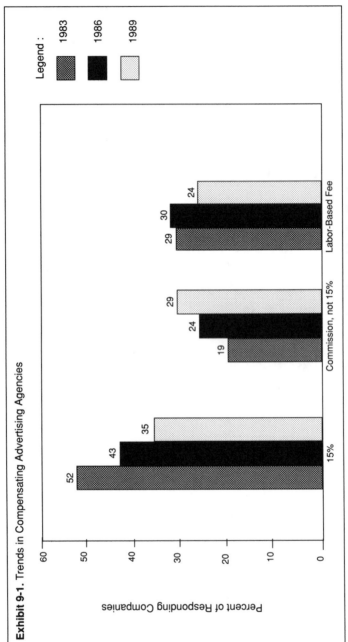

Exhibit 9-1. Trends in Compensating Advertising Agencies

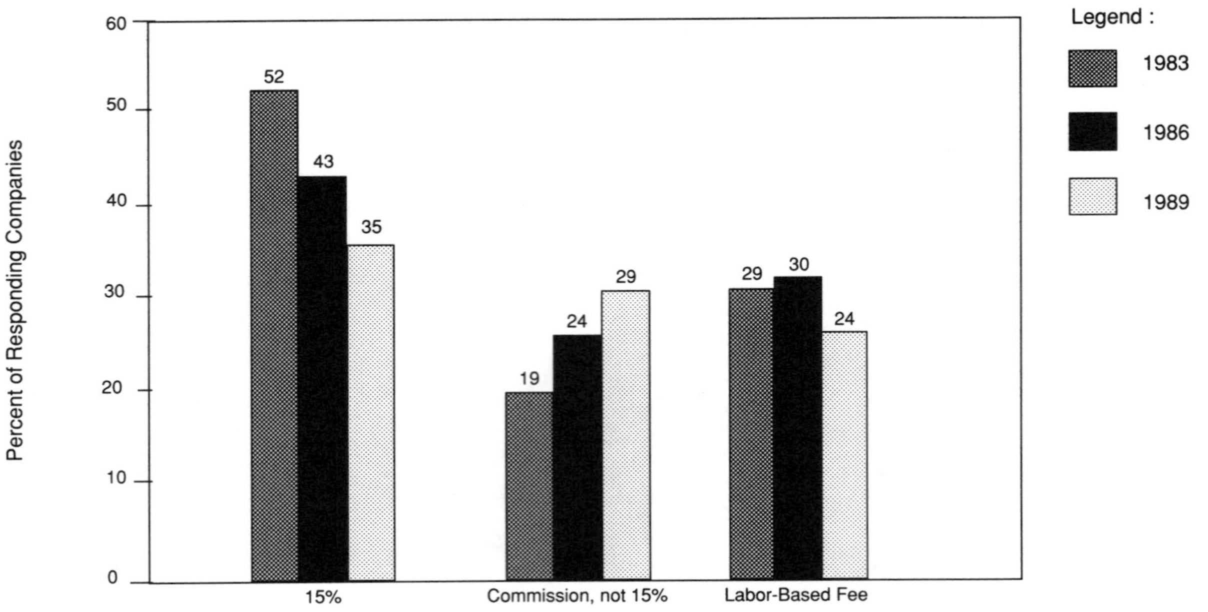
Percent of Responding Companies
60
50
40
30
20
10
0
52
43
35
19
24
29
29
30
24
15%
Commission, not 15%
Labor-Based Fee
Legend :
1983
1986
1989

Source: Association of National Advertisers, *Current Advertiser Practices in Compensating Their Advertising Agencies*, New York, 1989, p.7.

(Note: No answers and "others" were omitted from in the final figures.)

agencies to mark up production bills. Fifty-five percent of these permit the 17.65 percent markup; 2 percent pay more than 17.65 percent; and 35 percent pay less. (Eight percent of the respondents didn't answer the question.)

Variations in the Use of Compensation Methods

Most advertiser compensation agreements can be categorized into one of the three basic types described above. Yet there is a great variety in the detail of specific compensation agreements within each of these categories.

In traditional commission arrangements there are variations in production markups, in the amount of routine disclosure of accounting data about the advertising account by the agency to the advertiser, in the terms of the compensation agreement, and in the way in which the agreement may be terminated or renegotiated. In modified commission arrangements, all of these variations come into play, as well as variations in the level of fixed commissions paid or sliding scales applied to levels of billings. (See Chapter 10).

Fee agreements vary widely in respect to the bases and means of computing the labor cost component of the fee as well as in the details of overhead and profit markups that are permitted. (See Chapter 11). The richness of this variation within compensation methods is reflected in the fact that no 2 of the 167 compensation agreements studied by the ANA in 1989 were exactly the same.

Compensation Method Pros and Cons: Traditional and Modified Commissions

There is no one advertising agency compensation method that will satisfy the needs of all advertisers. Each of the methods described in Chapter 9 has strengths and weaknesses, and each is more likely to satisfy the needs of some kinds of advertisers than others. In this chapter the strengths and weaknesses of the commission methods—traditional and modified—will be outlined, with examples of alternative modified commission arrangements included.

In the following detailed discussion of advertising agency compensation systems, it is assumed that advertiser and agency genuinely desire to communicate frankly with each other about agency compensation and related issues. This implies a willingness on the agency's part to disclose costs, overhead factors, and profits. The majority of advertisers routinely receive such cost, overhead, and profit information from their agencies. It also implies a desire on the part of the advertiser that the agency be fairly compensated, including a reasonable profit.

The Traditional 15 Percent Commission

Strengths

The greatest strength of the traditional 15 percent commission system is its simplicity. The 15 percent commission system is easy to understand and is easy to apply in practice. Advertising agency employees are familiar with it and there are rarely any slip-ups in its implementation. This means that the 15 percent commission system is usually foolproof and hassle-free—there is little potential for arguments and/or recriminations about the exact nature and amount of agency charges.

Another strength of the traditional commission system is its wide acceptance in the advertising agency community. Agencies are, almost without exception, willing to be compensated by the 15 percent commission system, at least until their internal cost accounting records reveal that it is unprofitable to do so. If the advertiser desires a trouble-free financial relationship with its advertising agency, the use of the 15 percent commission system will virtually guarantee it.

Finally, many proponents of the 15 percent commission believe that it tends to provide an incentive for superior agency work. It does this in three ways.

1. It encourages the agency to produce superior work at lowest internal expense. Agencies tend to concentrate those people who are most likely to find superior advertising solutions against those advertising accounts with the greatest profit potential. Agency people believe that the best creative minds in an agency tend to find better solutions to advertising problems quicker than their less facile peers. It is only natural that agency managers are likely to put these superior creative talents to work on accounts where compensation is not based solely on work hours expended.

2. Many advertising people believe that there is usually a correlation between the excellence of advertising ideas and the size of advertising appropriations expended to support them. Also, really good advertising ideas tend to last a long time: It is cheaper for agencies to manage advertising ideas over a long life than it is continuously to create new advertising ideas.

3. As appropriations grow, economies of scale in agency operations are triggered. (See the first "weakness," following.)

Agencies thus tend, because of their own self-interest, as the argument goes, to do better work on traditional 15 percent commission accounts than on accounts with alternative compensation methods. It is simply more profitable to do so.

Weaknesses

Many advertisers believe that the most glaring weakness of the 15 percent commission method is that it ignores the possibility that there may be economies of scale in advertising agency operations. There are economies of scale in agency operations. In general, the agency costs tend to decline proportionately as the size of the advertising appropriation for a brand or an advertising account grows. If, for example, it costs an agency $1.2 million to service a $10 million account, it almost never costs $2.4 million to service the same account when its billings grow to $20 million.

This is because advertising agency service requires a minimum number of key advertising agency personnel—usually no more than seven or eight—who provide basic advertising agency service to each advertising account assigned to the agency. Two or three account executives, one or two senior creative people, a key media person, a senior production person, perhaps a senior researcher or planner—these people constitute the core group that services each agency account.

The number of people in this core group does not increase very much—if at all—as the media billings of the advertising account grow. The costs associated with the people in the core group may increase in two ways. When the billings on the account are relatively small, some members of this core group will not spend all of their time on the account. As billings grow some or all of these people will spend a greater proportion or all of their time servicing the account.

Also, as account billings grow, there is a tendency to assign better qualified, more senior, and better paid people to the account. Yet, no matter how large the advertising account becomes, costs tend to stabilize and then grow slowly, if at all, after the best people in the agency come to the point where they spend all or most of their time on it.

Thus, the 15 percent commission system has the fundamental weakness, at least from the standpoint of the advertiser, that is does not maintain a stable relationship between the flow of agency revenue and agency costs.

Another weakness of the 15 percent commission system is that it tends to remove the advertiser from the direct management of the *entire* advertising appropriation. The advertiser, under the 15 percent system, hires the agency to advise on the advertising ideas that will be used as a basis for spending 85 cents out of every advertising dollar. The remaining 15 cents reverts to the agency without either the overt concurrence or management control of the advertiser.

This is not a new issue. Writing in 1933, with what now seems to be considerable prescience, James Webb Young (then employed by the J. Walter Thompson advertising agency) had this to say:

[Advertisers] . . . see it as a defect in the structure that, having bought [advertising agency] service, the advertiser is asked to pay for it, not at a price determined by the quantity of the thing he buys, but at a price determined by the quantity of another thing—space—which has no necessary direct relation to what he wants and buys from the agency.[1]

---

[1]James Webb Young, *Advertising Agency Compensation* (Chicago: University of Chicago Press, 1933), p. 157.

More and more advertisers have, as we have seen, simply rejected this arrangement. "All of my advertising dollar belongs to me," they seem to be saying, "and it is my right and duty to manage that 15 cents on the dollar as vigorously as I manage the 85 cents that goes into the media."

The 15 Percent Media System in Practice

There are, by definition, no variations in the traditional 15 percent media commission. If the advertiser agrees to pay 15 percent, that is the end of the compensation question.

There are variations, as suggested in the preceding chapter, in the markups on production charges that 15 percent commission advertisers permit their agencies to charge. As the ANA 1989 study of agency compensation reported, 35 percent of all advertisers who permit their agencies to mark up productions bills allow a markup of less than the "traditional" 17.65 percent. A common alternative is a straight 15 percent markup on production bills, which yields a gross markup of 13.04 percent.

When to Use the 15 Percent Commission System

The traditional 15 percent commission system is ideal in those cases where it will cover the cost of the agency's critical service mass and yield a reasonable agency profit. It is important to recognize that such congruence of costs and revenues is not a likely event. In addition, the 15 percent commission system is best suited to advertisers whose budgets are relatively stable. If the 15 percent commission covers the cost of the agency's critical service mass and yields a reasonable profit, a drop in advertising budget will mean that the agency will begin to show a loss, and an increase in billings will lead to economy-of-scale-associated profit increases.

Modified Commission—Flat Rates below 15 Percent

The flat-rate commissions below 15 percent share some of the strengths and weaknesses of the 15 percent commission. Thus, the flat-rate method is simple and it may provide the agency with an incentive to produce superior work. It does not, however, recognize economies of scale in agency operations and it also tends to remove the advertiser from the direct management of the entire advertising appropriation.

A major question with flat-rate commissions is whether they are equitable to the agency. If the flat rate is set at a level that squeezes agency profits, it is likely that the agency will retaliate by cutting service costs and thus reduce either the amount or quality of service that the client receives. If either happens, the advertiser may have inadvertently lost more in agency service reduction than it has gained in reduction commissions.

A second major question with the flat-rate commission is whether the revenue it produces will permit the agency to make flexible responses to significant decreases in the advertiser's appropriation. If advertising appropriations decline, it is certain the level of service anticipated when the flat rate was determined must also decline. On the other hand, if advertising appropriations increase under the flat rate, the agency will tend to prosper because of the economies of scale.

The crucial consideration in setting a reduced flat rate of commission is communication between advertiser and agency. The advertiser must have a good knowledge of agency cost and profit expectations in setting the flat rate. In addition, there should be some ongoing system to monitor agency costs and service levels to ensure that the advertiser does not receive reduced or inadequate service as a result of the imposition of the flat rate. Finally, the enlightened advertiser establishes a minimum agency income so that agency service and profitability may be maintained even if there is a drop in media billings.

Modified Commissions—Flat-Rate Systems in Practice

The number of variations in flat-rate media commissions are obviously limited. In the first place, as noted in Chapter 9, almost no commission advertiser pays more than 15 percent in compensation for agency services.[2] The exact commission that is set below 15 percent depends upon two factors.

First, the advertiser's appropriation must be sufficiently large that economies in the scale of agency operations have been realized, The greater the economies of scale, the lower the flat-rate commission may be set. Second, advertiser service requirements also affect the level of flat-rate commissions. If the advertising appropriation is large and the level of agency service required by the advertiser is low, the flat-rate commission may be set at a lower level than if the appropriation is small and the service requirements are high.

---

[2]Some advertisers do, in fact, pay more for agency service than the traditional 15 percent commission. But these advertisers almost inevitably compensate their agencies with a labor-based fee. (See Chapter 11.)

The important point is, of course, that these are not matters that the advertiser should guess about. Flat-rate commissions below 15 percent should, to repeat, be set only after the advertiser has become thoroughly familiar with the agency cost structure and profit expectations.

The 1989 ANA study of advertiser compensation practices[3] reported the following examples of flat-rate commissions below 15 percent.

Type of Company	Billing Range	Commission Rate %
1. Package Goods	Over $100 million	10.75
2. Consumer Service	$20–49 million	12.5
3. Package Goods	$50–99 million	13.5
4. Corporate Image	$10–19 million	10.0
5. Consumer Durable	$5–9 million	14.0
6. Consumer Service	$50–99 million	12.0

When to Use the Flat-Rate Commission System

A flat-rate commission system is ideal in those cases where it will cover the cost of the agency's critical service mass and yield a reasonable profit to the agency. The use of a commission rate below 15 percent suggests that the advertising account to which it applies either has a higher level of billings or fewer service requirements than accounts which reach revenue-expense/profit equilibrium under a 15 percent commission. The circumstances under which a flat rate exactly achieves this equilibrium are as rare as the circumstances that produce such equilibrium under flat 15 percent.

Once again, a reduced flat rate implies stability in the advertising appropriation. If the appropriation is much reduced, an agency will begin to experience a profit squeeze and, if the appropriation is increased, there will be economy-of-scale-related profit increases.

Modified Commissions—The Sliding Scale

The sliding-scale commission system has the virtues of the traditional 15 percent commission without that system's insensitivity to agency econo-

---

[3]Association of National Advertisers, *Current Advertising Agency Practices in Compensating Their Agencies* (prepared by William M. Weilbacher), New York, 1989, p. 6.

mies of scale. Sliding scales are conceptually simple and usually easy to administer. Although a relatively recent development in agency compensation practice, it is not difficult to see why they are growing in popularity.

In developing a sliding scale, the most important consideration is making sure that the scale matches the economies of scale that the agency experiences in its operations.

It is not hard to conceptualize a billings chart that arrays agency billings along the left-hand or vertical axis and account-by-account direct labor cost along the horizontal axis. Presumably, as economies of scale set in, the direct labor will rise with billings, but not as fast, as hypothetically depicted in Exhibits 10–1 and 10–2. Exhibit 10–1 shows an economy-of-scale calculation that assumes that total direct-labor costs decline 5 percent with each billings increase of $12.5 million. Exhibit 10–2 assumes that labor costs decline 10 percent with each increment of $12.5 million in billings. As far as is known, no advertising agency has ever analyzed its costs in this way, at least for public consumption, but it seems certain that agencies will be encouraged to do so if and as the popularity of sliding-scale compensation systems continues to grow.

As is the case with any agency compensation system, the crucial requirement for success is full communication between advertiser and agency. The advertiser shouldn't be guessing what the agency's economy-of-scale curve looks like, and the agency should be in a position to document the revenue it needs to cover its legitimate costs and achieve a reasonable profit.

Modified Commissions—Sliding Scales in Practice

There is a wide variety of sliding scales in use. Unlike fixed-rate commission systems, traditional and modified, the sliding scale does not depend for its success upon finding the exact point where agency revenues and agency expense–profit balance. With the sliding scale, the hope is that the scale will generate revenues that track nicely with agency expenses, no matter what the level of the advertiser's appropriation.

The following examples of actual sliding scales should give a sense of the diversity of scales in use, rather than a specific idea of a particular scale that will work for a particular advertiser–agency relationship.

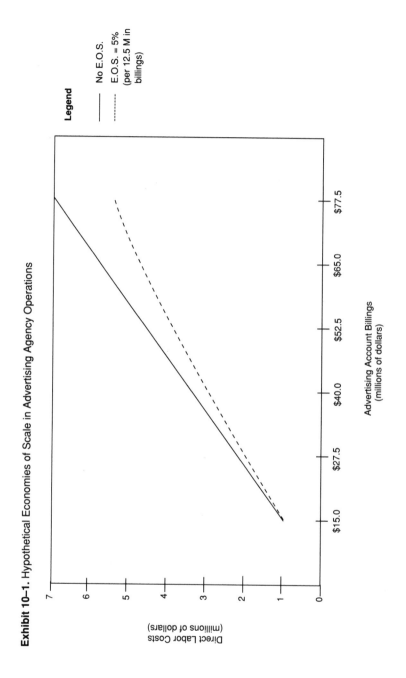

Exhibit 10–1. Hypothetical Economies of Scale in Advertising Agency Operations

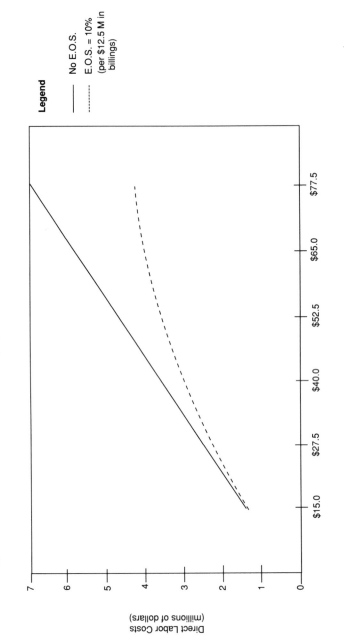

Exhibit 10–2. Hypothetical Economies of Scale in Advertising Agency Operations

Here are seven examples of sliding scales that were reported in the 1989 ANA agency compensation study.[4]

Type of Company	Billing Range	Sliding Scale
1. Package Goods	$20–49 million	15% to $10 million 13% $10–12 million 9.5% $12–30 million 9.0% $30–40 million 8.0% $40–50 million
2. Package Goods	$20–49 million	15% to $25 million 12.5% over $25 million
3. Corporate Image	$20–49 million	15% to $29 million 14% $29–34 million 13.2% over $34 million
4. Consumer Durable	$5–9 million	15% to $1.25 million 12.5% $1.25–2.5 million 10% $2.5–3.5 million 7% over $3.5 million
5. Consumer Service	$50–99 million	12.5% to $70 million 12% $70–80 million 11.5% $80–100 million
6. Package Goods	Over $100 million	15% to $5 million 14.5% $5–15 million 14% $15–25 million 13.5% $25–50 million 13% $50–100 million
7. Consumer Service	$20–49 million	11% to $20 million 15% over $20 million

When to Use a Sliding Scale

It seems clear that a sliding scale is ideal with advertising accounts that are large enough to produce economies of scale for the agencies that service them. The examples given above suggest that this threshold may vary widely.

The three package goods companies whose systems are profiled each pay 15 percent at the low end of the scale, but the first scale break point varies from $5 to $25 million. The corporate image account pays 15 percent up to $29 million. The consumer durable account pays 15 percent up to $1.25 million and breaks sharply downward after that level is reached.

[4]Ibid., p. 6.

Both service accounts pay less than 15 percent at the first point on the scale. One of these breaks slightly after the first plateau at $70 million is reached. The other increases the commission percentage from 11 percent to 15 percent when billings climb over $20 million, thus, presumably, providing the agency with an incentive to produce advertising that is so good that it will drive media billings above the $20 million level.

In conclusion, it is clear that a wide variety of sliding scales are in use. To what extent those shown above reflect a thorough study of agency costs and revenue is hard to say. Some probably represent no more than an advertiser guess, possibly informed, about agency scale economies that is not unacceptable to the agency. The one thing that is certain about sliding scales is that the better the agency knows its cost structure and profit needs and the more clearly it communicates these to its client, the more likely is the sliding scale to satisfy both parties over an extended period of time.

Compensation Method Pros and Cons: Labor-Based Fees

The commission methods of compensation are based on a percentage of media billings, with attendant strengths and weaknesses. The major alternative to the commission method of compensation is the labor-based fee. The essence of the labor-based fee is that agency compensation is based on the number of work hours that employees devote to the service of their client.

Strengths of Labor-Based Fees

1. The most compelling argument in favor of the labor-based fee is that under such arrangements the cost of agency service varies directly with the actual amount of service provided. As proponents of this method of compensation point out, this is the preferred method of compensation of many purveyors of professional services, including lawyers, architects, and accountants. Thus, the method is well-known and understood by a wide range of business persons.

Labor-based fees are rational. They are easy to understand, and unlike media commissions, relate directly to the work that the agency performs.

2. A second advantage of the labor-based fee is that it provides the advertiser with direct knowledge of and control over the actual cost of agency service. If the advertiser can agree with the agency on its service needs, it is a simple matter for the agency to convert this specification into a cost estimate for a month, a quarter, or a year.

Once such a cost estimate exists, it, in turn, becomes a yardstick against which the actual cost of agency service can be monitored. If the agency spends more time in servicing the account than has been estimated, the reasons can be determined and decisions made concerning the reasons for cost overruns as well as their implications for levels of agency service in the future.

Weaknesses of Labor-Based Fees

1. The labor-based fee method of agency compensation tends to be complicated and difficult to administer. The system requires elaborate record keeping and a continuing dialogue between advertiser and agency about the nature of agency costs, estimates of agency service, the conversion of such estimates into future cost estimates, and the eventual reconciliation of discrepancies between estimated costs and actual costs. All of this is a far cry from the uncomplicated and painless working of the traditional 15 percent commission system.

2. A second disadvantage of the labor-based fee is that it often leads to an intrusion by the advertiser into the realm of agency management. When an advertiser and its agency talk regularly about agency costs, overheads, and profit, there is a tendency for the advertiser to make requests and, even, demands that impair the agency management's responsibility to run its own business in a way that suits it rather than its clients. This tendency to control the prerogatives of agency managers becomes especially difficult for the agency that has a labor-based fee in place with several major clients at once.

Proponents of the labor-based fee believe that advertiser clients should not be required to pay for the cost of agency largesse and mismanagement. They also believe that competitive pressure will not hold agency costs down in the way that other costs incurred by the advertiser tend to be controlled. While both of these arguments have merit, they imply discussions between advertiser and agency managements that go to the heart of agency management responsibility to agency stockholders and employees.

For example, suppose that an agency's overhead escalates when it moves to new quarters. Should the agency's clients be able to criticize the agency management's decision to move because of its effect on agency costs, as they are translated into fees paid by the advertiser? Carried to an extreme, such criticisms of agency management can reduce that management to ineffectual toadies to their clients.

3. The labor-based fee system introduces an inflexibility into the provision of agency service. Opponents of the fee system point out that the par-

allel between advertising agency service and the services of lawyer, architects, and accountants is improperly drawn. Advertising agencies employ a much wider variety of talents than does the typical accounting, law, or architectural firm. The art of management in such firms is to get the right mix of talent against a particular professional problem. All the players have the same general kinds of training and skill: The trick is simply to deploy the right mix of experience and specialization within these general skills.

The art of advertising agency management is fundamentally different. The agency manager must deploy the wide range of professional talents—creative, production, research, executive, administrative, media, etc.—that is needed to service a particular account at a particular time. This ideal talent mix tends to change in both composition and size from day to day and year to year in most advertising accounts.

4. Labor-based fees also tend to direct the attention of both client and agency management away from advertising work to accounting definitions and processes. For example, in many fee arrangements there is a good deal of squabbling about what time should be charged to the client and whether the agency has the right to spend its time in the client's behalf in the way that the agency believes that it should. At their worst, fees have the effect of substituting the client's best financial interest for its best advertising interest.

5. Finally, the fee method of compensation may not reflect the way in which the best advertising ideas tend to be created. This method implicitly considers the creation of advertising ideas to be a long, drawn out, and formalized process. This may be one way to create "better" advertising ideas and, if so, it is well and properly rewarded by the labor-based fee.

However, many experienced advertising people have an inherent distrust of harnessed, analytical thought processes as a source of "better" advertising ideas. They believe the creative process to be essentially intuitive and neither totally controlled nor disciplined. Better advertising ideas, their experience suggests, are more likely to come in a blinding flash of creative insight than from a long, drawn out cognitive process shaped by rules and procedures.

The fee method of compensation is not well-suited to advertising ideas produced by such intuitive processes because the fee method has trouble isolating and compensating the incubation period that precedes the blinding flash of creative insight. In addition, the fee method clearly undercompensates the creator for those few moments during which the advertising idea actually comes into shape in his or her mind.

Thus, the labor-based fee tends to be favored by advertisers and agencies that believe that better advertising tends to be ground out through a lawyer-like immersion in a communications problem. On the other hand, the fee method of compensation is disliked by those agencies and advertisers that believe that better advertising ideas emerge from ill-defined yet immediate processes not unlike those that produce great ideas in the arts, science, and other facets of life in which unpremeditated creativity seems to generate the most valuable ideas.

The Labor-Based Fee System Mechanics

There are a wide variety of labor-based fee systems in use. In fact, it is probably safe to say that no two labor-based fees are exactly alike.

Budgeting of agency labor costs is inherent in labor-based fee arrangements. The agency is asked to predict the costs of its services for some future time, usually a year, with breakdowns by quarters. In building these cost estimates, the agency assumes a particular deployment of talent. Later, when actual costs are reconciled with budgeted costs, discrepancies are most likely to develop when a different talent mix has been required for the advertiser than the talent mix assumed in developing the original agency cost estimate. This process tends to inhibit agency management's flexibility in the day-to-day and month-to-month deployment of talent, no matter what the best advertising interests of their client may require.

The basic concept of the labor-based fee is that direct labor costs of servicing the advertiser's account are accumulated by the agency. To these direct labor costs, two additional items are added. One is a markup for the costs of agency overhead—rent, light, heat, power, wages of employees who do not keep time sheets (secretaries, receptionists, billing and research and media clerks, etc.), communications expense, and the like. The second markup is for agency profit.

This description of the process of computing labor-based fees is, however, oversimplified. It conceals a variety of additional questions—often vexing—that must be asked and answered before the mechanics of the fee method of compensation become clear.

What Is Direct Labor Cost?

Is direct labor cost only the cost of labor reflected in W-2 wages, reduced to an hourly rate, or does it also include such W-2 wage "followers" as unemployment insurance, group health and life insurance, F.I.C.A. contributions, payments into company-funded pension plans, and so forth?

Although many advertisers believe that direct labor cost should be defined as W-2 wages with "followers" assigned to agency overhead, the more enlightened, and widely held, view is that direct labor cost should be defined as W-2 wages plus any "following" payments that apply *equally to all employees*.

What Is the Total Number of Hours Worked in a Year?

The basis of all fee compensation systems is the calculation of each employee's "hourly rate." This is particularly important since many agency employees spread their time over two or more accounts and the dollar value of their time must be allocated amongst them.

The hourly rate calculation involves two distinct elements—annual wage and the total number of hours an employee works in a year, excluding paid holidays, vacations, and sick days. The commonly accepted number of hours in a year that is used in such calculations is 1,650. Thus, to calculate an employee's hourly rate, one divides his or her annual wage by 1,650.

For example, if an employee has a W-2 wage of $40,000, and if the "follower" costs are $10,000 per annum, the employee's hourly rate is:

$$\frac{\$50,000}{1,650} = \$30.30$$

What if the Employee Works More Than 1,650 Hours per Year?

The heart of the advertising agency time-cost accounting system is the employee time sheet. Each day the employee notes the number of hours worked on his or her time sheet, breaking the hours down by client or project. Hours are then totaled by account and the employee's hourly rate is applied. The result is a weekly, monthly, or other time period summation of the cost of that employee's time for each account on which he or she works.

Many advertising agency employees work long hours. This is especially true of those employees that are more responsible and involved with their client's business—that is, the agency employees who tend to be relatively highly paid. By the end of the year, such hardworking employees have usually accumulated many more hours than 1,650. It is not unusual, for example, for agency professional employees to log in 2,000 or 2,100 hours or more during the course of the year.

If our hypothetical employee with an hourly rate of $30.30 works a total of 2,000 hours and enters them all on his or her time sheet, and each of them is allocated to a fee account, the agency receives a total of $60,600 for the services of that employee even though he or she is only paid an annual wage of $40,000 plus $10,000 in salary followers. The possibility for excess agency income[1] that comes about as a result of the long hours worked by some employees has led many advertisers to require that agencies bill for employee time on the annual total of 1,650 hours, rather than simply to charge for total hours accumulated.

What Items Should Be Included in Agency Overhead?

Overhead is an amalgam of expense incurred by an agency that is not directly attributable to individual accounts. Everybody seems to agree that items like rent, heat, light, power, general administrative expenses, secretaries and clerks, sales taxes, communication expense, and the like are properly included in the expense pool that underlies the service that is provided to all agency clients.

There are, in addition, a group of other agency expenses that are not directly generated by the provision of agency service to clients but are, rather, incurred at the discretion of agency management. These other expenses include those associated with the solicitation of new business, write-offs that reflect agency mistakes in servicing certain clients, contributions to charities, executive bonuses beyond pension fund contributions, agency bad debts, and so forth. Many people argue that some or all of such expenses should not be included in agency overhead since they are properly viewed as expenses that reflect agency management decisions made about the disposition of operating profit.

If the bulk of such expenses are excluded from agency overhead, the typical agency overhead of direct labor costs will usually be between 100 and 125 percent. If the discretionary disbursements of operating profit are also included in overhead, agency overhead markups may exceed 150 percent.

There are variations in overhead from agency to agency because all agencies do not incur the same expenses in administering their business and serving their clients. There are, for example, variations in the rent that agencies pay, variations in the number of supernumery and support employees that an agency has, and variations in the fraction of top management salaries that are included in general and administrative expense.

---

[1] In the example, $10,600, but a total of $29,150. (Hourly time costs have been marked up by 120 percent for overhead and 25 percent for profit—see later.)

The overhead markup on direct labor cost that an agency charges is important to those advertisers who use a fee to compensate their agencies, since overhead charges are translated into a very significant multiplier of direct labor cost that usually exceeds the cost of the direct labor that is assigned to the advertiser's account. Thus, for example, if the cost of a direct labor hour is $30.30 and the overhead markup is 120 percent, the total cost of that direct labor hour after overhead, but before profit, is $66.66.

What Is a "Fair" Agency Profit?

Direct labor costs and agency overhead markups have a basis in tangible agency costs, but there is no tangible cost basis for agency profit. It is, rather, a subjective concept based on what a successful advertising agency should be expected to make as a result of acceptable service to its clients.

The American Association of Advertising Agencies (AAAA) has traditionally maintained that a "fair" level of profit on an advertising account is 25 percent of the total cost of running that account, or 20 percent of the gross cost of agency service to the advertiser.[2] In labor-based fee arrangements—following the AAAA guideline—the total direct agency costs plus overhead would be marked up an additional 25 percent. Thus, in the example of the employee whose direct labor cost is $30.30:

$$\$30.30 \ + \ 36.66 \ (\text{overhead}) \ + \ 25\% \ (\text{profit}) \ = \ \$83.32$$

It is important to recognize that account profit per unit of labor cost ($16.16 in this example) does not all go to agency profits before taxes. As discussed above, it is the prerogative and practice of agency management to disburse at least some of these funds as non-account related agency expenses (new business, charities, write-offs, etc.).

Labor-based fee compensation systems tend to focus the attention of both advertiser and agency on the profit the agency makes, as well as upon all the other agency direct labor and overhead costs. It is this emphasis on the cost/profit detail of the agency's operation that results in most of the perceived disadvantages of the fee method of compensation that are outlined above.

Perhaps the most pernicious effect of the labor-based fee method of

---

[2]Another way to think of this is by relating it back to the traditional 15 percent commission system. Twenty percent of 15 percent is 3 percent of gross media billings for agency profit. This yields a breakdown of 12 percent for agency cost and 3 percent for agency profit. Three percent is 25 percent of 12 percent.

compensation is in the area of agency profit determination. This compensation method makes it a legitimate area for negotiation. Yet experience suggests that nothing can cool the professional zest of an agency more quickly than an attack, arbitrary as it must be, on agency profits in an attempt to force them below levels that are accepted within the industry as a guideline.

Inherent in the idea of *negotiation* is the reality of compromise. Agency managers are almost inevitably forced to accept a profit level below 25 percent of costs, once the negotiation of profits is begun, *unless* the agency principal can defend that level of profits on the basis of the performance of the agency and the leverage of its creative work on its clients' sales and profits. The majority of agency managers have seemed unable or unwilling to mount such a defense in profit negotiations. They have, accordingly, often been forced to settle for agency profits below the suggested AAAA guideline.

Negotiating Labor-Based Fee Agreements

As the foregoing discussion suggests, four issues are routinely negotiated as labor-based fee agreements are developed between the advertiser and its agency.

Wage "Followers"

The first issue to be negotiated is what constitutes direct labor costs.

If, as is sometimes suggested, W-2 wages are used to determine hourly labor costs and one or more followers are relegated to overhead, this puts significant pressure on agency overhead, if it is to be held in the 100–125 percent range.

How Many Hours in a Work Year?

The question here is whether employee time is billed out on the basis of direct hours worked or recalculated on a basis that is proportional to the 1,650 hour standard work year. As we have seen, these hours in excess of the 1,650 hour work year can, if billed at the straight hourly rate, aggregate a significant amount of agency income, particularly if the agency's culture tends to encourage long hours of work.

What Is Included in Overhead?

The issue is what items are a legitimate part of the overhead expense incurred by the agency in directly serving its clients. The more discretionary expenses—those that are not directly related to the servicing of an account—are included in overhead, the higher the overhead markup will be.

What Is a Fair Level of Agency Profit?

Agency profit is always vulnerable in negotiations because it is an arbitrary figure that agency principles seem to have trouble defending. The more negotiating pressure that is brought to bear on agency profit, the less incentive agency management has for extraordinary professional effort in behalf of the advertiser's account. In fact, a fundamental object of agency compensation discussions boils down to agency incentive, and this issue is most likely to be exposed when a labor-based fee is negotiated.

It is well to remember that, in the final analysis, it is the agency management that determines the allocation of scarce agency resources among the agency's accounts. Accounts with marginal profits and an attitude of "squeeze the agency" are least likely to get the best people that an agency has to offer.

As one agency president recently remarked:

We give every one of our accounts super service. We couldn't survive in this business if we didn't. But, I must admit, we do have a second level of service. When we really care about an account, we really go the extra mile and in a business that is as intangible as the advertising agency business, that extra mile can be the difference between a winner and an also-ran.

The work of advertising agencies is, after all, not a commodity. There are good advertising campaigns and bad advertising campaigns and outstanding advertising campaigns. No one who understands how advertising agencies and advertising agency people work expect that outstanding advertising campaigns are likely to be routinely delivered to those clients who have driven their agencies to the very edge of profitability.

Labor-Based Fee Compensation Systems in Practice

There is no standard or typical labor-based fee compensation agreement. Every one tends to be different, and there is considerable variation from one fee system to another.

If there is a prototype labor-based fee system, it is probably very much like the direct hours with followers-overhead-profit system described in the preceding section. As that description makes clear, variation in the specific details can vary from agreement to agreement depending upon what is negotiated and how it is negotiated.

Thus, for example, this "prototype labor-based fee arrangement might produce three quite different fee arrangements.

	Examples 1	Example 2	Example 3
Direct Labor Cost Basis	W-2	W-2 plus "followers"	W-2 plus "followers"
Standard Hours	Prorated to 1,650	Prorated to 1,650	Total hours worked
Overhead	No management discretion items, wage followers, all standard items	No management discretion items, all standard items	All standard items, charity contributions, new business expenses
Overhead Cap	110%	125%	None
Profit Margin Cap	10%	15%	25%

Many labor-based fee arrangements, although reflecting characteristics of the prototypic arrangement, build in additional features. To suggest the diversity that may be introduced in addition to (or as an alternative to) the prototypic arrangements, consider the following descriptions of labor-based fee arrangements.

The BBDO Plan

BBDO has developed a plan that it calls the Efficiency Incentive Compensation Plan. Its intent is to control agency costs and provide the agency with a profit floor as well as a share of extraordinary profits. In essence, this plan is a guaranteed agency profit plan. It works like this:

• The agency receives as income the standard 15 percent commission, plus the 17.65 percent markup on agreed outside costs for production, collateral materials, etc.

• The agency computes direct salaries and associated costs, plus overhead, but not profit.

• A comparison is made between agency costs and agency income.

• The balance is agency *profit*. The agency believes that it should receive a profit of 2 percent of billings on each of its accounts. If the actual computed profit falls in the range of $1^1/_2$ to $2^1/_2$ percent of billings, this profit, under the Efficiency Incentive Compensation Plan, is retained by the agency and the matter is closed.

- If, however, profit exceeds $2^1/_2$ percent of billings, the balance is returned to the client. If profit is less than $1^1/_2$ percent, the client agrees to make up the difference.

This plan has many of the basic advantages of the fee arrangement. It motivates both agency and client to maximize agency profits. BBDO wants its profits to reach $2^1/_2$ percent of billings, if possible, and BBDO clients want agency profits to exceed $2^1/_2$ percent, if possible.

The plan does not force BBDO clients to specify their service needs in detail, as do fee arrangements that build up agency costs from the determination of personnel required to service the account. Yet the emphasis on the profit guarantee and its inherent incentive has the effect of focusing the attention of both BBDO and its clients on exactly which agency services are essential and which are not. Finally, this plan is simple and seems to guarantee a satisfactory price-value relationship between BBDO and its clients.

Commission-Based Profit Fees[3]

Another well-known fee arrangement is the Commission-Based Fee plan in which profits are computed as in the traditional 15 percent commission system. Its intention is to control agency costs as suggested by the prototypic plan outlined earlier, while guaranteeing the agency the same profit rate that they would make under a 15 percent commission system, according to the AAAA 20 percent of the total commission guideline. Here is how it works:

- Media commissions and production markups for an account are accrued in a "media rebate reserve."

- Advertiser and client agree on required agency services and build up a brand budget based on projected agency hours and labor rates, plus overhead.

- A profit of 3 percent of total billings (media and production) is added to the agency service budget, and this total is the agency compensation.

---

[3]An elegant version of the Commission-Based Profit Fee plan was in use by Richardson-Vicks, Inc., for many years before that company was acquired by Procter & Gamble.

- The agency is reimbursed from the media rebate reserve. The agency receives compensation either on budgeted or actual expenses, whichever are lower, unless overbudget expense has prior approval.

- If there is a surplus in the media rebate reserve after the agency has been compensated, the residue is used to support other brand advertising projects.

This system is a classic fee arrangement. It starts from a definition of advertiser service requirements. Agency costs are then computed. Agencies are expected to stay within their established budgets. Because agency profits are based on total billings, the traditional incentive of the commission system is built into this plan.

When to Use Labor-Based Fees

In one sense, the willingness of an advertiser to use a labor-based fee in compensating an advertising agency depends upon that advertiser's zest for bureaucratic processes and accounting detail. Some organizations seem to be particularly well-prepared to deal with the administrative burdens of a full-blown labor-based fee compensation system. Other organizations are more streamlined and more concerned with the strategic opportunities of tomorrow than with the tedious detail of the past. For these organizations, labor-based fees may seem too burdensome and inward looking.

There are two general situations in which labor-based fees are likely to work particularly well for advertisers.

1. Accounts with High Labor Intensity Relative to Billings

Accounts that require the preparation of a broad range of advertisements to run in a diverse group of low-cost media and/or non-commissionable media are logical candidates for labor-based fee compensation arrangements. Such accounts would include many business-to-business and professional products advertising activities that depend upon print advertising in small circulation or targeted advertising media across diverse audiences.

2. Advertising for Non-Advertising-Dependent Businesses

Labor-based fees may also be appropriate for business enterprises that are not dependent on advertising for the continuous stimulation of sales.

Companies that sponsor corporate advertising campaigns designed to foster a favorable reputation for the company as a whole rather than its individual products or services are a case in point.

The ratio of advertising to sales tends to be very small in such companies, and advertising programs tend to be conducted well beyond the mainstream of sales generating activities. In such circumstances, advertising agency service tends to be much more analogous to that provided by other outside professional firms like lawyers, accountants, and architects, and the labor-based fee is often best suited to the compensation of such firms' advertising agencies.

Incentive-Based Advertising Agency Compensation

Advertising agency service can be viewed in terms of what advertising agency service costs or what the agency contributes to the well-being of the advertiser. As the cost of agency service became a major preoccupation of advertisers in the late '70s and through the '80s, it seemed that far too little attention was directed to evaluating the specific contributions of the agency to the well-being of the advertiser's business.

There were three major reasons for this emphasis on the cost of agency service.

1. It began to dawn on advertisers that advertising agencies do have economies of scale in their operations and that, as the size of the advertising appropriation for an account grows, the account tends to become more and more profitable to the agency.

2. Costs are easier to measure than the contribution of the agency to its clients' well-being.

3. Corporate cultures, with their single-minded preoccupation with bottom-line results, tend to reward employees for tangible reductions in cost rather than for intangible contributions to corporate welfare.

The fundamental problem with this evolving state of affairs was that the emphasis on the cost of agency service coincided with a gradual decline in the creative effectiveness of advertising.[1] Advertising creativity would

---

[1] The long-term decline in the creative effectiveness of advertising is a theme that must be developed elsewhere. In short, the decline has come about for a variety of reasons, including the following:

- The tangible evidence of such a decline that I have observed in scores of agency new-business presentations viewed as an agency search consultant, over the past decade.

have probably declined no matter what in the 1980s, but the pressure on advertising agency profits certainly did nothing to reverse the trend.

The upshot of all this was that advertisers were sending the wrong signals to their advertising agencies. They seemed to be saying that they preferred cheap agency service rather than more expensive full value agency service. These signals were further confused by an advertiser preoccupation—in some cases downright paranoia—with the search for the perfect method of advertising agency compensation. As the foregoing chapters suggest, some methods of compensation usually work better in some situations than do others, but it is certain that there is no single, simple, all-purpose method that will solve, once and for all, the compensation problems of all advertisers and all advertising agencies.

Alternative Premises for Advertising Agency Compensation

There is nothing wrong with a legitimate advertiser desire to cut the cost of advertising agency service. The sticking point is to determine just where the best financial interest of the advertiser begins to jeopardize its best marketing/advertising interest. This is not an easy determination to make because in the end it depends upon a number of judgment issues that are not easily quantifiable.

Is the Advertising That the Agency Produces a Commodity or Is It a Differentiated Product?

If an advertiser can expect to receive equally effective advertising no matter what agency it chooses, a strong case can be made for the choice of agency on the basis of cost of advertising service. Yet there is really no

---

• The change in business orientation of advertising agency managements including, particularly, the publicly owned agencies, and those agencies that have been preoccupied with the creation of an accounting facade that would encourage their acquisition.
• The bureaucratization and rationalization of the marketing process that has occurred in business after business. This bureaucratization and rationalization focuses upon well-ordered process rather than the stimulation of creative insight.
• The proliferation of brands within product categories, with the consequent reduction in the average difference in brand characteristics from brand to brand. When brands become more and more alike, it is increasingly hard to differentiate brands through advertising.
• A decline in the ability of advertising agencies to attract and nurture genuinely creative young talent.
• The bad name that creativity for its own sake has given to calculated advertising risks.

question that the work of one advertising agency is almost always distinguishable from the work of other advertising agencies. Some agencies do consistently superior work on all their accounts. Some do consistently superior work on some, but not all, of their accounts. Others tend to produce mostly mediocre work, regardless of account.

To the extent that an advertiser believes that the work that it gets from its advertising agency is distinctive, it is likely to place less emphasis on lowering the cost of agency service.

How Important Is Advertising to the Success of the Advertiser's Business?

If advertising is a vital element in an advertiser's business—if it is expected to cause sales directly, as in direct response advertising, or to make a substantial contribution to sales, as in package goods advertising—the advertiser will want to do everything possible to assure that the agency deploys very strong talent against its advertising problems. When an advertiser judges that its advertising agency should place very talented people on its account, the advertiser is likely to place less emphasis on lowering the cost of agency service.

How Difficult Is It to Produce Outstanding Advertising Ideas in the Advertiser's Product Category?

Some product categories have generated a great deal of advertising over time, and have required a very large number of new advertising ideas—the breakfast food and packaged laundry product categories are good examples. Other product categories have less advertising history and/or less preoccupation with advertising as a marketing tool—new product categories of the 1980s, such as personal computers and the overnight delivery services, are good examples.

If the advertiser operates in a category or categories whose advertising ideas have been extensively mined over a period of time, it is more likely to be concerned with finding outstanding new advertising ideas than with the cost of generating them.

How Many Unprofitable Agency Activities Are Included in the Work Required by the Advertising Account?

Many advertising "accounts" involve a wide range of advertising activities and assignments. Heavy billing, nationally advertised consumer products and services are, for example, almost inevitably profitable to an advertising agency. But these profits are reduced, and often reduced severely, if the agency must also merchandise the advertising of the product or service to sales, dealer, or franchise organizations.

Similarly, if the account requires that one or more service offices be established in remote cities, or if the product or service must also be advertised internationally, especially if this must be done in a wide variety of smaller countries, profits will be adversely affected.

The more ancillary or support services that the advertiser requires the agency to provide, the less likely is the advertiser to emphasize reductions in the overall cost of agency service.

The advertiser's objective should be to pay an agency no more and no less than it costs to get the quality of agency service that its business requires. The upper limit for such payments is, in almost every advertiser-agency relationship, the traditional 15 percent commission.

As the data in Chapters 10 and 11 suggest, the level of commission may fall as low as 10 percent under fixed commissions and as low as 7 percent at the low end of sliding scales. Such variations illustrate the point that the advertiser must determine the final trade-off between the cost of advertising agency service and its perceived value to the advertiser.

Incentive Compensation Systems

One alluring solution to the dilemma of advertising agency compensation is incentive systems of agency compensation. The basic idea of such systems is that the agency should be fairly compensated for its work on the advertiser's behalf, but that, in addition, it should receive additional compensation if the advertising that it creates makes a demonstrable extra contribution to the success of that advertiser.

Such compensation systems seem to have the potential of separating the agency costs of providing service from the notion of providing the agency with an additional incentive to deliver superior, profit generating advertising to the advertiser. Implicit in this idea is the thought that ordinary advertising will probably maintain an advertised brand or service in marketing equilibrium, but that outstanding advertising will push the brand to new sales and profits heights.

In concept, such a compensation system seems to have several distinguishing characteristics.

1. When an incentive compensation system is introduced, it implies the possibility that the agency may earn, based on its performance, more

money than it is currently paid, if no other change in the compensation system is made. Thus, unless the whole compensation system is revised, with payments for basic agency service reduced, the overall cost of advertising agency service will increase when an incentive compensation system is introduced.

2. The use of an incentive system implies that the desirable effects of advertising can be measured in some way. This poses a considerable problem for incentive compensation systems, since almost everyone in advertising, except direct response specialists, seems to agree that it is almost always difficult to measure the specific effects of advertising. There will be a good deal more about these perceived difficulties of measurement of advertising effects in following paragraphs.

3. Incentive compensation systems are often confused with systems that control or contain agency costs or profits. For example, the BBDO plan, described in Chapter 11, gives the agency an incentive to cut its costs rather than an incentive to increase the effectiveness of the advertising that it produces for clients.

Genuine incentive systems are not a common feature of agency compensation arrangements. The 1989 ANA study was, as previously noted, based on a study of 167 separate compensation agreements. Of these, only four could be described as providing as genuine incentive for better advertising agency creative work. Here is how these four plans were described in the ANA study.[2]

Incentive bonus (10% or 20%) over base revenues. Bonus is based upon a performance evaluation using a 4 point scale. Highest rating earns 20% bonus, second highest earns 10% bonus. (Package goods, $100 million + .)

A fixed price is paid for each television commercial or print ad produced. Predetermined rates for each type are established every two years. Account service: a negotiated retainer. Media service: 2.5% of annual billing. The piece rate payment for television commercials and print ads provides an incentive to agency to get more creative product produced. As most of the account is corporate image advertising and creative driven, this encourages the agency to keep developing outstanding work that management will want to produce and thus increase agency compensation. (Corporate image, $50–99 million.)

Base compensation is increased based on achieving certain levels of performance. No minimum profit is guaranteed and there is no profit sharing. (Package goods, $20–49 million.)

---

[2]Association of National Advertisers, *Current Advertiser Practices in Compensating Their Advertising Agencies* (prepared by William M. Weilbacher), New York, 1989, p. 21.

Three percent of billings additional to basic compensation percent based on evaluation of superior creative work. (Package goods, $100 million + .)

Although these descriptions confirm that a genuine incentive for the agency is operative, they do not describe exactly how the advertiser decides that an incentive has been earned. Phrases like "performance evaluation using a 4 point scale" and "evaluation of superior creative work" suggest that the actual determination of incentive payments is somewhat, if not entirely, subjective.

Indeed, if the incentive is awarded as a result of some sort of souped-up evaluation of performance, nothing much new has been added to compensation practice. Advertisers are, or should be, continuously evaluating the performance of their advertising agencies. The question of how to base an incentive on some independent criterion or measurement is not answered by an intensified subjective evaluation, no matter how well-meaning it may be.

Does the Commission System Provide Agency Incentive?

Many advertisers, with the tacit endorsement of advertising agencies, argue that the commission system, and especially the commission system in its traditional 15 percent form, provides an effective incentive for advertising agencies. They base this argument on two points:

1. The better the advertising, the more money an advertiser is likely to spend in its support. Thus, the better the advertising, the higher the media billings, and thus the higher the agency income.
2. In addition, however, as media billings increase, agency economies of scale also tend to kick in, and agency income increases disproportionately with the increase in billings.

Thus, the traditional 15 percent commission provides agencies with all the incentive they could wish, and then some. This also tends to be true of all flat-rate commission systems, 15 percent or not. In every flat-rate commission system, the agencies make more money when billings go up both because of media dollar volume and economies of scale.

The sliding-scale commission systems tend to eliminate economies of scale incentives, but even the sliding scale provides an agency incentive based on increased billings, especially if those billings increases are significant. Note that this mechanism is implicit in the Commission-Based Profit compensation plan (see Chapter 10) with its guaranteed profit of 3 percent of total advertiser media billings.

The problem with commission-based incentive systems is that the phenomenon that triggers the incentive payment to agencies is an increase in media billings. But, here we are, once again, back at a fundamental sticking point in commission methods of compensation. The level of media billings may have little or nothing to do with the excellence of the work of an agency, or the absence of such excellence.

In fact, some advertisers would argue that the more one has to spend on media to accomplish an advertising result, the less effective the advertising that is carried by those media. Or, to put it another way, the objective of the agency should be to increase the productivity of a stable media budget, rather than to create advertising whose enhanced effect can only be realized through increased media appropriations.

How to Measure the Positive Effects of Advertising

If the advertiser insists upon an incentive plan, it must define the positive effects of advertising that it is prepared to award incentives to achieve.

There are two traditional measures of the specific effects of advertising content: studies of the immediate response of consumers when exposed to an advertisement (copy tests); and studies of the long-term changes in consumer knowledge and attitudes that have been induced by advertising (awareness and attitude tracking studies). Neither advertisers nor agencies have been especially inclined to base the final evaluation of agency performance on either copy tests or tracking studies. There are very good reasons for this reluctance.

Copy tests, whatever their other virtues, do not predict the sales productivity of specific advertisements nor of advertising campaigns. A copy test result that is twice as high as another does not mean that one advertisement will produce twice as many sales as the other, or even that there is any difference at all in the sales producing power of the tested advertisements. Worse, researchers know that when different copy testing systems are used with the same advertisements, there is little or no correlation in the test results. This means that the advertisement that is endorsed by one copy testing system may be rejected out of hand by another system.

Tracking studies usually measure some combination of the following:

• Consumer awareness of the advertised product/service and its competitors will

- Consumer knowledge of the content of the advertising of the product / service and its competitors
- Consumer attitudes toward multiple attributes of the product / service and its competitors[3]

The results produced by such measurements are usually not only all-encompassing but also redundant. This universality and redundancy makes it extraordinarily difficult, if not impossible, to isolate the specific sales producing effect of the advertising, if any. The advertising may be judged to have been successful in a general way, but it is difficult to discriminate among specific advertisements or campaigns on the basis of such tracking study results.

Everyone seems to agree that it cannot be bad to have high copy test scores and positive tracking results, but no one seems to want to depend upon them to assess the final contribution to sales of the agency's creative work. Thus, neither of the traditional methods of assessing advertising performance can or should be used as a basis for making incentive payments to agencies for superior work.

Non-Traditional Measures of Advertising Effect

The real question is whether other, *new* measures can be developed that can be used as a basis for incentive payments to advertising agencies. This question is not unlike the question that faces members of the legal profession as they prepare to present a case to a judge or jury. They are not very interested in using any evidence that happens to be merely relevant to the issue at hand. Rather, they want to find evidence, if, indeed, it exists at all, that will prove decisive in reaching the proper judgment.

There is an interesting issue here: Is marketing and advertising research, as now practiced, able to bear the burden that is implicit in an incentive plan that makes advertising research the final arbiter in agency incentive payments? Aside from media audience measurements that are used as a basis for buying and selling of much advertising space and time, there is little advertising and marketing research that provides the only or decisive basis for making marketing and advertising judgments.

There seems to be a hesitation to make such use of marketing or advertising research results both on the part of decision makers and research

---

[3]Tracking study results, of course, also reflect both the level of media expenditures and copy content. Yet the main thrust of tracking data is to reflect what consumers have learned from advertising content, independently of the level of advertising expenditures.

practitioners. This is one reason that researchers tend to design advertising and marketing research studies to make multiple and alternative measures of, for example, advertising induced changes in consumer knowledge and attitudes. The rule seems to be, for example, to measure awareness at several different levels (unaided, partially aided, fully aided) rather than at a single level, and to make attitude measurements across many different attributes.

The trade-off for this lack of specificity seems to be that the use of a variety of complementary, if not redundant, measures of advertising induced awareness and attitudes will produce a general, if fuzzy, understanding of the advertising's overall effects on consumers. This general understanding will, in turn, help marketing executives reach a consensus about what advertising or marketing decisions are most appropriate (or least threatening) to the continued well-being of the advertised product or service.

Yet, if there is to be a decisive measurement of the effects of advertising, it must focus on that single advertising contribution that, if achieved, all agree will cause sales to increase either immediately, or in the long run. If one is to look for that single, decisive, advertising induced effect, where is it most likely to be found? The short answer to the question is in the advertising strategy statement that advertiser and agency have, presumably, agreed to, long before the agency has tried to create advertising that will implement it.

Advertisers, presumably, approach the strategic planning process with the premise that the purpose of advertising is to make target consumers believe as the advertiser wishes them to believe and/or to make target consumers act as the advertiser wishes them to act, or both. The key strategic question is, then, what can advertising say about the product or service that will cause consumers to accept this belief or take action on it, or both?

If the strategic process has been refined to this point, it will tend to dictate exactly the single measurement that can be used to evaluate an advertising agency's work and serve as a basis for incentive payments to the agency. Take, as an example, an airline advertiser. Assume that research has demonstrated that most business travelers have developed a list of airlines that they are willing to fly as well as a list of airlines that they will fly on only if there is no other choice. Further assume that the price of airline service is either a matter of indifference to these business travelers, or that they assume that airlines generally match each other's fares so closely that a concern with price need not influence choice of airline.

Thus, under these assumptions, when a business traveler must fly between two cities, if one of his or her preferred airlines flies this route, it will be chosen by the traveler. If two or more of the preferred airlines fly the route, he or she will choose among them on the basis of the availability of non-stop flights, on the basis of departure time, on the basis of overall preference strength for an individual airline, on the basis of frequent flyer club membership, and so forth.

Given this situation, the unequivocal objective of airline advertising is to make business travelers believe that the advertiser's airline is worthy of membership in the business traveler's set of preferred airlines. If more business travelers are willing to fly on the airline as a result of the advertising, the advertising has been successful. Of course, all the other relevant marketing factors (schedule, airline image, frequent flyer club membership, etc.) may act in such a way as to negate the positive effect of the advertising, but *unless* the airline is, in the first instance, among those acceptable to the traveler, nothing but last resort will force him or her to fly that airline. Thus, the key research measurement is the change in the business traveler's willingness to fly an airline—that is, the acceptability score for the airline. Incentive payments to the advertising agency would be based, in this scenario, on increases in that score, no more, no less.

Note that the measurement described will not be appropriate to all airlines. If an airline has achieved a very high acceptability score, the next step for advertising is to find a way to increase business traveler preference for that airline among those airlines that are acceptable, no matter what other factors affect consumer preference for this airline. For this airline, the agency would receive incentive payments if advertising increased business traveler preference for it, no more, no less.

In most consumer goods categories, especially as undifferentiated brands increase in number, and as the patterns of brand loyalty are further shaken by consumer promotion, the concept of brand acceptability and, when acceptability has been well established, brand preference, may emerge as the crucial measures of the success of advertising.

In any event, it seems certain that no one universal measure of advertising effect will ever be found. Advertising effects must be situation specific, and the measurement of advertising effect must reflect this specificity. If incentive compensation systems are to be based on marketing/advertising research measurements, they must be based on those measurements, unlike those in common use today, that both advertiser and agency can agree, without reservation, show the unequivocal effect of advertising, positive or negative.

PART 4

Starting the New Agency Relationship

The Agency Contract

The relationship with the advertising agency should be formalized in a contract. In the absence of a formal contract, there are bound to be discussions, if not confrontations, about what exactly the advertising agency is supposed to do, how it is to be compensated, and how the relationship may be terminated.

There is substantial evidence that many advertisers, particularly larger advertisers, have a formal contract or memorandum of agreement with their agency. A question on this topic was included in the 1989 Association of National Advertisers' study of agency compensation,[1] and 89 percent of all companies responded that such a formal document existed. When a similar question was asked in 1979, 76 percent of the respondents said such a document existed.

It is always wise to have some sort of formal written contract between advertiser and agency. In addition, experience indicates that at least the broad outlines of this contract should be agreed upon *before* the formal appointment of an agency is publicly announced. This approach forces both sides to come to grips with important issues quickly, and this, in turn, tends to guarantee reasonable compromises in areas of disputes, as well as moderation on both side.

Nothing is worse than delaying discussion about a contract and then delegating it to staff attorneys or outside counsel, who have little understanding of either the issues involved, the discussions held, or explicit or implied agreements reached during the actual search process.

In the case of one packaged goods advertising account, negotiations about contracts were still going on between advertiser and agency two years after the original appointment. At various times the agency had been

---

[1]Association of National Advertisers, *Current Advertiser Practices in Compensating Their Advertising Agencies* (prepared by William M. Weilbacher), New York, 1989, p. 22.

represented in these discussions by three different senior account managers. The advertiser was represented by two different attorneys, both from the middle ranks of the in-house legal staff. Neither side felt any time pressure to reach agreement, and whenever an irreconcilable issue arose, the talks were halted for some weeks before beginning again. As the negotiations dragged on, the advertiser's lawyers demonstrated a total ignorance of the nature of advertiser–agency relations, trade practices in the field, and the nature of the advertising agency business. They were rigid and implacable and took virtually every agency proposal as unacceptable, if not totally offensive. Finally, the advertiser decided to terminate the agency's services because it was dissatisfied with its work. Although there was no contract, the negotiating teams were in place, and finally, with a clearcut mission, they quickly reached a termination agreement that was acceptable to both sides. All of the pointless contract negotiations could have been avoided if the advertiser had insisted on a memorandum of agreement covering the major issues of concern before the formal announcement of agency appointment.

The Major Issues between Advertisers and Agencies

No two advertiser–agency contracts are the same. There are matters that seem to be important to some advertisers and agencies, but are not to others. This is true, for example, in the case of cooperative advertising. If an advertiser has a cooperative advertising program, both advertiser and agency will want to be sure that the agency's participation in that program, if any, is clearly specified. Both sides also will want to clearly specify questions of agency compensation for its contributions to the cooperative advertising program.

The diversity of issues that can concern advertisers and agencies is clearly demonstrated in a 1963 ANA study. In that study, 109 advertisers submitted agency contracts for analysis. Collectively, these contracts contained 448 different kinds of contract clauses. No one contract contained all 448 clauses, of course, and many of the items reflected issues peculiar to a single advertiser or agency. But the diversity of advertiser-agency contract concerns is clearly indicated by the gross number of discrete contract clauses revealed by this study. It is unlikely that the number of topics covered by advertiser-agency contracts has declined since 1963.

Yet there are certain issues that should be covered in all advertiser–agency contracts. These include matters that are either of universal concern or likely to concern most advertisers and agencies, such as the following:

161

- The brands or products to be handled by the agency
- The agency's responsibilities
- The client's obligations to the agency
- Agency compensation
- Ownership of advertising prepared by the agency
- The term of the relationship
- Termination of the relationship

The exact content of each contract, as well as the specific wording of each provision, should be worked out with the guidance of legal counsel. Yet the advertiser and agency principals are competent and responsible enough to decide on the general outline of the formal agreement between their companies. The following paragraphs cover the essential elements that should be considered by these principals in reaching such agreement. Their understanding about each of these elements may then be summarized in a "memorandum of agreement," which may then guide the drafting of the formal agreement.

Products to Be Handled

There should be a statement as to exactly what advertising accounts the agency is retained to work on. If there are peculiarities or restrictions, they should be clearly stated. For example, if new or developmental products are involved, they should be identified. If only some fraction of the total advertising activity for the brand or product is covered by the agreement (e.g., limited geographic area, or creative and marketing but not media placement) this should also be specified.

Agency Responsibilities

The agreement should specify what the agency is supposed to do. Sometimes the agency responsibility is simply described as the provision of those services customarily rendered by an advertising agency. In other instances, a more detailed listing of exactly what the agency will do is provided. This would include topics such as:

- The study and analysis of client products and the markets for those products
- The study and analysis of distribution channels and methods and their relation to assigned products

• The study and analysis of advertising media and the determination of which media are especially adapted to the marketing of assigned products, considering their characteristics, markets, and methods of distribution

• The development of specific advertising plans, including recommended creative approaches, as well as detailed media programs

• The execution of the plan, when approved by the advertiser, to include specifically:

—The preparation of advertising messages in whatever form and for whatever media the plan specifies

—The physical production of advertising messages for use in specified advertising media

—The negotiation for favorable rates and the actual ordering of media space and time to carry the brand or product advertising messages

—The timely forwarding of advertising messages in proper form to specified media

—Checking and verifying that the advertising messages appeared as planned in the media space and time purchased in behalf of the client

—Confirmation of space and time charges submitted by the media and other authorized outside suppliers and payment of confirmed invoices

• Cooperation of advertising agency personnel with corporate employees not directly involved with advertising (sales, research and development, public relations, legal, accounting, etc.) to make advertising programs as effective as possible

• Agreement by the agency not to act as advertising agent for products that directly compete with those included in this assignment

• Agreement by the agency not to handle advertising accounts in a competing product category (e.g., automobiles or antacids) and/or any of the products of one or more specific competing companies (e.g., an agency of Procter & Gamble might agree not to handle any product manufactured by Lever Brothers or its subsidiaries)

• Agreement by the agency to act as agent of the advertiser in the purchase of services, including media services and materials required for advertising of the assigned products

• Agreement by the agency to secure the advertiser's approval prior to committing expenditures for media, advertising production, etc. (Often

163

advertisers require written approval for expenditure authorizations in excess of a particular amount and permit verbal authorizations for expenditures below the stipulated amount.)

- Agreement by the agency to take reasonable care in safeguarding the security of the advertiser's property given to the agency, including all reports, documents, statistical data, and other material

- Assurance by the agency that it will disclose its ownership position in any subcontractor it uses in satisfying the client's needs

- Agreement by the agency to ascertain the ownership of photographs, art work, copyrights, or other property rights that it uses in behalf of the advertiser, and a promise to obtain appropriate releases, licenses, or other authorization

- Agreement by the agency to carry advertising liability insurance or otherwise indemnify its client against expenses incurred due to legal claims arising from advertising materials prepared for its clients

- Agreement by the agency to carry out particular kinds of research work (Often this work is specifically required for the preparation and placement of advertising, such as copy pretesting and syndicated media research service purchase and analysis.)

Client Obligations

The advertiser may agree to any number of obligations requested by the agency. For example:

- The client may agree not to hire another advertising agency to work on the advertising account for the brands or products covered by the agreement without first obtaining agency consent.

- The client may agree to provide the agency with as much information as it needs to function as an advertising agency and to provide whatever other resources and aid are required by the agency to produce effective advertising.

- The client may agree that if advertising work in progress is canceled by the client, it will reimburse the agency for its out-of-pocket expenses and appropriate service charges for the canceled work.

- The client may agree to determine the ownership of any material provided to the agency to use in its advertising and to obtain appropriate licenses, releases, or other authorization.

- The advertiser may agree to indemnify the agency against expenses incurred due to legal claims arising from advertising approved by the advertiser and based on information provided by the advertiser.

• The advertiser may agree to indemnify the agency from legal claims that arise from distributor or third-party use of advertising, based on union codes or contracts covering commercial usage and talent compensation for such use.

• The advertiser may also agree, usually at the agency's request, that it will not require the agency to prepare advertising that the agency believes to be either deceitful or unlawful.

Agency Compensation

How the agency is to be compensated for its work should be determined in accordance with the following considerations.

• First, there will be an agreement as to how the agency is to be compensated for planning, producing, and placing advertising.
　—This may be by percentage commission.
　—Or by a fee.
　—Or by a combination of fee and commission.
　　Whatever the arrangement, the advertiser will agree to it, and a description of this compensation agreement will be included.

• Second, there will be an agreement on the reimbursement of the agency for its out-of-pocket costs for material, services, travel expenses of agency personnel, etc.
　—If the agency receives no markup on such costs, the agreement should say so.
　—If the agency receives a percentage markup on such services, the agreement will specify what it is. (For example, 17.65 percent of the net cost equals 15 percent of total cost. See Chapter 9.)

• The agreement may also specify how the client will qualify for cash discounts and how the agency will handle media rate adjustments.

• The method of compensating the agency for its participation in a cooperative advertising program, if it differs from compensation for agency service for other client advertising, will also be indicated.

• The agreement may specify how the agency will be compensated for special services not covered by the general agreement between the parties, such as package design, preparing of collateral material, or planning and executing special research studies, etc.

• If the parties agree to a minimum compensation or maximum compensation, this will be indicated.

• The agreement should specify what compensation the agency should receive, if any, when advertising created by the agency is placed, in the United States, by a third party. Such third-party placement could occur when regional sales organizations, franchisees, retailers, wholesalers, or others are given permission to place advertising that was originally created by the agency.

• The agreement may also detail how the agency is to be compensated, if at all, when advertising prepared by it appears outside the United States.

• The agreement may also specify a time frame within which the advertiser is expected to reimburse the agency for its various expenditures made in the client's behalf.

Advertising Ownership

Most agreements specify the ownership rights of the advertiser in advertising materials presented to it by the advertising agency. Usually, any material that is actually presented by the agency to its client becomes the client's property.

Term of Relationship

The agreement may specify that the relationship between advertiser and agency will exist until canceled by either party. Alternatively, the agreement may remain in force for a specified time period—often one year—and then be cancelable by either party. The agreement also may be written so that it remains in effect from year to year, with a specified annual date on which either party may cancel.

Finally, the agreement usually states how the parties will notify each other of their desire to terminate and when notice of termination must be given. For example, the agreement might specify the 90-day notice of termination period that is standard in the industry.

Termination of Relationship

In addition to agreement about termination notice periods, client and agency usually find it prudent to specify other details about how the agreement between them will be terminated. These may include the following.

• An agreement about how the agency will be compensated during the period of termination notice. Frequently, when the agency is compensated by commission, it is agreed that commissions will be paid on advertising placed for the advertiser during the termination period, regardless of whether it is placed by the terminated agency. Fee agreements usually remain substantially unchanged during the period of termination notice, although the agreement may specify that the advertiser reserves the right to reduce the agency service level (and thus the amount of fee compensation) during the period.

• The termination section may also specify the treatment of uncancelable contracts, subcontracted work in progress, and rate adjustments on advertising that has previously run.

• There may be an agreement about how the agency will return materials and other client property to the client.

• Finally, the agency may be asked to agree to cooperate with the new agency during the period of transition.

The discussions that lead to a basic understanding of the agreement between client and agency need not be lengthy or arduous. Many of the issues will be clear-cut at the beginning or may have been agreed on earlier in the agency search. (The basic method of compensation may have been a matter of such prior agreement. All finalist agencies may have agreed to the compensation method favored by the advertiser before becoming finalists, for example.) In addition, many of the issues in the agreement have come to be covered by standard contract language. Such standard clauses are likely to be agreeable to both sides. Specimens of such clauses are readily available from such trade associations as the American Association of Advertising Agencies or the Association of National Advertisers. Frequently, too, the agency will have a standard contract of its own that can serve as a starting point for discussions.

The objective of these discussions is to develop an understanding as to how the advertiser and agency will do business together, as a final part of the agency selection process. That is why it is important for the principals to reach a broad agreement on these matters—before the actual agency selection is made final and publicly announced.

First Steps in the
New Agency Relationship

It remains for the advertiser to announce the appointment and begin its relationship with the new agency.

Of course, there will be a great deal of urgency about getting started. First of all, the selection of the new agency marks the end of a long and expensive process for the advertiser. The advertiser's organization will be eager to have this process come to an end. Those who have been in the search group and those who have participated in the agency presentation will undoubtedly have had enough of this digression from their normal jobs. And the rest of the organization, more or less aware that a search for an advertising agency has been going on, will want to know how it has turned out.

Secondly, there will be a strong interest in getting the new agency to work on the advertising problem of the brand or brands to which it has been assigned. There will be a strong sense of anticipation as to what the new agency will recommend and how well it will perform. None of this anticipation can be satisfied until the agency actually goes to work, and this will create organizational pressure for the announcement to be made so that this work can begin.

All this pressure will be heightened even more if the incumbent agency has already been put on notice. Little will then be expected of the old agency; in fact, there will be no interest in it at all. Nor will the incumbent agency, once fired, be interested in doing anything more than the minimum required by the termination agreement. The change of agencies will create an advertising vacuum around the brands affected, and this vacuum will also encourage the advertiser to appoint the new advertising agency and let it get to work.

There is only one reason for hesitation in appointing the new agency. No appointment should be announced until general agreements have been reached about the method of compensation and the content of the contract. As Chapters 9 and 13 point out, it is imprudent to leave discussion of these matters until later. If the contract and compensation agreements are delayed, they will not be treated with the interest or intensity that their determination *before* the announcement will generate.

Once the general agreements about compensation and contract have been reached, however, it is in everybody's best interest to make the appointment of the new advertising agency as promptly as possible.

Who Should Be Notified?

It is easy enough to determine who should be notified: the winning agency, the losing agencies, the incumbent agency, the advertiser's employees, the trade with which the advertiser conducts business, the suppliers that may be interested in or affected by the agency change (including the media), the advertiser's other agencies, and the trade press.

Telling the winning agency that it has won the competition is almost always a pleasure, accompanied as it is by a request that the agency start work at once. Somewhat more difficult is notifying the other finalist agencies that they have lost. This should be done at the same time that the winning agency is notified. It should be done promptly, so that the losers do not get the word from a third party or as a result of street rumor.

There are many different ways to notify the agency finalists that they have lost. At one extreme, one advertiser, having requested and received speculative presentations from about 12 agencies, sent the 11 losers a curt telegram saying only that the appointment of another agency had been made. The losers were not even given the courtesy of knowing which agency had been appointed, and they did not find out until the winner was announced in the trade press. To the losing agencies, this seemed to be rather short shrift for the work and expense of preparing extensive presentations for which they received neither compensation nor thanks.

At the other extreme, a major packaged goods advertiser heard speculative presentations from three finalist agencies, each of which received $25,000 for its presentations—enough to win their heartfelt appreciation, even if their total costs were not fully recovered. The losing agencies were telephoned and tactfully informed of their loss before the winner was notified. Finally, the losing agencies were invited to a one-and-a-half hour debriefing session, attended by the three-man search group and headed by the executive vice president for marketing. Each agency was told exactly why the winner had won and what it was about the losers' work that led to

169

their failure. One of the agencies lost because of the quality of its creative work. The other agency failed because of a lack of good chemistry with two of the proposed account people and a lack of understanding of the key marketing issues.

If only as a matter of courtesy, it is also important to inform the incumbent agency about the identity of the new agency. If the incumbent agency is already on notice, it must be told who they will work with in transferring the advertising account. If the incumbent agency is not on formal notice, it is hard to believe that it will be unaware that its advertising account has been the subject of a search for a new agency. The formal appointment will then precipitate the formal termination notice and direction from the advertiser to the old agency about transferring the account.

Finally, some sort of announcement should be made to advertiser employees, the trade, interested suppliers, and the trade press. These notices will inevitably be less personal than those sent to the agencies involved, but they should, as a matter of good public relations, be handled as promptly and gracefully as possible.

Some advertisers make an occasion of the appointment of an advertising agency. They may hold a formal press conference with principals of the agency to announce the appointment. They may host an entertainment for the new agency—a breakfast or luncheon—so that the employees of both organizations may start their relationship in a more or less relaxed, non-business environment.

No matter how the appointment is made, the next order of business is to get the agency working. As the new agency is initiated into this work process, the advertiser should do everything to make certain that the agency is brought on board as skillfully as possible. The advertiser's actions in the first days and weeks that the new agency is starting to work will often be decisive in determining how well the agency performs for the advertiser. To this problem, inherent in this transition, we now turn.

Getting off the Ground

Presumably, by this point, both advertiser and agency agree about the exact nature of the agency's work for the advertiser. The understanding should have been reached during the compensation and contract discussions that preceded the formal announcement. Both advertiser and agency must now implement this understanding.

First, the agency must identify the whole team that will work on the new account. Before this, the agency will have identified key members of the team, and they usually will have performed in the formal presentation. Now it is necessary for the agency to identify all of the people in the agency who will be responsible for working on the new account. In addition, the agency must fill in the account management and creative depth chart indicating who will serve below those key account and creative people.

Meanwhile, the nature of the relationship and specific responsibilities of the new agency should be made known to all advertiser personnel who will work with the new agency. The extent to which the new agency's duties are different from those of the previous agency should be spelled out in considerable detail to the advertiser's employees. This is often the case when an advertiser has switched from the commission to the labor-based fee method of compensation.

Because the commission system tends to leave the boundaries of agency service rather vague, advertisers frequently become dependent on the agency for many advertising and non-advertising services. Multiple marketing and media analyses may be routinely supplied by the agency, for example, whether necessary or not, simply because the client requires them. And the agency may be called on to supply extensive entertainment to individual advertiser employees, simply because it has gradually slipped into this posture of accommodation over the years. A switch to the labor-based fee method of compensation may reduce these kinds of agency services, which may come as a shock to advertiser employees who have become dependent on the old agency. It is important, therefore, that all advertiser employees be fully briefed on what the new agency will and will not provide under the new arrangement.

Once the agency team has been assembled and the advertiser employees know how the agency will work in the advertiser's behalf, it is important that individuals in both organizations get to know each other. The development of interfaces between the account managers on the agency side and the product managers on the client side will obviously take place quickly. It is also important that functional personnel in accounting, marketing research, legal, etc., get to know each other at a relatively early stage in the relationship. It is the responsibility of the senior agency account manager to see to it that such contacts occur and that the proper persons from both sides meet.

Next, possibly even before all of the necessary advertiser-agency interfaces have been established, the agency should be formally briefed by the research and development or technical people about the specific characteristics of the product or service for which the agency has been retained. This may also include a briefing by advertiser legal personnel on the rules that they wish to be followed in the preparation of advertising. These

171

briefings are vital to the advertising agency and will critically affect the quality of the work that is ultimately produced.

In addition, the advertiser should arrange for appropriate agency personnel—usually account managers—to become acquainted with those trade elements, systems, and practices that affect the advertiser product or service sales. Agency personnel should be encouraged to meet trade buyers and other trade intermediaries, and they should spend time traveling with members of the client sales organization. It is important that agency employees become thoroughly familiar with all the institutions existing between the advertiser and the ultimate consumer. This understanding will not only provide valuable background in the preparation of advertising, but may also enable the agency to make contributions beyond advertising to the client's line selling operation.

Finally, the advertiser and agency must consider how they will communicate with each other. Some advertisers and agencies agree to arrange meetings as they go along, discussing issues informally on the telephone between meetings. Frequently, however, especially when they are separated by a considerable distance, advertisers and agencies set up a more formal schedule of meetings, with the understanding that any meeting can be canceled if there is nothing to talk about.

No matter how often or in what way the client and agency meet, it is important to obtain a formal record of agreements reached. In most relationships, it is the agency's responsibility to provide a historical record of meetings and the decisions that they generate. This record is usually called a "call report" or a "conference report." It is important for advertiser and agency to agree that such reports *must* be continuously generated by the agency. These reports will provide a basis for adjudicating later disputes about such matters as billings, agency fees and projects, and the authorization for the agency to make specific commitments in behalf of the advertiser. A clear and comprehensive series of conference reports is an indispensable ingredient in an effective, continuing relationship between advertiser and agency.

How to Avoid Dissatisfaction

The appointment of a new advertising agency provides an appropriate time for reflection about what went wrong in the relationship with the old agency and how it may be prevented with the new agency. Prevention of the old problems will not automatically occur with the appointment of the new agency. If discontent with agency performance is not to surface anew, it is up to the advertiser to focus on this issue and consciously identify what must change in the new agency relationship. The final chapters of this book discuss advertiser–agency relationships and the steps that advertisers and agencies can take to make them both harmonious and productive.

PART 5

Effective Advertiser–Agency Working Relationships

Effective Advertiser–Agency Relationships—I

Once the advertising agency has been chosen and the compensation plan worked out, one major issue remains—the development of an effective working relationship with the new agency.

The first and most important principle in developing an effective agency relationship is to recognize that it is a two-way street—both sides, client and agency, must work hard and continuously if the relationship is to succeed. The two-way street concept sometimes seems difficult for advertisers to understand. No matter how much talk there is about an advertiser–agency "partnership," the advertiser is always the dominant partner in the relationship. The agency serves at the advertiser's pleasure.

Given this reality, it is not unusual for the advertiser to more or less leave it up to the agency to make the relationship "work." And, although few agency people would disagree that this is the client's prerogative, they would also point out that great advertising is rarely created in a vacuum. The two-way street notion will be covered in depth in this and the next chapter. Unless both sides work hard at the relationship from the beginning, the advertiser is likely to end up right back where it began in Chapter 1 of this book—wondering whether to start looking for a new advertising agency.

The second important thing to understand in building an effective advertiser–agency relationship is that such relationships may founder in many different ways. A successful relationship requires a wide variety of successful interactions. Many people are involved on both sides and they represent many different levels of experience and expertise.

There are no two or three major causes of client dissatisfaction with the advertiser–agency relationship. Instead, there are more than fifty individual factors—some on the advertiser side and some on the agency side—that can cause a relationship to go sour.

Although it is unusual for a single factor to cause a break in the relationship, this sometimes happens. It is much more usual, however, for three or four or more factors, usually interrelated, to gradually cause friction and, ultimately, dissatisfaction, on one side of the relationship or the other.

When an advertiser becomes totally dissatisfied, it is likely to start looking for a new agency. When the dissatisfaction is on the agency side, it rarely causes the agency to break off the relationship. Rather, the agency dissatisfaction usually leads to a general deterioration of agency service as the agency's problems with the advertiser grow. This in turn leads, sooner or later, to advertiser dissatisfaction and to an agency review.

There are six fundamental areas of advertiser–agency interaction that require attention if the relationship is to be as effective and productive as it should and must be. Each of these six areas contain a variety of specific factors that, collectively, determine the health of the relationship. In this chapter, three of these six basic areas will be considered. These areas, which reflect the ways in which advertiser and agency are organized and staffed, are specification of the roles of client and agency in the relationship, making sure that the agency creative product is promptly reviewed by senior advertiser personnel, and making sure that the advertiser and agency personnel are well-chosen and managed as the advertising process unfolds.

Specifying the Roles of Advertiser and Agency

The first thing that must happen in an effective advertiser–agency relationship is that both parties must understand exactly what they are supposed to do and how and when they are supposed to do it.

Advertisers Should Articulate Advertising and Marketing Policies That Affect the Advertising Agency's Work

It is a truism that businesses do not run themselves. Every business has a set of policies—implicit or explicit—that determine how that business will deal with situations and issues that arise as it develops and sells its products or services.

Thus, for example, businesses will have policies about product quality, customer service, trade relations, terms of payment, supplier bidding procedures, advertising claims, media vehicle suitability, and on and on. Everywhere one looks in a business there are policies that guide the day-to-day performance of the business. Much of the work of executives in any company has to do with formulating new policies or reformulating old policies as situations unfold that cannot be handled by application of existing policies.

The first responsibility of the advertiser to its new advertising agency is to brief the agency about company policies that are related to the way it advertises and markets the products and/or services that it produces.

Companies Should Articulate Policies about the Division of Labor between Company and Agency

There is a good deal of marketing and advertising work in the typical advertiser–agency relationship that could be handled by either the advertiser or the agency. To be sure, the agency will create the advertisements, and, to be sure, the company will either approve them or not. But, in between and around these decisive activities, there is much work to be done and there must be policies that spell out whether the advertiser or the agency is to do it. In most mature companies, this kind of rule making was undertaken years ago with little change over time, unless the original policies run up against changed situations that require modification. The ideal division of labor between advertiser and agency is as follows:

• The advertiser and agency are jointly responsible for the brand's basic marketing and advertising strategies and for long-term planning that will lead to basic changes in marketing variables to improve future sales and profits.

• The advertiser organization sets the business and financial goals for the brand; is responsible for the execution of basic changes in non-advertising-related marketing variables; and conducts all brand-related marketing research except that concerned with advertising.

• The agency is responsible for the planning and development of copy and media executions that spring from agreed-upon marketing and advertising strategies.

Sometimes, the advertiser may specify exactly how advertising executions are to be developed so that they can be quickly and comfortably appraised by the advertiser. Usually such specification has to do with the way in which advertising strategies are developed by the agency and approved by the advertiser. Once approved advertising strategies exist, advertisers may then set up rules that ensure that advertising copy and media executions explicitly reflect these strategies.

As one executive in a large package goods company expressed the problem:

The only really serious problem that I have with my advertising agencies is that they sometimes seem to get carried away in their creative work or media plans, and ignore the basic strategy agreements that we are all supposed to be working under. I now insist that they restate our strategic agreements before I even look at their creative or media work.

The Agency Should Specify Its Role in the Relationship

Most advertising agency people expect that the role they will play in their relationship with each of their clients will be specified by their clients and that it is the agency's responsibility to accede and adhere to this role exactly as specified. But the advertising agency is a business organization, too, and, as such, it must develop its own policies to direct the course of its enterprise. One area in which agency policies may affect the agency role in the relationship is personnel.

Most agencies have very similar personnel policies, so most advertisers find a similarity in the general availability of agency personnel to serve them. However, agencies may have personnel policies that will have a distinct impact on the way in which clients are served.

Some of these policies are more or less trivial. For example, most New York agencies now close at noon or 1 P.M. on Fridays during the summer months between Memorial Day and Labor Day. This policy is generally in force, even though agency clients are normally open for business on Friday afternoons in the summer.

The policy was adopted by most New York agencies in the early 1970s, primarily to keep young, socially mobile employees happy. It was, in addition, a *de facto* recognition on the part of one or two pioneering agencies that their key personnel left at noon on summer Fridays anyway, and the formal extension of this practice into an agency-wide rule simply extended reality to the entire work force. Once one or two agencies did this, all were forced to follow in order to remain competitive in the labor marketplace.

Another agency personnel policy, considerably more profound in its effect upon how clients are serviced, has to do with how agencies organize their staffs to handle clients' business. The traditional agency account management organization has tended to mirror the client organization. Thus, there is an agency account person designated as an opposite to every

179

client marketing person. Since advertiser marketing organizations tend to be four or five layers deep on every marketed brand or service, agency account groups also tend to be four or five persons deep.

Meanwhile, the agency's functional departments also tend to be organized in hierarchies, with three or four layers of responsibility for each functional activity. Agency personnel tend to interface with their hierarchical peers both within the account group and at the client.

The inevitable result of hierarchical organizations within the agency is a good deal of up and down communication before meetings between account people and creative or media or research department people occur. Then there is further communication across hierarchies within the agency before formal contact between agency and client occur.

Agencies organized like this tend to act slowly and ponderously. Decisions on agency copy or media plans tend to be made, refined, and remade within the agencies as work moves up and down and then between the hierarchies. Decisions are then made, refined, and remade as the agency work is presented, with recommendations, to the client.

This kind of organizational structure on both the client and agency side tends to be relatively foolproof—few mistakes are made by either agency or client because there are so many internal and external watchers of the agency's work. However, such organizations are criticized as slow moving, inflexible, and hostile to unusual or particularly creative ideas.

Some agencies believe that there is a better way. These agencies think that it is better to have a few first-rate people devoting a significant portion of their time, in a close-knit group, to the advertising problems of their clients. They prefer this smaller, more dedicated group to a much larger group of relatively junior people organized in hierarchies, spending proportionately less of their total time against a particular client's advertising problems. For that is what tends to happen in agency hierarchies—more people and more junior people spend less time on a greater number of accounts.

There is good reason to believe that clients receive better service from the dedicated group within an agency than from more fractional people across the hierarchy. Clients receive more attention from relatively senior people, service is quicker and more flexible, points of view are clearer.

Finally, the general run of advertising ideas is probably of a higher order, because each idea reaches the client in a purer, less masticated form. Agency managements like the dedicated group system too, because it tends to cost less to provide service of this kind than to provide service based on account and departmental hierarchies.

Yet, having said all this, such a revised organization will affect the client–agency relationship. The client gets a different kind of service, as individuals within the client organization are less likely to have a dedicated peer at the agency. There will be less contact with agency people, less client hand-holding, less agency support for the way in which individuals in the advertiser organization do their jobs. This will be true whether the agency commits itself to a full-blown implementation of the dedicated-group system or moves toward it in a gradual way, shortening or breaking down the hierarchies over a period of time.

No matter how beneficial the effect of such an organizational change may be on the work of the agency, the decision to move toward dedicated groups must be balanced by a consideration of how each client prefers to be served by the agency. Agencies may make organizational moves that appear to them to be in the best interest of client and agency, only to find these moves rejected by clients because it appears that the levels of agency service to which the client is accustomed have been emasculated.

When Is the Best Time to Specify the Agency and Advertiser Roles?

Changes in the specified roles of advertiser and agency can, of course, be made at any time. However, such changes in role specification tend to occur as part of a more general redefinition of agency and client relationships rather than as an off-shoot of day-to-day activities. Thus, there seem to be three occasions when changes in the specification of client and agency roles are most likely to occur.

First, of course, is when a new agency is hired. Both client and agency have a clean slate. This is the point at which it is not only likely but imperative that some sort of role definition for both agency and advertiser must occur.

A second occasion on which the redefinition of client and advertiser roles usually occurs is when a new agency compensation agreement is worked out. As previous chapters have suggested, discussions about agency compensation are likely to cover topics such as the work that is required from the agency, the staffing levels that are required to provide such work, and/or the staffing levels that are preferred by the advertiser. This kind of discussion leads, inevitably, to a discussion of the exact roles that agency and advertiser must play in the relationship.

Third, many advertisers make a periodic, formal appraisal of the work done by their agencies. (See Chapter 16.) The fundamental weakness in most such appraisals is that they are too one-sided. They deal too much with what the agency does for the advertiser and too little with how the advertiser interacts with the agency.

Nevertheless, any discussion of agency performance, no matter how one-sided, is bound to lead to topics that involve the advertiser and agency roles in the relationship. It is desirable that, if necessary, such discussions lead, in turn, to a redefinition of the roles of both advertiser and agency in order to overcome weaknesses in the relationship.

Clarifying How the Creative Work of the Agency Will Be Judged

Closely allied to the question of what roles will be played by advertiser and agency is the fundamental question of just how the agency's work will be judged. This issue involves both the strategic work of the agency for creative and media as well as the tactical or executional work within creative campaigns and media plans.

Multiple Approvals of Agency Work

No matter how the agency organizes itself, by hierarchy or dedicated group, it must still contend with the reality that most advertisers are organized in hierarchies. The further reality is that everyone in the advertiser hierarchy would like to get a crack at evaluating the work of the agency.

This poses two distinct questions of concern to the agency: How many times will their work be evaluated? And, what level of advertiser sophistication will be brought to each of these evaluations?

Clearly, from the standpoint of the agency, the ideal is to have all work evaluated once by a single person whose advertising judgment the agency respects and whose advertising sophistication the agency admires. However, most advertisers perceive it to be in their best interest to have important advertising decisions reviewed at several levels within their organization so that the possibility of error or oversight is reduced to as close to zero as possible.

These two points of view are basically incompatible. The advertising agency wants sensitive review of its work at the highest level because it believes that this is the only way in which the creative essence of the work is likely to be preserved. But it is the risk inherent in highly unusual creative approaches that the advertiser's personnel hierarchy has been created to minimize.

It is probably inevitable that most important agency work will be reviewed by two, three, or more layers at the client organization. What can the advertiser do to ensure that genuinely creative ideas receive a profound and professional review within the organization as well as a wide ranging appraisal? Many advertisers believe that there are two interlocking solutions to this problem.

First, the final decision about key agency strategic, creative, and media recommendations should be made by a senior advertiser executive who has a recognized ability to make mature advertising judgments. The talent of this individual and his or her ability to command the respect of the agency is a critical element in the effectiveness of the advertiser-agency relationship.

Second, the rule should be established that other individuals in the advertiser organization may make any comments on the advertising that they wish. These comments will be reviewed by the senior advertising evaluator *before* he or she passes final judgment on the agency's work. However, no other person in the advertiser organization has the authority to reject agency work or to require that revisions in it be made *before* the senior advertising evaluator reviews it.

These rules tend to accomplish two important objectives.

The agency is guaranteed that its work will be reviewed and accepted or rejected by a mature marketing executive whose judgment the agency will either respect, or, at least, be willing to live with. Under this arrangement, the agency is assured that its basic ideas will not be picked to death by marketing underlings before they are finally reviewed.

These rules also protect the advertiser since they assure that the agency only brings forward ideas to which it is firmly and finally committed. This procedure does not permit the agency to propose a wide variety of ideas to lower levels of the advertiser hierarchy in order to see which ideas is most likely to "fly" as it moves up the hierarchy. It is now the responsibility of the agency to explore creative alternatives as broadly as possible; to expose them to full internal agency exploration and consideration; and to make recommendations that are based on the broad base of agency professional expertise.

Agency Participation in Client Marketing Deliberations

The process that has just been described—disposition of agency recommendations by a senior marketing person, no authority to change agency recommendations at lower client levels—can only work well if the advertiser involves the agency in all of its marketing deliberations and decision making. Somehow or other, the agency must become fully informed about all of the marketing considerations that will affect the advertising that it creates, and to which this advertising must respond. Without this immersion, the agency cannot prepare itself to make final advertising recommendations only at the most senior marketing level in the advertiser's organization.

One of the benefits of the agency hierarchy to client hierarchy interaction with continuous review of agency work at multiple levels within the advertiser organization is that this process tends to inform and immerse the agency in the marketing thought of the advertiser organization. As pointed out above, many advertising people believe that this is a cumbersome and inefficient method to deal with advertising agencies, and a method that tends to eviscerate the best agency creative ideas. The only point is that one benefit of this hierarchy-to-hierarchy interaction is to immerse the agency in client marketing thought. If this process is attenuated or canceled, its positive effects must be created in some other way.

The issue has been illuminated by the management consulting firm, Booz, Allen & Hamilton:

The most successful client-agency relationship appears to result from a meeting of the minds of marketing management and agency management on broad strategy and "product positioning"—in advance of the work of company and agency people on marketing programs and advertising executions.[1]

Managing the Advertising Process

After the respective roles of advertiser and agency have been specified and after attention has been paid to how agency work will be reviewed to ensure its acceptability, it remains to make sure that both advertiser and agency successfully manage the process of creating and placing advertising. This is the nitty-gritty, day-to-day side of the advertiser–agency relationship. It is also the side of the relationship that defines its reality.

Filling Jobs with Knowledgeable People—Advertiser. The first issue, for both advertiser and agency, is to staff their respective organizations with people who know what their jobs are and who have enough experience to perform at a high level.

On the advertiser side, this has two implications. First of all, the ad-

---

[1]Booz, Allen & Hamilton, *Management and Advertising Problems in the Advertiser–Agency Relationship,* Association of National Advertisers, New York, 1965, p. 60.

vertiser's people must know how to manage the advertising process. They must have a sense of the time frame which exists for the creation and execution of advertising programs and they must know what decisions this process requires, and when these decisions must be made in accordance with the overall time frame.

Nothing can gum up the advertising process and emasculate the agency more effectively than an advertiser who is indifferent to or ignorant of the details of how advertising comes into being. There should be no amateurs or dilettantes on the advertiser's side of the relationship.

The other essential skill for advertisers is to know how to get the best work out of an advertising agency. Making sure that only a respected senior advertiser has the responsiblity to accept or reject agency recommendations, and especially creative recommendations, is, as we have seen, one important aspect of the relationship.

But there is also the question of how this senior advertiser person and, indeed, all advertiser personnel, deal with the agency over the short term and over the long term. In the first place, both sides of the relationship must recognize that its only purpose is to produce consistently superior advertising for the advertiser. The purpose of the relationship is not to give advertiser personnel an opportunity to exploit or harass agency personnel, nor is it to provide a consumately pleasurable work experience for employees of the agency.

Having said all this, it remains to suggest what kinds of advertiser attitudes toward the agency are most likely to inspire agency employees to excel consistently in behalf of the advertiser. Advertisers will serve their own interests best when they routinely hold these attitudes about their agency.

• Nothing inspires agency people more than a client who clearly expects that everything that an agency does will be worthy of its admiration. The client may not, in the final analysis, like or approve specific pieces of an agency's work, but the attitude from the start should be one of respectful expectation.

On the other hand, nothing can damage agency morale more surely than the client who acts as if the agency can do nothing right and that the next proposal or recommendation is certain to be worse than the last.

• The advertiser should always tell the agency why it finds particular agency work unacceptable. Many clients seem to be unable to articulate just why it is that they have reservations about particular agency proposals or recommendations.

Professional agency people yearn for thoughtful examination of their work and a candid explanation of why the client thinks it is flawed or un-

185

acceptable. A two-way street between client and agency implies that, if nothing else, there will be a constructive and positive dialogue about the work of the agency and its strengths and weaknesses.

• The agency must have adaquate time in which to excel. Advertiser employees who are not good managers of the advertising process tend to show their ineptness by imposing arbitrary and/or impossible deadlines on advertising agency employees.

Agency professionals, perhaps more than most people, tend to delay the execution of work until the last minute, sometimes because they are lazy and sometimes because they want to make sure that they have spent as much time as they can to think through the problem at hand to its best solution.

In spite of all this, it is the wise client that understands that superior work requires adequate time, and tries to provide the agency with enough time to do the job, if for no other reason than by doing so the advertising agency will not have the excuse of insufficient time if its work turns out to be unacceptable.

• Advertiser–agency relationships should always be conducted at a professional level. The *only* reason that an advertiser–agency relation exists is to produce first-rate advertising work. Smart clients never forget this. They never let personal interests or reactions or political considerations enter into their relationships with agency employees.

Admittedly, human beings are human beings and most seem incapable of limiting or eliminating the personal or political from their relations with others, in the workplace or elsewhere. Yet, the creation of superior advertising is solely a professional matter, and the advertiser who can minimize or excise the personal and political from the agency relationship will have taken an important step toward maximizing its effectiveness.

Filling Jobs with Competent People—Agency. Agency principals often say, privately, that if client people are good, the agency counterparts must be better. And there is substantial truth to this. After all, the advertiser is the dominant partner in the relationship and, in the end, the agency must staff itself to make sure that whatever the advertiser wants, it gets. The only way to make sure that this happens is to staff the advertiser's account with advertising practitioners whose credentials, professionalism, and work style are beyond reproach. To be better than their clients, agency people have to excel in specific areas.

• First, they must know at least as much about the process of advertising as their clients. The agency person—account, creative, or media—

must understand the imperatives of the advertising process so well that he or she is always anticipating the client's needs.

The great advertiser–agency relationships have a positive and constructive tension about them. Both sides have such an intrinsic understanding of what must be done to produce superior advertising and when it must be done that the relationships seem to move forward almost in spite of themselves. This only happens because the agency professionals understand the process of advertising at least a little bit better than do their client counterparts.

• Good agency people always put the professional needs and interest of their clients before anything else. Good agency people understand that they are in a service business. This means that nothing can come between the agency employee and the most professional possible performance. Personal considerations are forgotten—There can be no negative reaction to client insensitivity or arrogance. The only basis for what the agency does or thinks is the professional need dictated by the best interest of the client.

Unhappily, of course, the people who work in advertising agencies are human, and few if any of them are capable of becoming the service-before-all automatons that is implied in the preceding paragraph. If client service at all cost is an ideal that most intelligent and conscientious agency people have a little trouble achieving, it is still an ideal to which the very best agency people aspire. And excellence in client service is, after all, what clients should, and do, expect from their agencies. Sometimes clients may be unreasonable about their demands, but first-rate agency people know that this is what the advertising agency business is all about. They also know that if they cannot prosper in such a client-service-dedicated environment, the advertising agency business is not for them.

• Good advertising agency people are not arrogant. There is a certain potential explosiveness in an organization that, as a matter of policy, staffs itself with smart people who accept the client–agency service work ethic. If agency people are as good as they should be, they may come to believe that they are better than others, including even their clients.

Arrogance is the antithesis of client service and it is unusual to find it among account service people. Yet some agencies, at least some of the time, have employed creative people, media people, and/or research people who are flat-out arrogant in their dealings with clients. This arrogance develops because these people are not only good at their jobs, they are also at the very pinnacle of professional accomplishment.

Some agency people may be so good at what they do, and consistently so much better than their peers, that they can get away with such

187

arrogance—some creative "superstars" are a case in point. Every client and every agency must deal with such extraordinary execellence on its own terms. A certain amount of arrogance may be a small price to pay if such people really are as good as they think they are.

The real problem of arrogance is not with agency people who are so good that they earn their right to it, but with people who are not sublimely talented, but who believe themselves to be. Arrogance from people who are wrong at least some of the time is unacceptable. Clients don't have to put up with it, and agency managers have the unyielding responsibility to get rid of such people before their poison spreads throughout the agency.

• Finally, superior advertising agency people have good work habits. This is almost the logical consequence of people who are smart, knowledgeable about the advertising process, client-service-oriented, and humble. One can be all of these things and still be sloppy, however.

Good agency people are not sloppy about meeting client deadlines; they always listen to what their clients have to say; always ask the right questions; write timely, succinct, and accurate conference reports; do their "homework" on every topic that affects their client; are on time for meetings; never forget a commitment or a promise. In short, good agency people don't make mistakes in the mechanics of servicing their clients on a day-in and day-out basis. They are masters of the nitty-gritty.

Personnel Problems for Both Agencies and Advertisers. Some personnel problems are apparently endemic to the advertising business. They affect advertisers and their agencies, alike. Two areas come to mind.

• First, there is a good deal of turnover in agency ranks, particularly at junior levels in the organization. Such turnover is not limited to agencies, however—many advertisers have significant turnover within their organizations too.

There are two generally acknowledged reasons for such turnover. In the first place, there is a genuine need to train younger advertising people and to encourage them to think positively about their future in the organization. Providing a variety of experience to such beginners is one way to accomplish this.

However, the need to keep young people interested in their assignments within an advertiser or agency organization can lead to nothing but turnover on both sides of the relationship. Seemingly, this is a no-win situation for both advertiser and agency: If they don't move their junior people around, they'll lose them anyway.

Probably the only way to reduce the effects of this vicious circle is to impose minimum assignment times for younger people. Under this approach, a rule is set that everyone must spend a minimum amount of time—a year, a year and one half—in every assignment before moving on to the next.

But such rules do nothing to reduce the second cause of high turnover among advertising people, agency and client. The field is notorious for its transferability. Job-hopping is part of the culture, especially if the new job pays more than the old and offers more responsibility or opportunity. Agencies are especially susceptible to this kind of personnel turnover. For example, one way in which agencies expand their staff to handle new business is to hire experienced people away from other agencies or advertisers.

Whether the problem of personnel turnover is easy to solve, it is a source of irritation in advertiser–agency relationships. High turnover of advertiser or agency people will inevitably make the relationship less effective.

• Both advertisers and agencies tend to overstaff their operations. Advertisers tend to develop bureaucracies as a device to make sure that their organization does not make mistakes. As we have seen, advertising agencies often staff their own organizations so that they match, function by function and responsibility by responsibility, the organization of their client.

As noted above, at least some agencies are doing their best to get away from hierarchical, mirror-image staffing because they think it impedes creativity, is wasteful, and reduces profitability. This tendency has been especially prevalent in recent years as client interest in agency compensation has increased.

On the other hand, advertisers have the same cost sensitivity as do agencies, and some have abandoned their own hierarchical staffing, slimming down their operations, expecting their agency to pick up the slack. When such advertiser action occurs, the agency tends to become more of a "partner" in the relationship, but this maneuver can only really work when agency compensation is maintained or increased.

A good deal of the trouble in the staffing area relates to the issue of defining advertiser and agency roles properly and to the need for advertisers to view their agency relationship as a two-way street. In the end, the advertiser and its agency must work together to make sure that the required work is done, and done extremely well. Both should want this work to be performed as efficiently as possible, and the advertiser should want to make sure that the agency is adequately compensated to provide the staff needed to make the whole enterprise productive.

Effective Advertiser–Agency Relationships—II

The preceding chapter considered organization and staffing issues that affect the relationship between advertiser and agency. These topics—specifying the roles of advertiser and agency, organizing to review agency creative work at a senior level, and staffing the two sides of the relationship—depend upon management decisions in the advertiser and agency organizations.

The issues that remain are less matters of organization control than of the way the relationship between advertiser and agency works out in practice. Every advertiser–agency relationship takes on a character of its own that reflects not only the organizational decisions that have been made about it, but also the way that all of the people-to-people relations develop and evolve as time passes.

Three areas reflect these people-to-people interactions: the way the organizations communicate with each other, the top management interaction that characterizes the relationship, and the informal and formal bases on which the advertiser evaluates the agency's work. The balance of this chapter is concerned with these matters.

Interactive Communication

An advertiser–agency relationship cannot work well unless there is effective communication between the two organizations. "Communication" is a peculiar concept. Instead of meaning something specific, it is often used in a generic way to describe why organizations are not productive or why organizations do not interact effectively with each other. The term *communication failure* is thus used to describe any organizational failure whether or not it can be attributed to an actual communication shortcoming. In this chapter "communication failure" refers only to a failure that can be repaired by some change or improvement in the communications within or between organizations, and nothing else.

People communicate with each other in writing and verbally, either on the telephone or face-to-face. Communications occur *within* advertiser organizations and *within* agency organizations through written communication (memoranda, reports, other documents); through telephone conversations with two or more people; and in meetings of two or more people. Similarly, communications *between* advertiser and agency proceed similarly with the addition of communications that summarize the interaction of advertiser and agency (conference reports, work project lists and reports, etc.).

Communication failures occur either because the communication process is, itself, flawed or because the process is not used as it was intended to be used.

The Communication Process: Keeping the Advertising Program Moving

The appropriate means of communication within and between advertiser and agency must be clearly specified. If a communication fails to be made within the advertiser or agency organization, that particular communication probably cannot and will not be made *between* the organizations.

Written communications are easiest to control and direct. One cannot assume that a communication has been made unless it has been made in writing.

Every member of the advertiser and agency staffs should know exactly who in their organizations must be informed in writing about the advertising program in all of its detail. Similarly, everyone in each organization should know who in the other organization should be informed in writing about developments in the advertising program that have originated in their organization. This is what standard carbon copy or routing lists are for. They should reflect, precisely, everyone within the two organizations who has or shares any responsibility for the planning and execution of the advertising program in all of its ramifications.

Developing effective communication within the advertiser organization, within the agency organization, and between the two is a tricky business. Not everyone in both organizations need know *everything* that affects the advertising process, but everyone must know all the things that are likely to affect the performance of his or her job. It is not easy to set up a

191

communications system that guarantees that each person has all the information that he or she requires about the advertising program, but no more.

In advertising agencies, it is the responsibility of the senior account executive to manage the information flow so that every person in the organization receives no more information than necessary to do his or her own job well. The media and creative departments do not, for example, need detailed information about what happens within each other's departments, but they do need to be informed regarding developments in general.

In the advertiser's organization, the senior marketing executive for the particular advertising assignment has a similar responsibility for making sure that all advertiser people are supplied with the information they need.

It is the agency's responsibility to develop and disseminate reports on the interactions that occur between the two organizations. Only if the agency assumes this responsibility can it be sure that communications between agency and advertiser will be fully reported.

When advertiser and agency meet, everything agreed upon—all understandings, decisions, and directions to agency and advertiser for future activity—are documented by the agency in a formal report, sometimes called a "conference" report, a "meeting" report, or a "call" report.

What follows is a discussion of the many ways communication systems of this kind can break down.

It Is Not Clear Who Should Communicate with Whom. For this kind of system to work, every member of both organizations must understand his or her responsibility, if any, to communicate with every other member of both organizations. The understanding must include not only whether to communicate but also what to communicate.

Some Individuals May Consciously Subvert the System. An individual's power within any business organization usually depends upon what the individual knows. It is possible for some individuals to increase their own power and diminish that of others by manipulating the flow of information. Whatever the personal gain that is sought by such individuals, it is clear that whenever the system does not work as planned, either the total efficiency of the advertiser organization, the agency organization, or both, is affected.

The best way to control such manipulation of the communication system is to formalize the system rather than let it depend upon the whims and instincts of individual employees. The more formal and overt the system and the more it depends on written communication, the more difficult it is to manipulate.

There Is No Formal Indoctrination of New Employees about How to Communicate. As we have seen, one of the problems in advertiser–agency relationships is that there is often considerable personnel turnover within the organizations. Such turnover can seriously affect communications if there is no formal indoctrination of new employees concerning the communication system. If new employees are left to their own devices to figure out how the system works and how to participate in it, it is almost inevitable that the system will break down to some degree.

In the end, it is the responsibility of the advertiser's senior marketing person and the agency's senior account executive to make sure that the communication system that underlies the relationship is clearly specified and that it works, and continues to work. Nothing can lead to a breakdown in the effectiveness of the advertiser–agency relationship quicker than a breakdown in the communication system that it depends upon.

How Much Does the Agency Need to Know?

Another issue affecting the success of advertiser–agency communication is the appropriate degree of knowledge the agency should have concerning the advertiser's business and who within the agency should have this knowledge.

From the perspective of the agency, it is extremely important that it know everything about its client's business that is necessary to produce superior advertising. A definition of "everything" has often led to problems in the advertiser–agency relationship.

In the first place, everyone seems to agree that the agency should know everything about the client's product or service that might effect the content of the advertising. This obviously means product specifications, performance test reports, competitive evaluations, results of consumer use and reaction tests, and the like. Does this mean, however, that everyone in the agency should know *everything* there is to know about the advertiser's product? What about weaknesses of the product or competitive shortcomings? What about advertiser trade secrets? What about the economic underpinnings of the product or service—its costs, its profitability, breakeven points, etc.?

From the advertiser's viewpoint there are two distinct issues here. The first has to do with the relevance of the specific information to the development of advertising programs. The closer the feeling of "partnership" between advertiser and agency, the more likely that the agency will be privy to advertiser information that is questionable in its relevance to advertising, no matter how relevant it is to an overall appreciation of the advertiser's business.

If, however, the advertiser views the agency as just another vendor of services, the agency is less likely to know much intimate detail about the operations of the company that seem to have nothing to do with advertising.

And, in the final analysis, no matter how intimate the relationship, it is certain that some information, including much that is potentially relevant to advertising, must and will be withheld. For example, it is virtually certain that The Coca-Cola Company has never revealed the formula for any of its cola products to its advertising agencies.

The second issue that concerns advertisers in deciding what the agency should know is the security with which the agency holds confidential information.

There is a certain nervousness among advertisers about agency security. This seems to reflect two distinct advertiser beliefs: They believe that agency personnel turnover is excessive and that advertiser secrets will not be secure with people who have left an agency to go elsewhere, often to work on a competitive account.

They also believe that many agency employees are, by the nature of their personality, indifferent to the security of client secrets no matter how sacred they are to the advertiser.

There is probably a little truth in both of these concerns. Agency employees do turn over and they may even turn over at a faster rate than the advertiser's own employees. And some agency employees are a little blasé and indifferent to the concerns of the stark and unforgiving world as perceived by advertisers.

On the other hand, there is some question as to how much advertiser knowledge is really of the kind that will hurt the advertiser when it ends up in the hands of a competitor. As Marvin Bower, then a director of McKinsey and Company, remarked: "As a matter of realism, the interests of competing clients would not be harmed by an almost complete exchange of information among the people serving two competing companies."[1]

An additional reality is that if the advertiser cannot trust its agency's security, it has the alternative of finding an agency with a security program that it does respect.

If the agency is given the information that it needs to produce first-

---

[1] William M. Weilbacher, *Auditing Productivity,* Association of National Advertisers, New York, 1981, p.58.

rate advertising, well and good. If the client holds back information that could be used to produce such advertising, the advertiser–agency relationship will not be as effective as it should be.

Are Employees Indifferent to Effective Communication?

There is a final problem that may upset communication channels. The channels may be well-defined. Their use may be understood and endorsed by all employees, new and old. The client may agree, at least in principle, to convey to the agency everything that it should know to produce excellent advertising. The only thing that can now go wrong with the system is that advertiser and/or agency people, or both, may simply not use it or fail to use it all of the time.

Such failures have nothing to do with employees who wish consciously to subvert the system. Rather, it has to do with employee indifference and laziness. What employees should know may be communicated *at* them, but may not consciously be received *by* them. The communication receiving mechanisms of these employees simply do not work as it has been assumed that they will. Such laziness, indifference, or lack of motivation may occur for at least three separate reasons.

• Some people have never learned the discipline of reading or listening, attentively and accurately. They are permanently out to lunch when others try to communicate to them.

• Some people may not read/listen because they are apprehensive of what they will learn and what it will mean for them: hard work, lost weekends, difficult personality interfaces, or other unpleasant prospects.

• Some people do not read or listen because they have an inherent arrogance toward new information. They know it all, and there is nothing more that anyone can convey to them that will be useful to them in any way.

People who do not participate in the communication process for any of these reasons are not very good employees. They should be replaced by those who are willing and eager to communicate according to the rules.

The Tone of Effective Advertising Relationships Is Set at the Top

Effective advertiser–agency relationships are almost always based on positive involvement of the top executives of the two organizations. This involvement is usually at the board chairperson or president level, and it is always at a level where the executives involved can make decisions that are binding on their respective organizations.

If the relationship between the senior executive is cordial and strong, the relationship between the organizations is likely to prosper and prevail over a long period of time. If, however, the relationship between these people is flawed or unsatisfactory, it is usually certain that the relationship will soon come to an end.

A strong relationship between the top executives confirms that the business relationship between their firms is an important one—a relationship that is worth nurturing.

The chairperson or president of the advertiser company will want to achieve six objectives in the relationship with senior agency management.

1. The advertiser will want to provide a public endorsement of the advertising agency. Such an endorsement of the agency has the effect of making the agency directly responsible to the advertiser's top management for the quality of its work. This endorsement cannot be delegated to others in the advertiser's organization if it is to be totally effective.

2. Access to agency top management gives the advertiser an opportunity to present and explain key goals, philosophies, and policies of the company to the agency.

3. The relationship with agency top management gives the advertiser an opportunity to assess the quality of the senior agency manager as well as the agency's commitment to the advertiser's business.

4. The relationship also provides the advertiser with the opportunity for an independent, objective appraisal of the advertiser's organization by the agency. This is likely to be important to the advertiser, since few if any other outsiders have the opportunity to interact intimately with the advertiser's organization. The agency has a unique exposure to the structure, personnel, and operating style of the advertiser, and the advertiser can learn a great deal about itself from the agency.

5. The advertiser executive's relation with the agency provides the advertiser with a continuing opportunity to convey to the agency the advertiser's assessment of its work. Praise from the senior advertising executive is music to an agency's ears and no criticism will be more quickly and effectively dealt with than criticism from the very top of the client's organization.

6. Finally, this relationship provides the ideal forum in which to discuss the value of the agency's efforts in behalf of the advertiser, and the fairness or adequacy of the compensation that the agency receives for its services.

Meanwhile, the senior agency executive will have a specific agenda for the relationship with the client counterpart. It will include the following objectives:

1. The top agency manager will want to establish a positive presence with the client's top executive. The agency manager will become, in many ways, a symbol of the agency in the client's mind. The relationship with the senior client executive provides an opportunity to invest this symbol with strong and positive meanings and associations.

2. The top agency manager will use the relationship to reinforce the agency's image of integrity. It is paramount that every client believe that its agency is totally committed to the idea that its best interests can only be achieved if it unfailingly pursues the best interests of its clients.

3. The top agency executive should become the client's primary source of information about effective communication with consumers and about the entire advertising industry in its largest sense. The top executive of the client should feel that the agency counterpart's points of view about consumer communication and advertising are both totally informed and totally sophisticated.

4. The agency executive should develop a dialogue with the client about agency compensation and how it can be made equitable to advertiser and agency alike. The agency executive must be the prime spokesperson for the quality and value of the work that is provided to the advertiser by the agency.

5. Similarly, the agency executive must develop a dialogue with the senior client about the overall performance of the agency. This should be a frank and constructive interchange about how the advertiser's organization can make better use of the agency as well as how the agency can better serve the advertiser.

6. Finally, the agency executive should use the access to the client to reaffirm that the agency has the courage of its convictions no matter how unpopular they may be with the advertiser.

If the top executives of the client and the advertiser do not establish their own relationship or, once established, do not use it to pursue the goals outlined above, the relationship between the companies will become amorphous and directionless and its effectiveness will be undermined.

The Advertiser's Continuing Formal Evaluation of the Agency

The advertiser organization usually will review and evaluate the agency's work as, day-by-day, the relationship unfolds. It is important that an agency feel that it is judged on every recommendation that it makes, and for every advertisement that it produces. Such continuing appraisal tends to maintain the tone of positive and effective client service in agency operations, and it is fundamental to the success of the relationship.

In addition, each advertiser–agency relationship should be subjected to a more formal, periodic appraisal that is distinctly independent of the normal day-to-day appraisal of agency operations. It is customary to make such formal assessments of the agency either annually or semiannually. Such appraisals usually have several objectives. What follows is a discussion of several of them.

How Good Is the Agency Product?

A primary objective of the formal agency evaluation is to appraise the effectiveness of the agency's work in behalf of the advertiser. This topic is intimately related to the discussion of incentive compensation in Chapter 12.

Recall that, in that discussion, it was pointed out that advertising agency work may be evaluated either subjectively or objectively. In the vast majority of instances, it appears that the final evaluation of agency work is subjective, reflecting the overall satisfaction of the advertiser with the agency. The subjective appraisal may be buttressed by copy test results and/or tracking studies of advertising induced brand awareness and attitudes. Such research may contribute to a general advertiser feeling of well-being about the agency's product, but it will usually not produce a single, decisive measurement of the effectiveness of the agency's work that is accepted by both advertiser and agency.

If the advertiser and agency both agree that the pursuit of such a single, decisive measurement is fruitless, this leaves unanswered what the advertiser should do to invigorate their subjective appraisals to make them more objective and dependable. There are four steps that an advertiser can take to increase such objectivity.

• The advertiser should maintain continuing pressure on the agency to document the effectiveness of its work. Advertising agencies are, after all, the experts about advertising. It is their responsibility to defend their work and, ultimately, to demonstrate its effectiveness in an objective way. Advertisers should never let their agencies forget that it is part of their job to prove that advertising has a positive effect on the sales and profits of their clients.

• Advertisers should be willing to experiment to find better measurements of advertising effectiveness. The problem of measuring advertising effects is unlikely to be solved by intellectualizing or philosophizing about it. Sooner or later the effects of advertising will be measured in the marketplace, and advertisers should welcome experimental projects in the real world that show promise of moving in this direction.

• The ultimate objective of advertising strategy should be to define the advertising effect that will justify a particular level of advertising expenditure. As suggested in Chapter 12, the heart of the problem of advertising effectiveness lies in the determination of advertising strategy. Advertising strategies should always focus single-mindly on the way advertising can cause the effect desired by the advertiser.

• Advertisers should conduct post mortem examinations on past advertising successes and failures. One source of knowledge about the effects of advertising is what has happened in the past. There should be more formal study of what seemed to be effective in the past and why, and of what seemed to fail, and why.

How Good Is Agency Service?

A second area for appraisal is advertising agency service. Agency "service" covers, of course, everything that an agency does in its client's behalf. In the context of agency appraisal, "service" means the day-to-day efficiency of the agency operation in meeting deadlines and other commitments; the quality of the agency's work product in support of final, finished advertisements and media executions; the quality and profundity of the agency's thinking about the client's marketing and advertising problems; the initiative and proactivity of the agency in interaction with the advertiser; and the compatibility and effectiveness of agency employees in interaction with advertiser employees.

Formal agency evaluations normally include a number of specific bases of evaluation that reflect back on these appraisal factors. Such evaluative items are usually organized under broad topic areas including:

• Does the agency organize itself to work effectively with the advertiser's organization?

• Does it staff the account with compatible, productive people?

- Does the advertising process and its attendant work flow move smoothly ahead?
- Does the agency remove irritants in the relationship as they appear?
- Is there evidence of agency involvement in and powerful thinking about the client's business?
- Does the agency's creative and media work respond to perceptions and needs of the client organization?
- Does creative and media work proceed smoothly through the advertiser's review processes, or is there continuous bickering about the quality of the agency's work?
- Do all of the agency's departments make a distinct contribution to the advertiser, or are some of the departments inept or ineffective?

Rating scales are usually developed for such client service factors—often several scales within each general area. Concerned individuals within the advertiser's organization—usually everyone who has responsibility in the advertising process—are asked to rate the agency on each of the scales, and composite scores are calculated. These scores become the basis for a dialogue with the agency about the quality of its service and how it might be improved.

Are the Agency's Books and Financial Accounts in Order?

Finally, periodic agency appraisals inevitably include an audit of agency management of its fiscal affairs. Are client funds expended as agreed? Are the bills paid, and paid when they should be paid? Are expenditures substantiated and discrepancies between agency estimates and actual expenditures promptly reconciled? Are agency time records properly maintained and compiled?

In summary, the financial audit is aimed at confirming that the agency runs a tight ship for the client's money. Of course, the financial audits are not generally made by the advertiser's marketing personnel. Rather, they are conducted by the advertiser's financial executives according to accepted auditing principles, and the results are turned over to marketing officials for discussion with the agency.

Is the Formal Assessment of Agency Work All That Is Needed to Maintain an Effective Relationship?

Formal appraisals of the work of the agency such as those described in the preceeding paragraphs are an important ingredient in maintaining the ongoing effectiveness of an advertiser–agency relationship. The question is whether such periodic appraisals are enough.

A basic premise of the discussion in this and the preceding chapter about how to build an effective advertiser–agency relationship is that the relationship must truly be a two-way street. As we have analyzed factors that contribute to the effectiveness of these relationships, it has been clear that both the advertiser and the agency must contribute to the relationship if it is to remain healthy. This suggests that a one-sided, advertiser-controlled appraisal of agency performance is not enough to reach conclusions about the overall effectiveness of the total relationship.

Such appraisals, important as they may be in their own right, have two fundamental weaknesses.

1. They usually ignore those factors that reflect the contribution of the advertiser to the relationship, as well as factors for which advertiser and agency have joint responsibility. For example, such appraisals rarely concentrate upon the review process in which the advertiser assesses agency creative work. Neither do such appraisals review an area of joint responsibility such as the quality of the interaction between senior advertiser and agency executives.

2. In most of these appraisals, the only people doing the appraising are advertiser personnel. Lip service may be paid to agency participation in such appraisals, but such participation is really meaningless if the appraisal itself is limited to the performance and work of the agency.

What is needed is a more broadly based review that deals not only with the work of the agency but also with the contribution of the advertiser to the relationship. More broadly based reviews should cover not only the topics that are normally included in an agency appraisal but also all of the other factors that can affect the advertiser–agency relationship, as outlined in this and the preceding chapter.

It is certain that the advertiser loses as much or more as the agency when the relationship does not work well. If it is incumbent on the agency to do its job so well that the question of termination never arises, it is to the advertiser's advantage to go its half of the way to achieve the same end. And, having just lived through the inconvenience of firing one agency and hiring another, the advertiser should do its best to make sure its shortcomings in the previous relationship are not repeated with the new agency. If the advertiser is certain that it is blameless when an agency misperforms, then the advertiser can also be certain that the appointment of a new agency holds out the promise of actually maximizing the productivity of the new relationship.

Index